Rediscovering the Lost Body-Connection Within Christian Spirituality

Rediscovering the Lost Body-Connection Within Christian Spirituality

*The Missing Link for Experiencing Yourself
in the Body of the Whole Christ
is a Changing Relationship to Your Own Body*

Edwin M. McMahon, Ph.D.
Peter A. Campbell, Ph.D.

■ **Practical Body-Learnings and Exercises** *that Transform
Your Awareness of Who Christ is Today and Who You are in Christ
by Developing a New Habit of Noticing and Nurturing
Your Important Feelings*

Copyright © 2010 by Edwin M. McMahon, Ph.D. & Peter A. Campbell, Ph.D.

All Rights Reserved.

Tasora Books
5120 Cedar Lake Road
Minneapolis, MN 55416
(952) 345-4488

Distributed by Itasca Books
Printed in the U.S.A.

Cover and interior design by Elizabeth Edwards

All rights reserved. No part of this publication may be reproduced, stored in a retrieval system, or transmitted, in any form or by any means, electronic, mechanical, photocopying, recording, or otherwise, without the written prior permission of the authors.

ISBN – 978-1-934960-37-6

Book sales for North America and International:
Itasca Books, 3501 Highway 100 South, Suite 220
Minneapolis, MN 55416

To Order: Phone: 952-345-4488 (toll free 1-800-901-3480): Fax: 952-920-0541; email to orders@itascabooks.com

For a small quantity discount of 20% for individual customers (5 or more books), or for larger orders, contact Itasca Books by phone, fax or email.
Quantity discounts are not processed on the website.

Contents

Authors' Preface   **xiii**

Why This Book?   xvi

An Historic Interchange   *xviii*

Living a New Christian Paradigm   *xxiv*

Reinventing a More Ancient Way of Knowing for Today's World   *xxviii*

Remarkable Pieces of Interdisciplinary Research will Reveal
   More of the Lost Body-Connection Within Christian Spirituality   *xxxii*

A Suggested Exercise to Help You Acquire the Habit of Noticing
   and Nurturing Your Important Feelings After Reading These Pages   *xxxv*

A Few Further Suggestions for Using This Workbook   *xxxvi*

Personal Notes   *xl*

A **First** Body-Learning   Noticing

Changing the Relationship To Your Own Body by Noticing
Your Feelings and How You Treat Them

Chapter 1
Why Pay Attention to Feelings?   1

The Hawk Story   *1*

Six Fundamentals About Body-Knowing and Learning   *4*

Some Basics About Developing the Habit
   of Noticing and Nurturing Your Important Feelings   *6*

Inviting Children to Listen to All Their Important Feelings   *8*

Personal Notes   *10*

Chapter 2
An Exercise
'What Would it Have Felt Like if...?'   11

Personal Notes   *15*

> *A **Second** Body-Learning* Nurturing
> Growing Into An Inside, Physical Presence
> That Helps You Care For The Burden And Pain
> Your Body Carries Around Difficult Feelings
> When You Make Them Into Enemies

Chapter 3
A Story for the Hiding Child in All of Us   17

    An Introduction to Transformational Knowing   17

    'The Little Bird Who Found Herself'—
        A Tale for Both Children and Adults   21

    An Exercise After Reading, 'The Little Bird Story'   25

    Personal Notes   26

Chapter 4
Journeying into Your Own Inner World of Felt-Sensing   27

    Entering into and Through Your Feelings   29

    How Symbols Work   32

    Symbol as Metaphor   33

    Personal Notes   36

Chapter 5
Easing into Steps that will Help You Develop a Caring Relationship With Your Body's Ordinary Physical and Emotional Discomforts   37

    An Exercise   37

    Why Develop These Steps as a Habit   39

    Relevance for Christian Faith   41

    Personal Notes   44

Chapter 6
The Master Key for Opening Up a Potential You Already Possess for Taking Care of Your Difficult Feelings   45

    Don't Throw the Baby Out With the Dirty Bath Water   47

    The Paradox Hidden Within a New Perspective   48

    Approaches that Get Us Off Track   49

    Personal Notes   52

Chapter 7
A New BioSpiritual Way of Loving, Guided by Your Affection Teacher Through, '...the Eyes of your Heart' (Ephesians 1:18) — 53

   Exploring Untapped Potential Within Your Capacity for Affection   54

   An Affection Teacher Exercise   55

   Extending the Exercise   57

   Learning From Your Affection Teacher   57

   Lessons From My Grandmother's Lap   59

   Ed's Story of Yet Another Affection Teacher
      that may Call Forth the Body-Feel of One in Your Own Life   64

   Decades Later an Affection Teacher Returns   67

   A Brief Summary: Why are We Asking You to Go
      Into Your Own Experience of 'Affection Teachers?'   70

   Exercise: Time to Recall an Affection Teacher of Your Own   71

   Personal Notes   72

Chapter 8
Daily Check-In Exercises for Noticing and Nurturing Your Important Feelings and Helping Others to Do the Same — 73

   Some Helpful Guides for Companioning Yourself and Others   73

   The Basics of a Personal Check-In   75

   If You Get Stuck   77

   Helping Children Develop the Habit
      of 'Noticing' and 'Nurturing' Their Important Feelings   78

   Suggestions for Developing in Very Young Children
      the Habit of a 'Caring Presence' for Their Important Feelings   80

   Some Suggestions for Companioning   81

   Personal Notes   87

> *A **Third** Body-Learning* Balancing the Difference Between What Your Head Knows About the Body of the Whole Christ and How Your Body Feels It
>
> *Developing the Habit of Noticing and Nurturing Your
> Felt-Senses Builds this Missing Body-Connection.*
>
> *Christians Need to Build a Felt Bridge Between What Their Minds
> Can Grasp Intellectually About a Teaching, Like St. Paul's Meaning of 'in Christ,'
> and How Their Body Actually Experiences This Same Teaching
> Through the Gift of Their Living Faith.*
>
> *This Habit Opens the Door of Christian Awareness into the Wider, Gifting World
> of Grace and Spirit in the Body of the Whole Christ, so that Even Difficult Feelings
> Become an Integral Part, not an Obstacle on Your Journey into God.*

Chapter 9
Ancient and Modern Intimations of a Larger Body— But How Do We Connect?   **89**

- Children Teach Us to Decipher the Hidden Language of God   89
- Building the Body-Bridge of Christian Faith   91
- A Curious Parallel Within the Structure of Scientific Revolutions   93
- Reading Through the Eyes of Your Body-Knowing   96
- Body, Flesh and Spirit in the Writings of St. Paul   96
- Paul's Creative Efforts to Show His Experience
  of Living Within the Body of the Whole Christ   100
- Going Shopping for Inside Metaphors
  Within the Mystery of Your Body's Knowing   105
- Membranes Within the Body of Christ   108
- The Miracle of Yet-To-Be Discovered Blessings   109
- Ed's Suggestion for a Simple Morning Exercise   111
- Personal Notes   115

Chapter 10
Clues Unearthed During the Last Century by Scientists From Various Fields Who Discerned the Larger Body Within which We Live   **116**

- Some Outstanding 20th Century Explorers   *116*
- A New Kind of Interiority for Human Beings   *120*
- Growing into a New Habit Within Your Own Body's Knowing   *122*
- An Old Fashioned Lesson from a Pre-Digital Darkroom   *124*
- Learning the Body-Language of Agápe   *125*
- A Prayer Based on Ephesians 3:14–19   *130*
- Personal Notes   *132*

Chapter 11
Agápe in the Light of Carl Rogers' Research   **133**

- Ed's Reflection on Experiencing Dr. Carl Rogers   *133*
- Agápe Love as an Expanding Sense of Identity   *136*
- Three Psychological Characteristics of Agápe   *137*
- An Example of Companioning Presence   *143*
- An Exercise You Can Often Return To   *145*
- Personal Notes   *146*

Chapter 12
Exploring Agápe Love from Inside Your Body's Knowing   **147**

- The Body-Life of Agápe Love   *147*
- Helping Our Children Recognize God's Presence as They Grow in the Gift of Agápe Love   *148*
- Our Violent World Cries Out for an Experience of God-with-us in our Hurting Bodies   *154*
- Another Pauline Prayer from Inside Your Body's Knowing Based Upon Ephesians 1:18–19   *156*
- A Brief Reminder—An Exercise After Reading This Chapter   *156*
- Personal Notes   *157*

> *A **Fourth** Body-Learning* Living Christ's
> New Commandment of Loving as God Loves
>
> *Maturing into the Gift and Freedom
> of Loving as God Loves Transforms
> Our Self-Awareness of Who Christ Really is Today
> and Who We are in Christ*

Chapter 13
Loving God or Loving as God Loves?   **159**

- *A Special Little Boy*   159
- *Things are not What They at First Appear to Be
  What Does it Really Mean—to be Human?*   162
- *A Compelling Realization of Who You are 'in Christ'*   164
- *Christ's New Commandment*   167
- *One Woman's Journey into Loving as God Loves*   173
- *A Brief Reminder Exercise After Reading This Chapter*   178
- *Personal Notes*   179

> *A **Fifth** Body-Learning* Process-Skipping
>
> *Growing Beyond Process-Skipping Habits Which Lock In
> Addictive Patterns, Blocking the Body-Feel of Grace
> and The Experience of Living Within the Larger Body 'In Christ'*

Chapter 14
What is Process-Skipping and How do We Grow Beyond it into Loving as God Loves?   **181**

- *Pete's Process-Skipping Story*   181
- *Why Have We Placed Process-Skipping
  Toward the End of Our Programs?*   185
- *Repairing the Relationship to Our Difficult Feelings*   188
- *Deliberately Noticing Your Process-Skipping Patterns*   190
- *The Flinch*   191
- *Growing Beyond Process-Skipping—An Exercise*   194
- *Personal Notes*   196

Chapter 15
Paul's Astonishing Discovery 'in Christ'— 'When I am Weak Then I am Strong...' (2 Cor. 12:7–10)   **197**

    Opening a Door on 'Inner Dwelling'   197

    Puzzling Interactions   199

    Paul's Process-Skipping Experience   200

    '...When I am Weak, Then I am Strong...' (2 Cor. 12:7–10)   203

    Five Questions that Will Help You Evaluate the
       Psychological Health of Spiritual and Growth Practices   208

    Personal Notes   211

Chapter 16
The Habit of Noticing and Nurturing Your Important Feelings 'in Christ' Enables You to Mature Beyond Addictive Spiritualities   **212**

    The Origins of Addiction in Spirituality   213

    Areas of Addictive Behaviors   218

    Some Characteristics of an Addictive use of Spirituality and Religion   220

    The Road to Recovery   227

    Beyond the Stumbling Block of Fear and Pain Lies Hope-Filled Paradox   229

    A Closing Exercise   236

    Personal Notes   237

A Sixth Body-Learning   Creating Families and Groups of Companions in Christ—as Cellular Models for Living— Christ's New Commandment to Love as God Loves

---

Chapter 17
Recovering the Lost Biology of Christian Spirituality   **239**

    Looking Back Over Your Body's Journey into Finding God in All Things   239

    Bringing Change to the Serious Systemic Problem of Process-
       Skipping—by Creating Small Groups of 'Companions in Christ'   244

    A Closing Exercise   250

    Personal Notes   251

Afterword   **252**
Notes   **255**

Authors' Preface

BY INTRODUCING THE HUMAN BODY and its unique way of knowing into Christian spirituality, this workbook offers all Christians an inviting path beyond their often divisive debates and poisoned histories. Many Christians today want more than religious information. They seek *a transformational, new reformation.* Longing for a spirituality no longer disconnected from what their body knows, they cry out for help in changing the relationship to their own body's feelings. They search this fresh, holy ground to rediscover their own body within the Body of the Whole Christ. By slowly journeying at your own pace through the body-learnings and exercises in this workbook—whether alone, with a companion or in a small group—your steps in personal wholeness and the body-feel of grace open as one, unifying, organic experience. The implications for building peace-filled communities and a dedication to the global common good are enormous.

■

During more than 45 years of our team research, we have discovered that the way in which people treat their own bodies and feelings becomes a reliable predictor of how they will then treat and interact with those around them. It offers a window on how they will fashion the social and political structures in their societies, their business communities, systems of economics and education, even how they will design and live out their religious aspirations. In our view, the missing link in our all too human educational efforts for world peace lies in our lack of fully comprehending the structure and functioning of *a biospiritual pedagogy* which can lead individuals and societies into their shared body-knowing as an opening doorway along the path of achieving an enduring, global peace. But how can we actually teach this? How do we pass such experience on to the next generation? The overlooked key, of course, is that you cannot do this as an idea or information in the mind alone. It must somehow be passed on *within the body's consciousness of being a living cell within a Larger Body.* But how?

Authors' Preface

The above observation has boundless global implications for our future understanding of the body's key role in Christian spiritual development. Over the last 30 years, a recurring experience which stands out for us has been the number of people in so many different cultures and countries, who have attended our programs and thanked us for *the inner biospiritual process* they learned. For many, it became the principal support for how they carried the stress of life and aging, how they functioned constructively in trauma, as well as becoming their most effective approach, routinely used in spiritual companioning, ministry and pastoral work.

What they continued to ask, however, was for the inner body-process they were learning to be integrated *experientially* into a unified, Christian spirituality. We could not attend to this full-time until we began developing a three month transformational living program which then gradually evolved into this workbook—*Rediscovering the Lost Body-Connection Within Christian Spirituality*—an easily learnable body-process *as itself* an experience of their Christian faith. The workbook now serves as the primary resource, both psychological and theological, as well as the experiential format through body-learnings and exercises, for a program in Christian transformational living. The program can be adapted for 3–5 year olds in the home or preschool as well as for retirement communities and special needs groups—grief and chronic pain groups, marriage preparation, adolescent support groups and pastoral care in high schools and universities—as well as in the training of seminarians and novices within religious communities.

If Christians cannot help one another to *experience* their bodies as *living membranes* within the Body of the Whole Christ, giving witness by their organic presence in the world as the Continuing Incarnation of God "in Christ," then Christianity will be experienced as increasingly irrelevant within the lives of those suffering the pain of aging, physical trauma or those carrying the insecurity and emotional-physical impact of violence, as well as the inevitable dying we all go through.

Our important feelings try to express so many levels of felt-meaning that are vital for a religion built around the Incarnation of God in Christ. It is crucial that Christianity be experienced *within the human organism itself,* living in Christ's Body through our own bodies as a profoundly meaning-filled, Christ-revealing resource and healing way of carrying our fears, anger, low self-esteem, chronic pain, grief, helplessness, loneliness, hopelessness and loss of loved ones. Otherwise, Christianity will inevitably be sensed as missing the mark and feel more and more disconnected from everyday life.

The research and experience of our long lives has taught us that now is the time for Christian communities to rediscover who Christ really is today by changing the relationship most of us have to our own body. We need travel no further than inside ourselves. May this workbook be a loving companion for you and those with whom you might share this journey.

Edwin M. McMahon, Ph.D.
Peter A. Campbell, Ph.D.
Sonora, California
July 2010

Why This Book?

*"When we try to pick out anything by itself,
we find it hitched to everything else in the Universe."*
   John Muir, My First Summer in the Sierra, 1911[1]

*"Religion and science are the two conjugated faces or phases
of one and the same act of complete knowledge—the only one
which can embrace the past and future of evolution
so as to contemplate, measure and fulfill them."*
   Pierre Teilhard de Chardin, The Phenomenon of Man, 1959[2]

A whole school of psychologists now believe that
"spiritual values" are in the organism, so much a part
of the well-functioning organism as to be sine qua non
"defining-characteristics" of it.
   Abraham H. Maslow, Religions Values and Peak Experiences, 1964[3]

*"The only security for a growing person is
stability in the process of human wholeness itself."*
   Carl R. Rogers, from a Private Conversation, 1970[4]

*"Your physically felt body is in fact part of a gigantic system
of here and other places, now and other times,
you and other people—in fact, the whole universe.
This sense of being bodily alive in a vast system
is the body as it is felt from inside."*
   Eugene T. Gendlin, Focusing, 1978[5]

*"The path forward is about becoming more human,
not just more clever. It is about transcending our fears of vulnerability,
not finding new ways of protecting ourselves. It is about
discovering how to act in the service of the whole,
not just in the service of our own interests."*
   **Peter M. Senge, Foreword to "Solving Tough Problems"
by Adam Kahane, 2004**[6]

Rediscovering the Lost Body-Connection

SIX DIFFERENT QUOTATIONS, from six individuals using six radically diverse perspectives, and yet whose striking conclusions fuse together, less by reason of any overlapping information but more because some common *body-learning* and perspective has led this distinguished group of researchers to explore distinct, yet complementary facets of one and the same embodied, human experience. Each of their statements expresses part of a leap forward in our experience of what it means to be human.

We all know we have bodies. But how many of us consciously recognize in the very marrow of our bones that we each exist as an integral participant within a much Larger Whole, some Greater Living Organism? This book offers a potential experience of your own body as the missing link enabling you to mature into just such a *felt organic awareness*. Your mind obviously has a role to play when learning to drive a car, but your body gives you *a feel for the road*. Each of us needs to develop our own unique body-sense for being part of something greater than ourselves. Without some actual *in-the-body-experience* of this Greater Whole, we're left with nothing more than abstract definitions, ideas and cognitive analyses in our minds. We lack some tangible anchor within our own physical organism that can ground our experience, our wondering and our deepest spiritual longing. In his novel, *Nausea* (1964), Jean-Paul Sartre reminds us, "…the world of explanations and reasons is not the world of existence." [7]

A massage therapist who helps in our programs once told us:

> I have a client who has *fought* cancer for some years. Last week during treatment I helped him listen to some tears that had leaked from the eye corners. Suddenly, he realized how harshly he had pushed against the cancer when what he most needed was to hold in a loving way how his body carried the cancer. In that moment of realization his entire body relaxed and a pain that had been felt in his shoulder for years lessened dramatically. We can now not only achieve very satisfying treatment results, but continue an inner journey that was blocked because of fighting vs holding in a loving way how his body carried the cancer.[8]

The issues are in your tissues. The answers you seek hide quietly in your own backyard. The failure to include what your body knows

Why This Book?

masks the missing link. This workbook brings that neglected piece of awareness back into your everyday faith experience.

An Historic Interchange

Many years ago, during our search for a more embodied approach to helping Christians experience themselves in the Body of the Whole Christ, we found that wisdom and learnings in the writings of Joseph Campbell, an American author, scholar and professor of comparative religion, enabled us to realize how myth and legend brought powerful, *bodily-felt* purpose and meaning into the lives of ancient, preliterate peoples all over the world. Campbell also shared how all of us today need this same *embodied* sense for life-meaning and a felt awareness of purpose in order to have our own lives make any sense, especially in our heady, informational, wired-up world.

Both of us were fortunate to have been invited during the 1970's to attend a series of summer conferences on Voluntary Control of Internal States of Consciousness sponsored by the Menninger Foundation and led by Elmer and Alyce Greene, well known pioneers in the field of biofeedback research. Like ourselves, Joseph Campbell was an invitee. He spent many long hours sharing with Ed because he was fascinated with our search for a healthy, more transformational body-spirituality that could fill a growing void within first world cultures. As we expand beyond our more familiar tribal, monarchical, ethnic and even national identities and their myths which have held societies together in the past, the body-experience of being an integral, living membrane of some Larger Body begins to fade. At least in the past, people had a body-sense for the common good of their tribe, and it was integral to their spirituality.

Joseph and Ed often discussed how it seemed our very survival depends upon an ability to rediscover this Larger Body Experience beyond such limited tribal identities, as well as their religious, cultural and historical divisions and differences. These still continue to feed most of the senseless wars which destroy us as our technologies of global destruction clearly outpace our exploration into *a unifying inner process of peace-making* that results in an embodied sense of the global common good. Walking in the evenings together, Ed and Joseph wondered whether a more interior process of unification common to all humans really existed within each person. Furthermore, does the development of this inner process need to *precede*, or at least *accompany* efforts at peacemaking in the politico-social world, in order to achieve any enduring diminishment of violence?

Dr. Campbell thoroughly understood that in our time, most of the old myths we have inherited today become at best what he called, *artificial*. They no longer provide the meaningful *body-connections* which draw us into a sense for some physically-felt Larger Cosmic Body or Presence at work in our modern-day lives. The leftover residue of such myths tend to support survival of institutions crafted from and for the past, instead of nurturing greater wholeness and a sense for the global common good in people living within those institutions today.

However, the main issue which always surfaced in their discussions invariably came back to the same question: "Can some universal, yet personal *inner human process* that lies beyond all the historically conditioned, male dominated, tribal and institutional traditions enable each individual to discover his or her own fresh, new *personal metaphors* and unique body-sense for living within a Larger Presence and its unifying common good?"

Such an inner process, while not new in human experience may be quite new within our ordinary, everyday awareness of it—becoming a puzzle only because we don't know how to access and attend to it. That then leads to the more pointed question, "What holds us back from even being able to notice what our bodies already know so we can then act upon what they tell us?" Here, finally, we come to grips with the problem:

> ...recognizing something new does not necessarily lead to acting differently. For that to happen, we need a deeper level of attention, one that allows people to step outside their traditional experience and truly *feel* beyond the mind. For example, countless businesses have been unable to change in response to changes in their environments even though they recognize those changes intellectually. Why? As Arie de Geus, author and former planning coordinator at Royal Dutch Shell, says, "the signals of a new reality simply could not penetrate the corporate immune system." Conversely, when people living inside a shifting reality begin

Why This Book?

to "see" what was previously unseen *and* see *their own part* in maintaining the old and inhibiting or denying the new, the dam starts to break. This can happen in a company or a country.[9]

And, we would add, by necessity within churches and spiritual traditions as well. If nothing else, in our experience many Christians today sense some need for developing new eyes to see and ears to hear. Feeling beyond the mind today has become not an idle luxury but a stark necessity for finding our way forward by learning how to peer over the next horizon. In his Foreword to, *Theory U,*[10] a book on the social technology of Presencing, Peter Senge writes of the author, Otto Scharmer's vision that:

> Virtually all well-known theories of learning focus on learning from the past: how we can learn from what has already happened. Though this type of learning is always important, it is not enough when we are moving into a future that differs profoundly from the past. Then a second, much less well recognized, type of learning must come into play. This is what Scharmer calls "learning from the future as it emerges."[11]

Ed shared with Joseph our own personal and professional search for just such a new way of learning by sharing our experience working with an inner process of unification which the American psychologist, Dr. Carl Rogers had called, *congruence*, and which his former graduate student, Dr. Eugene Gendlin, was further exploring through a teachable process called, *Focusing*. This approach, in our view, offered the best potential for opening up a profound, meaning-filled and readily-experienced process within personal, *human growth itself* as the inner global metaphor opening a new doorway for future psychological exploration as well as discovering ourselves within the Mystery of God-with-us. Perhaps just such a process and metaphor might introduce an enormous breakthrough stretching well beyond tribalism and the *strong man* or *old boys club* mentality, with its religious, racial, ethnic and social tensions still locked in place on a globe rapidly becoming economically and ecologically interdependent.

For Rogers, the word, *congruence*, simply meant being able to feel your feelings physiologically and allowing them to symbolize themselves accurately. While the description may seem relatively easy to

Rediscovering the Lost Body-Connection

grasp theoretically, growing into such an experience as an actual *habit* within your own body in most self-escaping cultures like our own becomes quite another matter. It means sailing across uncharted waters within cultures where institutional religion and education generally ignore the body's vital contribution to personal and spiritual meaning.

In the light of Gendlin's research, *meaning* not only expresses itself through the mind. It rises up from within the body as well. Moreover, such *felt-meaning* animates the power of myth, legend and metaphor. Ed told Joseph that if the combination of Rogers' and Gendlin's findings could move out into the global body, especially into any of the world's great religions, it would model an evolutionary step for the rest of humankind. Joseph smiled knowingly and pointedly asked Ed, "Is this what you and Pete are trying to do for Christianity as psychologists of religion?"

Ed answered, "Yes. We've been collecting pieces of this puzzle that we feel may fit together. By trial and error, we are slowly learning how to pass this missing link on to those who find themselves hungry for experience and not just more talk or ideas about God but rather, in the words of St. Luke, that they would,

> ...seek, reach out for, and perhaps find the One who is really not far from any of us—the One in whom we live and move and have our very being...*(Acts 17:27–28 TIB)*

One of the important pieces of this search has certainly been Joseph's research on the central role of *metaphor*. For our introductory purpose here, it can help to recall that metaphor may be defined, in general, as a comparison of two unrelated things without using the words *like* or *as*—which if employed would create a *simile*. The simile would be, "Muriel runs like a deer." The metaphor: "Muriel is a deer." This simple description, however, only explains the linguistic *structure* of metaphor, not its more profound *embodied function* in human life and spiritual development. The latter, more functional investigation and research, has challenged the two of us for more than 40 years.

Ancient Hebrew teachers realized that including the body's knowing was integral to effective communication of the Word of God for an illiterate people. Information alone can never successfully convey the

Why This Book?

total message. Knowledge of God somehow thrusts deeper roots within the human organism itself even beyond the mind's ability to think and analyze. These teachers, therefore, sought a more efficacious way to enter into the body's knowing as well as into the mind thinking. This accounts for the *metaphoric* flavor present in so much of Hebrew midrashic teaching.

Experiencing this more *embodied function* of metaphor in healthy spiritual growth reaches deep within the human body's knowing. Symbolic language interacts with the body's awareness in a way that introduces a knowing that reaches well beyond conceptual thinking and information. Symbols touch and interact with a meaningful sense felt in the body even when the content of such experience cannot yet be articulated in concepts and words. The world which Eugene Gendlin has entered into and explored throughout his years of research into Focusing has opened a vast frontier for future exploration which still continues to this day.

Joseph Campbell introduces this deeper world of personal felt-meaning carried within the human body as follows:

> Let me begin by explaining the history of my impulse to place metaphor at the center of our exploration of Western spirituality...(12)
>
> Failure to appreciate the metaphorical nature of religious literature and discourse has led to numerous embarrassing crusades or expeditions to defend the biblical accounts of creation...Men mount expensive expeditions to locate the remains of Noah's ark on Mt. Ararat but, of course, they never find it...The ark, however, can be found easily and without travel by those who understand that it is a mythological vessel in an extraordinary story whose point is not historical documentation but spiritual enlightenment. To appreciate Genesis as myth is not to destroy that book but to discover again its spiritual vitality and relevance.(13)

In his Editor's Foreword, Eugene Kennedy further clarifies these remarks by commenting that Joseph Campbell clearly understood how metaphoric function played a central role in the creative efforts of our species to evolve human awareness beyond outworn ways of patterned thinking and perceiving that no longer work for us. In Kennedy's words, Joseph Campbell was:

...preoccupied with solving the enormous problems that flow from institutional religion's ongoing misinterpretation of spiritual metaphors as historical facts. Metaphor comes from the Greek *meta*, a passing over, or a going from one place to another, and *phorein*, to move or to carry. Metaphors carry us from one place to another, they enable us to cross boundaries that would otherwise be closed to us.(14)

Too many people today find themselves in a psycho-spiritual vacuum of purposeless disconnection where no embodied sense can mature in the awareness of our responsibility and accountability for a common good. Our bodies ache with an inner knowing that boundaries yet lie waiting to be crossed and grown beyond inside ourselves and our societies. Yet, media marketing and entertainment run 24 hours a day, distracting with products that simply turn us into a mirror image of what we buy—and still this never satisfies. Some missing link fails to connect. Our sense of *interdependence* with all that sustains life on this earth disappears beneath a wave of unsettling and addictive diversion so perceptively identified in Alcoholics Anonymous as— endless talking the talk without ever walking the walk.

This workbook represents our attempt to fill that void which Joseph Campbell urged the two of us to pursue. Our goal in these pages is to give you a support structure within which the development of a body-habit of noticing and nurturing your important feelings can become the *doorway* into a life-long metaphoric process through which you become more fully yourself within this Larger Body we all share in as interconnected, living cells. St. Paul calls this Body, the Body of Christ.

A fresh horizon opens out before us within just such faith experiencing. But this challenging new frontier rises up in a form as ancient as the origins of religion itself. Symbol and metaphor offer a transformational key into the human body and heart with profound spiritual significance. Unlocking an inner door we find ourselves poised at the edge of our own creative human potential, being drawn forward as an integral part of something far greater than ourselves, along with the exciting possibility that such experience introduces an entirely new personal and social order. The Kingdom of Heaven truly does

Why This Book?

rest within each of us. It does not lie buried beneath frozen heights of the windswept Mt. Ararats of this earth. Our generation and those to come now face the stimulating challenge of reentering the tribal religious night, but this time with our body's spiritual eyes wide open.

Living a New Christian Paradigm

The real challenge for any of us can never be overcome by merely *explaining* this interior process more clearly. Rather, the path becomes more evident as you learn how to put one foot in front of the other and walk your own, unique inner body-path of actually living your life forward as you develop a new habit of being open and attending to what your body knows and not solely to what your mind thinks. This maturing experience holds the key for discovering yourself as an integral part of something greater than yourself. By the repetitious practice of simple exercises in this book you can develop the habit of noticing and nurturing what your own body has to tell you about the Larger Body within which we all, "…live and move and have our being…" (Acts 17:28 RSV)

The price? Commitment, patience and time because we expend so much effort being entertained and acquiring new *information* that little space is left for achieving any real *transformation* in our everyday living. We sense some further step waiting to be taken inside ourselves, yet life slips by without our ever learning how to access, cooperate with, follow or even *allow* such hidden longing to guide us. We don't know how to make space for some deeper hunger that our own bodies attempt to reveal through barely noticed inner yearning or spontaneous flashes of realization that seep through the preoccupying busyness of our everyday, problem-solving lives.

Yet, surely the very meaning of God's Self-Revelation in Christ tells us with no uncertain clarity that a Continuing Incarnation of the Divine Presence becomes possible *through* our ongoing, embodied experience of transformation. In fact, such transformation unveils the core witness and meaning of Christian life itself.

This dilemma feels even more urgent today because it seems so strange that it has taken nearly 2000 years to begin discovering teachable body-learnings which can lead Christians into the Body of Christ

Rediscovering the Lost Body-Connection

by entering *through* the ordinary feelings and daily experiences which arise from within their own bodies.

In this book we have gathered together a basic pedagogy for noticing and caring for just such feelings. We make this available for Christian communities so they may begin helping themselves and one another to enter *together* into an inner world of felt meaning that the philosopher and psychologist, Eugene Gendlin, has called, our *felt-senses*.

"Felt," because you feel it in your body. "Sense," not like the five senses but more like, "She makes good sense," where *sense* is a *meaning* word. Felt-senses flow from physical links and connections as your body relates and interacts, whether in the present moment or with reference to some past or future event. You often experience the body-sense of a meaning that you feel long before being able to express exactly *what* you experience in more precise words and concepts.

Felt-Sensing reveals much more than recovering something forgotten, like when you say, "It's right on the tip of my tongue." Felt-Senses express your body-awareness of *meaning-filled body-connections*. But even more, felt-senses often carry an entirely fresh knowing never thought of nor learned before. Your body knows such meaning in an *implicit* way even though you may not yet be able to think about nor express it through *explicit* words, concepts, gestures or other actions.

What yet awaits our further exploration, and which this book introduces in a practical, down-to-earth manner that ordinary people can begin integrating into their everyday lives, may be found in the opening quotation from Gendlin describing how your physically felt body is part of a gigantic system that includes here and other places, now and other times, you and other people—in fact, the whole universe. This felt-sense of being bodily alive in a vast system emerges, in Gendlin's view, from your body "…as it is felt from inside."

The spiritual implication of such a statement for both the Christian community—as well as other spiritual traditions—lies hidden within the almost casual statement, "…your body as it is felt from inside." This realm of *felt-sense meaning* can take us on that metaphoric leap into a much deeper story about *ourselves-in-God*. One finds here not

Why This Book?

merely greater depth and understanding, but more far-reaching connections and barely noticed interactions which unveil *your body's experience of grace* along with a body-sense for being part of something Greater than yourself.

In our experience, few Christians realize that not only do meaning-filled feelings and felt-senses offer a precious invitation and doorway into a deeper relationship to God in Christ, but that practical, simple steps have already been developed which enable even small children to begin this journey. In fact, St. Paul seemed to realize that once this process had been experienced in our bodies it was meant to become the very center of Christian prayer. Our human organism itself offers an often surprising path, a physically felt, meaning-filled truth, and a largely unexplored way of living that can help to sustain each believer's own unique journey into the Body of the Whole Christ. If we learn the art of growing into this *new paradigm* within ourselves, we can begin to develop a quality of presence and caring which in time will impact all our relationships. But what do we mean by, *"growing into a new paradigm?"*

Let's briefly try to understand the significance and power which your own body offers as a new way of experiencing the future of Christian living. Winston Churchill once remarked that we build buildings and then the buildings build us. Architecture is not just something we live in. It eventually shapes our perceptions, our perspectives, and our expectations. The same may be said of paradigms. They function as a kind of *built-in psychological architecture* within our everyday outlook on the world and, most of all, in how we experience and feel about ourselves.

Paradigms, therefore, are ever-changing ways of viewing ourselves, other people, places, things, and relationships. A paradigm does two things. It lays down clear boundaries for thought and action, while at the same time defining the rules of engagement or interaction that lead to productive and successful relationships within those boundaries.

A tennis court is a good example of a paradigm. It has clear boundaries, the net and lines painted on the ground. It also sets down rules for the players on how they are to interact within those boundaries—like being able to determine whether the ball hits in or out of the court. Everything works fine until something unexpected happens that raises questions and shakes the old paradigm as, for example, during an earthquake in the middle of a game. When the earth shakes and your ball lands close to a line, determining whether it fell in or out of the court becomes difficult.

Something like this happened when Galileo and Copernicus turned everything topsy-turvy by upsetting the serene, stable order of a geocentric universe. By *changing the relationships* between sun, moon, stars, and our planet earth, they challenged and realigned all the old boundaries and rules of the game. They introduced a perception-shattering *new paradigm* which demanded a fresh habit and novel perspective on the universe, but most of all, a whole new way of experiencing ourselves within the universe. We were no longer the center of everything, and developing new eyes to see and ears to hear did not just stop with the sun, moon and stars. This powerful new experience would eventually thrust itself deep within the communal body of humankind transforming and challenging even our most intimate inner sense of ourselves. *"When we try to pick out anything by itself we find it hitched to everything else in the Universe."*

The swirling winds of this more potent new paradigm revolution now sweep with growing intensity throughout the cloistered halls and chambers of religion itself, challenging Christians to discover themselves in an entirely new way while still asking the same age-old questions posed by St. Paul, "Who is Christ today, and who are we *now, in Christ*?"

Learning to notice and nurture your own story-filled and therefore important feelings offers the first giant step toward experiencing yourself within the Larger Living Body which, for Christians, St. Paul named the Body of *Christ*. The firm foundation and starting point for living a physically balanced and healthy emotional and spiritual life depends upon developing the body-habit of noticing and nurturing your important feelings. When you find yourself out of sync with your body's felt-sense-knowing and its forward movement, healthy human growth rapidly deteriorates.

When there are no institutional resources, such as parenting programs, schools or institutionalized religion able to help us grow into an inner environmental balance—an inside ecology that can then flow into healthy, life-sustaining relationships within the

Why This Book?

world around us—then some form of violence and breakdown will inevitably occur.

Reinventing a More Ancient Way of Knowing for Today's World

We find it fascinating that a group of social scientists gathered around Dr. C. Otto Scharmer and the Society for Organizational Learning at MIT seem to have arrived at a similar point where we found ourselves 35 years ago when we left teaching in grad school in order to help found the Institute for BioSpiritual Research, Inc.[15] As Peter Senge, one of the MIT group has written in his Foreword to Dr. Scharmer's book, *Theory U—Learning from the Future as It Emerges*, "What we pay attention to and how we attend—both individually and collectively—is key to what we create."[16]

From our own research perspective, when Christians don't pay attention to their bodies' inner process of wholeness, they end up creating a spirituality of pious, intellectual theologizing and disconnected ritual adrift in an ever-changing world. We unintentionally become enablers of the view that Christ and Christianity seem impotent and irrelevant in the face of all the multi-converging crises that feed hopelessness and violence today. The Body of God on Earth remains abandoned and alone in the flight from our own difficult feelings, leaving us with our hunger for the meaning of life yet unsatisfied and the *living felt-presence of God's healing power within us in Christ* still not recognized and experienced in our bodies.

Instead, what pours into billions of living rooms all over the globe are the talking heads of both political and religious leaders bemoaning, scolding, blaming, warning and leaving us only more words and promises of either a brighter future if they are elected or hope in the afterlife while new crises continue to break out everywhere. We are confronted with extreme inequalities in healthcare, unending wars, economic and energy challenges, toxic water and air pollution, drug abuse, global warming, extreme imbalances in ecologies and excessive wealth, corruption in food-relief distribution, inadequate education and job losses. All these situations overwhelm people with wrenching feelings which paradoxically, as we shall see, hold the potential to unveil the undiscovered doorways into their resolution if only we know where and how to look inside our own bodies *in God* for balance within us and direction for resolution and hope outside us.

If the very core of Christian spirituality does not include an experience of discovering ourselves as living membranes within the Body of the Whole Christ whenever we are most overwhelmed, filled with fear and hurting, then we miss the essence of St. Paul's unceasing prayer that we come to know in our own bodies the reality of who we really are within the suffering *and* healing Body of the Resurrected Whole Christ. All this demands up-front, first and foremost, that we find our way back into a more ancient body-way of knowing which, finally, can draw us beyond the limitations of our more conceptual, modern-day habit of always trying to resolve every problem with our minds alone.

We are intrigued, as believing Christians and psychologists of religion, that within a secular research setting (MIT and their Presencing Institute supported by patrons like Ford, Boeing, AT&T, Shell and Nissan), our seemingly insoluble global, environmental, political, social, economic, religious and organizational problems are forcing some researchers to burrow more deeply *into human behavior itself* for answers. They have come to believe that this approach offers the only way to discover what prevents us from attending to those inner places in our own bodies' consciousness out of which each of us operates, whether in a peacemaking, creative and life-giving way that cares for the common good, or in a dominative, ultimately destructive and violent manner with the potential to destroy us all.

We have found that an inner structure which Eugene Gendlin has named, *process-skipping*,[17] which we shall examine more closely later in the book, feeds the addictive habits that keep us out of touch with our feelings and their deeper felt meanings—making them so resistant to change. Acknowledging these ingrained habits casts further light on our understanding of what we actually do inside ourselves in order to numb our body's knowing whenever we skip over the process of noticing and nurturing our important feelings. After finally learning how to recognize the myriad ways through which we remain out of touch with what our bodies know, we can then begin unearthing helpful clues which guide us toward a clear path of knowing how to *grow beyond* such an enslaving routine.

Why This Book?

Adam Kahane from the MIT group mentioned above offers a further direction to explore in our quest for a more embodied sense for participation within something greater than ourselves:

> When we talk about 'solving a problem,' we imply that we stand apart from the problem and can study it objectively and control it mechanically, with cause producing effect, as we would with a broken-down car. But this isn't a good model of our increasingly complex and interdependent and rapidly changing world. There is not 'a' problem out there that we can react to and fix. There is a 'problem situation' of which each of us is a part, the way an organ is part of the body...
>
> But this way of understanding the world...has serious consequences. If we admit that we are part of co-creating the way things are, then we are also co-responsible for the way things are. This is the moral and political challenge implicit in the comment...that if you're not part of the problem, you can't be part of the solution.
>
> And this way of understanding the world has another implication that is even more deeply challenging. This world is too complex and interdependent and rapidly changing for us to be able to reason through everything that is going on. We can no longer rely only on making sense of the whole of what is going on: we also have to sense it. This requires us to access a deeper, non-rational, more ancient way of knowing.[18]

But how do we access this *more ancient way of knowing?* That brings us to the heart of the matter in this book. "Who is Christ *today*, and who are we *in Christ*?" The writings of St. John and the Apostle Paul tell us, even to this day, that we must still access a more primal mode of awareness in order to experience ourselves alive within the Body of Christ. So much of St. Paul's strange, often enigmatic writing and exclamatory outbursts beg to be translated into a living, sensed experience of being part of something greater than ourselves *as this can be experienced from within our own bodies.*

> I can do all things in him who strengthens me. *(Phil 4:13 RSV)*

> Hence I am well content, for Christ's sake, with weakness, contempt, persecution, hardship, and frustration; for when I am weak, then I am strong. *(2 Cor 12:10 NEB)*

Rediscovering the Lost Body-Connection

> May the eyes of your hearts (ὀφθαλμοὺς τῆς καρδίας) be enlightened, that you may know what is the hope that belongs to his call. *(Eph 1:18 NAB) (Greek translation insert ours)*
>
> Now you are Christ's body, and each of you a limb or organ of it. *(1 Cor 12:27 NEB)*
>
> For to me to live is Christ. *(Phil 1:21 RSV)*

Strange language? Yes and no, depending upon whether you can read not only the words but also the inner body experience which Paul attempts to describe. Your own physical organism still remains the master key for unlocking this experienced sense for membership—or better, *membraneship* within some Greater Whole. At the same time, your body also serves you well as teacher, guide and best friend for learning how to grow beyond whatever obstacles get in the way of your attending to blocked inner experiences. Your physical organism can guide you in learning how to care for all those neglected, disregarded and buried feelings which long to be heard and freed so they may finally share their as yet untold stories.

Integral to finding your way into the Body of Christ means learning to become more human. Your own body offers the best path forward on this journey of *Continuing Incarnation* which challenges the entire Christian community to lead a world veering dangerously toward self-destruction into a changed relationship first to our own bodies, and then from that experience into a life-affirming, unifying, peace-filled relationship to all that exists.

Enough pieces of the puzzle have finally come together in our time that we can now deliberately choose to companion one another from early childhood into acquiring the inner habit of a loving relationship to how our own bodies carry our tears and fears. Our frailties and weaknesses, along with ordinary human limitations and incompleteness, may now become the real, honest and healthy stepping stones for our exploration into the Body of God *in Christ*. Ironically, for most Christians, such experience casts surprising new light on an ancient theme already laid down for us by the Apostle Paul when he cried out for help from the depth of his own frailty and imperfections, and the following reply was his answer:

Why This Book?

> My grace is sufficient for you, for my power is made perfect in weakness. *(2 Cor 12:9)*

To which Paul then exclaimed:

> I will all the more gladly boast of my weaknesses, that the power of Christ *(the tangible Larger Body of Loving Presence)* may dwell in me…For the sake of Christ, then, I am content with weaknesses, insults, hardships, persecutions, and frustration; for when I am weak, then I am strong. *(2 Cor 12:10). (Comment insert ours)*

Until we, too, learn to companion ourselves and one another on this journey into a personal *body-experience* of living within this Greater Body of Love, a Body which can carry us beyond the confusion generated by this seeming paradox of weak vs strong, we will just prolong our failure to recognize the hidden, missing psychological experience of being linked into a Greater Wholeness within the Common Body we all share. Such experience offers the vital and necessary ingredient for organically knowing in our bones that living in societies which constitutionally protect every citizen's rights, presupposes that citizens profoundly know in their bodies that they are endowed with a sacred trust and *responsibility* to care for the common good that sustains all life. Because this body-experience is largely missing today, democracies find themselves at a crossroads. The choice which each of us makes will be the legacy we leave to our children and their children for many generations to come.

Remarkable Pieces of Interdisciplinary Research Will in the Future Reveal More and More of the Lost Body-Connection Within Christian Spirituality

As a medical researcher, Henry S. Lodge, M.D., co-author of the New York Times bestseller, *Younger Next Year*,[19] and a clinical faculty member of Columbia University College of Physicians and Surgeons, develops a perspective on the human body with far-reaching implications for the BioSpirituality which we develop in this book. He writes in a popular manner for nonprofessional medical readers about the relatively little known interaction between psychological processes and the body's nervous and immune systems which raise implications for emotional and spiritual health. This interdisciplinary field of research has been given the name, *psychoneuroimmunology*, because it studies, for example, relationships between our feelings and neurology, immunology, molecular biology, physiology, etc.

Lodge's interdisciplinary insight into the nature of human emotion (we use the terms, *feelings* and *emotions* synonymously), together with its impact on your body's health, offers promising medical motivation for developing the habit of what we call *noticing and nurturing your important feelings*. Within our programs and through the guidance this book offers our readers, we have found that when feelings can tell you their stories and be heard, they then change in the way they feel inside and how you carry them in your body. Muscles and breathing become more loosened and physically felt pain diminishes rather than staying stuck, tight and hurting. When noticed and nurtured, feelings of depression and loneliness often diminish and more homeostasis (balance) is felt and can be observed. As the habit of noticing and nurturing grows, *the relationship*, and therefore the *interacting* with important feelings changes. The limbic brain, to use Dr. Lodge's term, *resonates* and responds to your own caring presence, and this message of caring appears to be communicated to every cell in the body as a signal to live and grow in a healthy way. Lodge summarized his research in an article on the role of emotion for physical health:

> Startling new images from MRI and PET scans show that emotion is at the physical center of our brains. Emotion is not nature's afterthought; it is one of the master regulators of health and happiness in every corner of your body. You have trillions of emotional signals moving around your brain and body every day. You can't shut emotions off. Like it or not, you are an emotional animal. It's as much a part of you as breathing. If you understand this—and take advantage of it—your life will be better and longer. [20]

The body-habit we teach in this book encourages an open dialogue, a *limbic resonating* with your own body and the important ingredient in its language—your feelings—ensuring that your body's knowing becomes a healthy part of all your daily living and decision-making, a resonating integrally woven into your growing self-identity in a Larger

Why This Book?

Body of Life and Love—expressed in St. Paul's experience as the Body of the Whole Christ. This more embodied sense of self then becomes essential to Christian faith as *a felt-sense way of praying, in Christ*.

In another article, Dr. Lodge describes how your body has two master signals to its cells telling them to grow or decay. Motion or exercise controls the first system. Then he writes:

> The other master signal to our cells—equal and, in some respects, even more important than exercise—is emotion. One of the most fascinating revelations of the last decade is that emotions change our cells through the same molecular pathways as exercise. Anger, stress and loneliness are signals for "starvation" and chronic danger. They "melt" our bodies as surely as sedentary living. Optimism, love and community trigger the process of growth, building our bodies, hearts and minds. ... Everywhere you look, you see the role of emotion in our biology. Like exercise, it's a choice. ...Deep in our cells, down at the level of molecular genetics, we are wired to exercise and to care. Start today. Your cells are listening.[21]

Such a caring, even loving presence must first develop in your body as an established habit, not only when directed toward others and all that sustains life, but in the relationship to your own body's feelings as well in order for you to become a more fully healthy human in your physical, emotional and spiritual growth.

A careful study of letters from St. John and St. Paul reveals an amazing and exciting convergence with this growing body of data from psychoneuroimmunology as well as psychotherapy. Healthy spirituality is meant to grow within a loving relationship that embraces *self*, others and the environment. For Christians, this has a very deep and special faith-meaning because John describes God *as a Loving Presence*, a special kind of loving interaction—*agápe*—and Paul describes us as living cells within this Body of the Whole Christ, gifted with His Spirit so that change is possible. Dr. Lodge has also noted that, "Love, friendship and community can't be written out on a prescription pad, but they should be."[22]

This book represents our attempt to pull some of these scattered resources together, writing out that prescription for the Christian community as a workbook, starting with learning how to take care of the painful, health-damaging burden we create inside ourselves when we turn negative feelings into our enemies.

A healthier, creative and hope-filled psychological, neurobiological and embodied spirituality can then emerge. It resonates with what Saints John and Paul attempted to articulate from within their own deeply felt experience as living cells within the Body of Christ. This awareness grew out of their sense for God as *agápe*, a loving presence animating all their relationships within the Body of the Whole Christ. As best they could, each struggled to put into words some primitive description of *a body-connection within Christian faith* which, tragically, has been ignored.

This book makes available practical body-learnings which we have evaluated over many decades. We have concluded, after working with countless groups and individuals in many countries, that they can guide you into a new experience of presence to yourself and the world around you. You can begin to experience an expanding capacity for presence within your own personal identity, not merely as a separate, autonomous individual, but as an integral living cell within a Greater Body. This fills your body's cells with meaning, faith and hope because of their experience of the love you bring to them. Mostly hidden in modern cultures, this transforming body experience reveals who you really are within this Larger Body of Love, a Body waiting to greet you with a warm and heartfelt, "Welcome home. You yourself are the hope you have been longing for—and you are never, ever alone."

A Suggested Exercise to Help You Acquire the Habit of Noticing and Nurturing Your Important Feelings After Reading These Pages

You already know what you feel like inside when moved to tears while watching a movie, a well-dramatized play, or simply reading or viewing on TV some heart-wrenching personal account. But how often do you take even a brief moment either during the experience, or perhaps later when you have more time, to pause and notice where your body most feels this experience? How does *your body* sense whatever it is that so touches you?

From personal experience you probably relish those precious moments alone, while quietly reading or when something deeply affects

Why This Book?

you and you physically feel some new realization in your body. You know how you often instinctively pause to look up from further reading or close your eyes to turn inward toward how your body knows something deeper which you wish you could connect with. Sometimes, when watching a play or movie, your body just wants to yell out, "Stop, so I can be with what I'm feeling right now and let it speak to me." But instead the film just keeps on going. How frustrating that feels inside— unless a TV commercial breaks in and you can *hit the mute button*, dropping down inside to listen and take care of your own unique relationship to whatever just occurred.

Our point, for helping you gain more from your reading here, beyond simply harvesting the printed information on these pages, would be that you deliberately begin making an effort to heighten your alertness for whenever your body reacts to something in your reading. For example, a story, some illustration, a novel idea or original perspective jumps out at you, hitting home in a way that your body responds. Such moments call out for inner space and time, for inviting *your felt-reaction itself* onto center stage to tell you its story.

So, before going any further in this book, take some time to notice how you feel right now about what you have just read. Where do you feel it in your body? Then, if you notice how your body carries something from your reading, respect this enough to say, "Hi," and then hold how your body carries this feeling in a caring, open, listening way so if it's ready, some of the deeper meaning within this feeling might break through in a memory, image, word, tears, joy, sadness, gratitude, fear, regret... something that feels connected to the way your body now carries this feeling. If you are able to spare the time now, allow whatever your body knows about what you have just read some space to be noticed and cared for.

A Few Further Suggestions for Using This Workbook

If at all possible, go through this workbook with another person or several people so you can all learn together as you experience the exercises, discussing, sharing and companioning one another. Replacing old habits in your body that no longer work for you with healthier ones will be greatly facilitated by the presence of another caring person or group who, like yourself choose to experience (in their own unique way) what you each commit yourselves to as an inner journey into the Body of the Whole Christ through your own body.

For everyone who risks growth and change, this kind of group learning can become a powerful teacher and inspiration. As we find ourselves more free to change inside, the quality of our presence to one another changes as well. This transformation in your companioning together can be physically felt, becoming mutually hope-filled and encouraging to all involved, even awesome in its community-building potential. A very different experience from going to a class or lectures where only information is exchanged.

Through the body-exercises in this book, you help one another learn a quality of caring presence inside yourselves by attending to how your body carries its fears and tears. You learn the art of waiting for feelings to tell their stories. Together, you help one another grow into a new habit of what we will come to describe as a sacred availability to the body-feel of grace.

So, if you are learning together with another person or a group, everyone will need their own copy of this workbook in order to read agreed upon chapters at home and for repeating needed exercises in between regular get-togethers. Set your own schedule and agree upon how much to read before the next meeting and then go through the exercises at home as best you can. At the meeting, make time to share any personal connections that have touched you the most, and then discuss any questions or problems doing the exercise at home.

When it is appropriate to do an exercise in the group, various formats are available. For example, let one member of the group volunteer to lead the rest through the exercises, or perhaps rotate the larger group companion for each session. Another option, you could break into smaller dyads or triads, exchanging companioning and being companioned by one another. Be sure to allow time for sharing anything around the exercise experience for those who might want to do so. Proceed according to a comfortable pace that seems to fit the needs of the group or fits your own needs if you learn the process by yourself.

In a larger group, if someone has more difficulty than others, perhaps needing extra time, our experience has been that as the group

Why This Book?

moves further into more of the body-learnings, something usually seems to *prime the pump,* so to speak, and the logjam often opens up on its own. Learning the process just takes more time for certain people. If this should happen, try to arrange additional one-to-one help from a group volunteer working outside the regular meeting times, even using the telephone or an Internet voice/video program like free software Skype (www.skype.com), which we have found works very well. For all of us, changing old patterns takes time, so don't rush through these exercises. The goal is not memorizing information, but developing a new habit in your body that changes the way you relate to your important feelings as they surface in daily life. Only as this capability and habit matures, becoming a regular practice, will you fully appreciate the impact it can have on all your relationships.

In our regular training programs from which this material has been taken, we spend three months from mid-September to mid-December meeting once a week in two hour sessions; half this time we spend in small groups of three learner participants together with a more experienced companion, working our way through the exercises together. We then augment this experience with time spent alone at home, daily repeating the same exercise in between sessions.

We are in no way suggesting this as the only way for you to use this book. However, our program schedule outlined above will give you some sense for the actual amount of time we have found it takes in order to help adults develop a physical sense for this new habit beginning to develop in their own bodies.

This workbook has been created so that each reader may, with the practical support of these pages, take themselves through their own body-learnings within the convenience of their own home, either with or without family members or nearby colleagues or friends being involved. Learning this process alone often becomes a necessity, because of the time, expense and energy it sometimes requires to travel distances regularly.

We began to format this workbook some years ago, using our living room to meet with mothers of very young children once a week in the mornings after they had just dropped their kids off at a preschool, minutes from our home. These young moms loved being offered a quiet place to gather away from their children for two hours, knowing everyone was safe, and meeting other young women with whom they shared so much in common. At the same time, they found themselves being supported and companioned into growing and discovering themselves in God through all their feelings that were often so overwhelming they had no idea what to do with them. We hope you will find as many ways to adapt, reorganize, re-express and re-teach the body-learnings in these pages, as there are many young and old people around you right now whose lives you could change forever with the help of this workbook.

Children and youth of different ages and adults with various levels of education and ethnic background will all require creative adaptation for effective learning. However, the format of this basic workbook will, hopefully, offer enough support to those open and ready to receive it as a blessing, that their experience of its inner process will stir their Christian faith to reach out by companioning others into their own body's personal experience of God's loving presence. Learning the process will take commitment and time. But ask yourself, "Doesn't my inner longing for an experience of God as close to me as I can become aware of my own body's feelings seem like an investment worth trying?" ■

Personal Notes

*A **First** Body-Learning*

■

Noticing

**Changing the Relationship
To Your Own Body by Noticing
Your Feelings and How You Treat Them**

Chapter 1

Why Pay Attention to Feelings?

IN OPENING THIS CHAPTER, Pete wants to share a little story for both children and adults—a story about learning how to become a teacher by listening to what your body knows. It describes an experience he had one bright, sunny morning, a long, long time ago.

The Hawk Story

Our former home office in California overlooked a beautiful mountain meadow with a stream meandering through that emptied into a jewel-like little lake. During Spring and Summer ducks and geese made their homes here, and red-tailed hawks hunted for small prey along the grassy shoreline. I had been blessed to live there for many years, and imagined that I knew all there was to know about this precious little corner of my world. But I was wrong. For there was a surprise yet in store for me. A surprise that would teach me much about the meadow, but eventually even far more about myself as well.

That surprise came one fresh Summer morning as I looked up from my desk and noticed, far down the meadow, a red-tailed hawk high in the sky drifting slowly down toward our lake. As it veered in front of my office, turning toward it's eventual hunting position along the far shore, I could see all the individual wing-tip feathers extended like out-stretching fingers, delicately balancing the bird in flight.

As it sank slowly toward the water, for a moment I thought the bird's sharp eyes might be searching for unsuspecting fish warming themselves near the surface. But in a very determined and purposeful way it continued gliding toward the farther shore where I assumed it might seek out small rodents and other prey along the water's edge.

Then came the surprise. Just as it crossed the shoreline, without ever flapping its great wings, the bird was suddenly lifted straight up in the air. Banking sharply, while deliberately holding itself within a small tight circle, it spiraled gracefully skyward, never once flapping its wings.

Why Pay Attention to Feelings?

In that instant, I immediately understood. This point on the shoreline marked a powerful, invisible updraft. From past experience the hawk knew precisely where this convenient column of rising air originated. Deliberately aiming for the familiar spot along the shore and entering the steadily rising current, it knew instinctively how to remain within the updraft, banking in a tight upwardly spiraling circle to keep within the narrow column lifting it skyward.

I watched with awe at this skilled act of survival, filled with such grace and near effortless movement unfolding before my eyes. Deliberately, without ever flapping its wings, the great bird spiraled upward until reaching some chosen height where it finally drifted out of the column, coasting slowly away from me and back down the meadow from whence it had come.

My desk work lay forgotten as I returned indoors, sitting for a moment in a kind of reverie with my memory of the experience. I had known this small meadow valley for years, almost like the back of my own hand. Every rock, stone, and tree, I knew where they all stood, and the old fence posts rotting in the rich soil. I knew where cattle crossed the stream and deer fed in the evening. But I knew absolutely nothing about this particular column of air. From more careful observation I soon learned there were even more, spread out along the far edge of the lake like convenient elevators rising high in the Sierra sky. I had discovered an invisible, hidden world of moving air that I might never have noticed without a leaf being driven into it by some random breeze, or a hawk deliberately hitching a ride skyward in its sure and steady embrace.

I carried this experience inside for days. Even now, years later the memory comes back vivid, fresh, and compelling in the lessons it bore for me—because there is more to this story. A delightful postscript that helped shape my perspective and set my life in a new direction.

A week or so later, I was again at my desk, when from outside through the open door I heard a tremendous squawking and calling back and forth of birds. Looking up, I again saw the hawk beginning its slow, graceful descent toward the lake. This time, however, right behind the parent hawk flew a little baby hawk, furiously flapping its small wings, trying to keep up with mom or dad and, to my ears, complaining mightily about the entire enterprise.

Quickly, I got up and walked outside, already anticipating what might come next. The parent hawk flew directly toward the invisible column of air, coasting gracefully into it and immediately rose upward. The little one, too, plunged forward, flapping furiously and was caught by the column, likewise rising skyward. Struggling to follow the tight spiraling turn of its parent above, the little one managed to make the first, and even the second sharp turn. But at that point, it lost control and fell out of the column, drifting back down toward the lake. The larger hawk, viewing all this from above, quickly abandoned the column of rising air, diving downward to position itself once more in front of the little one, leading it again back into the rising column. The lesson was repeated several times. In the end they both rose skyward together, eventually drifting out of the updraft and away back down the valley, hunting along the way.

I carried this experience inside for a long time, gradually coming to recognize that hidden, invisible currents were very active in my own life as well. Grace-filled surprise and opportunity, new directions, and fresh meanings were continually emerging from inside my own bodily knowing. Hunches, intuitions, vague yearnings and often surprising, unexpected inspiration—much more than purely cognitive, reasoned thinking.

Each of us has been blessed with our very own inner world, much like the small valley I have just described. Yet, an entire universe of unexamined possibility lies hidden there. I often imagine my private inner world to be filled with upward spiraling columns of gift and surprise. Such a resource lies waiting to be discovered within every person's body. The challenge, of course, is learning how to notice, nurture and in turn be nurtured by such hidden possibilities.

To this day, I remain impressed with the parent hawk. The older bird had no way to sit the little one down in their nest and give it a lecture on rising thermal currents. The parent simply had to lead the younger bird directly into the rising air so it could get a feel in it's own smaller body for the invisible power and supporting presence that lay hidden at the edge of our lake. A critical skill for survival could then pass from body to body, and generation to generation. Once we develop the body-feel for grace, then we too can pass this on to the next generation, helping each other as adults to rediscover it. That is why we share this workbook with you.

Why Pay Attention to Feelings?

Hidden deep within our bones lies an unrecognized capacity just waiting to be found. We each exist as an integral part of something greater than ourselves. Our bodies already know this even before our minds can think it. And within just such knowing lies the key, finally, to experiencing what it really means to be human. Can we make time to begin this sacred, inward journey, discovering hidden possibilities inside ourselves just waiting to surprise us?

Six Fundamentals about Body-Knowing and Learning

Your first step toward developing a new body-habit around feelings helps you notice when you have them. Most people don't even recognize when their feelings rise up because they're generally too preoccupied with instant reacting to them—especially when their experience surfaces difficult, scary or lonely feelings.

This first chapter offers a simple step toward noticing your feelings by summarizing a few basics that may have *motivational value* for committing yourself to the more challenging task of actually becoming aware of your feelings as they unfold—noticing their appearance right away instead of spontaneously hanging back or running away from them.

In the next chapter, you will have an opportunity to go through a useful exercise that helps you recall and work with some remembering from your childhood which we have found can give you a body-sense for how you carry feelings within your own physical organism. For right now, however, here are some basics you can start with.

1. We all know we have feelings. What most of us don't realize is that more than 50% of human knowledge is learned from our body's ability to know, rather than through our mind's capacity to think. This is another way of saying that most of us use only a self-restricting amount of our knowing potential throughout life. As a species, we have barely begun to recognize the depth and hidden potential in what our bodies will teach us—if we can only learn how to listen to them.

2. Every good coach knows that students learn swimming or any sport, typing, singing, dance, or carpentry from *the body-feel* of doing it correctly. They need more than outside information. They must enter directly into the process of learning from *inside* their own bodies.

Acquiring this *how-in-the-bones* enables each generation to pass special ways of body-knowing on to the next, but in a manner quite different from communicating information through concepts and ideas that our intellects can grasp.

3. The human body has a unique way of felt-knowing quite different from any thinking, analyzing, or reasoning. Your body spontaneously senses the relational whole of a situation or experience, embracing the entire interacting web of complex linking and connecting which goes along with each and every part. Your body knows in a great gulp, while your mind must systematically chew its way through every individual piece. Our human species has been blessed with two entirely different but complementary ways of knowing. Our challenge lies in developing the habit of using the two together in a balanced and interacting practice. Discovering and implementing a simple, effective way to teach our children and youth how to connect with and learn from the important stories in their own feelings represents our next forward step in what it means to be human.

4. The ancient Greeks recognized at least five different kinds of knowledge: scientific knowing, wisdom, opinion, faith, and an esoteric experience called *gnosis*. Among the five, however, only *scientific knowing* referred to informational knowledge in the mind. The other four pointed to special ways of knowing in your body. This is the world of hunch, intuition, creativity, inspiration, revelation and, most of all, the wisdom that comes from experience in living your life.

   Wisdom always expresses far more than information. It gives voice to your felt body-connections. The wisdom of Solomon shown in 1 Kings 3:16–28 is a case in point. Two new mothers who live together approach the King, one carrying a dead infant and the other a live baby boy. Both claim the living newborn. After some deliberation, the king calls for his sword and declares that the only fair solution is to cut the baby in half, giving a portion to each woman. The true mother, wanting to keep her son alive, cries out in anguish to the king to give her newborn to the other woman. Solomon, immediately recognizing the true mother, gives the baby back to her. He drew upon a deeper knowing felt within the heart of a mother, something beyond logic and law, analysis, reason and hard thinking. The king constructed a situation wherein something within the body would cry out and reveal the true situation. Your body speaks the truth when your mind cannot even begin thinking about what to do or say.

5. Everyday feelings, emotions, and physical sensations represent an important first step into the world of felt body connections—your felt-senses. Such body-links bring their own special meaning into your life, a meaning you feel rather than think. *All feelings*, whether positive or negative, express an important part of your body's intelligence because they introduce you to deeper felt meanings at work in your life. In this workbook, noticing and nurturing important feelings so they can tell you their stories describes an habitual process you can grow into within your own body as it is felt from inside.

6. *Most people don't realize how values, basic human goodness, and a positive sense of self are all learned in and acquired through our body and our body's knowing.* Such valuing does not mature in us because we follow some external list of do's and don'ts. Nor do we discover this through various religious or ethical interpretations. Rather, it arrives through our body's ability to become aware of its innumerable connections as well as an even more compelling invitation that lies within such linking. Since the body knows through felt relationships, it also knows that each of us is part of some Greater Body or Larger Whole.

Most children absorb their parents' values through ordinary, everyday experiences of interacting with them. The old adage, "Examples speak louder than words," reveals how valuing is primarily a body awareness and habit—not a piece of analytic information arrived at logically in the mind. Effective parenting instructs, models and leads through body knowing as well as through lecture and commands. The parent hawk offers a striking metaphor for guiding us into this more integral manner of educating. The baby hawk learned by experiencing a body-sense for what the parent was teaching.

Some Basics about Developing the Habit of Noticing and Nurturing Your Important Feelings

The dictionary defines *habit* as "…an acquired pattern of behavior that has become almost involuntary as a result of frequent repetition."

Parents and child caregivers need to know that most habits are accompanied by an *acquired neural patterning in the brain* as well, a patterning that both stimulates and reenforces habitual behavior.

The first six years of human life are most important for the development of our brains. During this period, neural patterns are laid down. In other words, the switchboard is being designed and soldered into place that will determine much of our behavior in later years. This is true, especially, of our neural patterns and habits of *openness* to learn from new experience, or our tendency to *resist* such experience when we perceive it as somehow threatening. This tendency includes attitudes toward feelings as well as for other experiences in the child's world.

If a child feels humiliation or pain from attempting something new, and then failing or being ridiculed, there is a natural pulling in for protection and security—a cutting back on risk. A *habit* of withdrawing begins to grow. Neural patterning in the brain becomes established and reenforced. On the other hand, if a child experiences encouragement and support for discovering *the personal meaning* in an experience, even in the face of set-back, fear, and pain, an entirely different *habit* and neural brain patterning can emerge.

Feelings are like the phone ringing. A message is trying to get through. We don't have phones in our offices or homes just to make noise. They ring to alert us that some information is waiting. The problem for many, however, is that when the phone of their feelings rings, trying to get a message through, a habit of blocking the message kicks in. People respond to the ring of their feeling by turning on the TV, music or pouring themselves a drink. They go to the refrigerator or their computer, they pick up a magazine, daydream, go shopping, text their friends etc. They escape, they numb, they avoid, or substitute something they enjoy in place of what they perceive as fearful or a hurting attack and threat. The neural response in their brain stimulates and reinforces their particular habit of avoidance. We will have more to say about how to change these patterns in a chapter further on about *process-skipping*.

It helps for parents and teachers to learn and recognize the major differences between a child *owning and processing* their feelings, versus *acting them out* in a destructive way that demands intervention.

Why Pay Attention to Feelings?

Learning the habit of noticing and nurturing important feelings as a first step toward processing potentially destructive feelings diminishes the child's need to act them out in a destructive way.

The growth issue, both for adults and children, does not lie in whether we interpret a feeling as being socially, spiritually or culturally *good* or *bad*. Rather, it depends upon whether a person can own and process his or her feelings in a way that allows the inner felt meanings within them to unfold and be heard. Morally speaking, feelings are neither *good* nor *bad* in themselves. They simply happen. Acting them out in a destructive way that harms self or others is where moral and social accountability come into play. Children need support and mentoring in order not to be afraid of their feelings. They learn this by watching the ways in which their parents, teachers and the important people in their lives model the processing of their own difficult feelings.

Inviting Children to Listen to All Their Important Feelings

Children should learn from a very early age that every important feeling offers an opportunity for new adventures, or finding a hidden treasure. By taking time to help them notice such feelings and learn how to care for them, they are invited to embark upon a discovery trip inside themselves. Feelings can express themselves like the stories in a book. Further pages always wait to be turned and new discoveries lie hidden around every corner. Children, as well as most adults, value and look forward to what's next in a story, on a walk, or when they are exploring. So, in order to reach and get closer to children, adults need to set *noticing* and *nurturing* an important feeling as though it were an important adventure you take together with a child. The adventure motivates learning, and results in the development of a lifelong habit of listening to what their body tells them as part of their own unfolding personal story.

Adults, too, can discover a more positive way of relating to their own feelings which may be quite different from what they learned as children. We can develop a patient, listening and caring attitude toward how our bodies carry feelings, especially where we still live with unfinished business inside ourselves. As feelings are heard and change in how we carry them, so too can outworn, growth-blocking neural patterns in the brain change. This builds body-links of hope for development and transformation. It frees us from the prison of old, stuck patterns that obstruct continuing growth in wholeness no matter what happens to us or how we feel about it. Child caregivers often play a special role in helping to create more positive patterning in a young person's life.

All of us, especially children, must be encouraged to listen to *our bodies as teachers* and not as enemies. Our bodies speak through important feelings and the deeper felt meanings within them. Experiencing this inner resource generates courage, self-confidence, and a creative human spirit.

When adults learn to help children listen into the stories, the personal meaning and life direction hidden within their feelings, it gives the child's spirit a chance to blossom. Kids end up feeling good about who they are, no matter what their feelings may be or what is happening in their lives. They recognize that feelings are only *the tip of the iceberg,* and that a deeper story lies waiting beneath every feeling they learn to access.

Children learn self-esteem and caring for their feelings when adults respond to such feelings with respect, teaching them to notice, nurture, and learn from them. This book can be a guide for parents, grandparents, teachers, counselors, and caregivers, helping them learn how to do this. The foundation for a healthy spirituality grows from just this kind of body-learning and knowing. ∎

Personal Notes

Chapter 2

An Exercise
'What Would it Have Felt Like if…?'

THE FOLLOWING EXERCISE provides an opportunity for you to begin exploring deeper into how your body's knowing remains recorded within the feeling side of your memories. A powerful component within any remembering brings back not only thoughts but old feelings and physical sensations as well. The sound of children at recess in your old schoolyard or a bubbling brook in a favored place where you liked to rest can summon memories and feelings associated with such experiences. The clickity-clack of a passing train as you visit your old neighborhood, the sighing of wind through the trees or crackling of dry leaves underfoot in the Fall recall *meaning-filled felt-senses* of more youthful years, all still alive within your body's knowing, accessible in one form or another.

Our "What if…?" exercise invites the *felt meaning* side of your remembering into awareness, to be noticed in a caring way that often allows such memories to become unique and meaning-filled personal metaphors for you. Recall the earlier comment of Eugene Kennedy on the meaning of metaphor. Whenever we approach the unopened door of attending to the felt meaning in our remembering, this allows our inner metaphors to:

> …carry us from one place to another, they enable us to cross boundaries that would otherwise be closed to us.[1]

The following exercise unfolds in four parts, with simple directions to guide your quiet inner remembering within each part.

■

(A) What would it have felt like in your body if, from the time you were very small until you grew up and moved away from home, your Mom or Dad, or both, day in and day out had consistently responded to your tears

'What Would it Have Felt Like if...?'

and fears, your excitement, your curiosity, shared dreams, hurts, confusion or, perhaps, a passion for sports, music, or whatever with an invitation in words like these…

- "That sounds like there's an important story inside those feelings trying to break through inside you…"

- "Is there some place in your body where you especially feel this… *(fill in your…excitement, hurt, sadness, fear, curiosity, wondering, challenge, etc. …?)*"

- "Would you like me to sit with you while you move your awareness into your body where you feel all this the most?"

- "Stay inside with how your body feels—as best you can. Try to be there in a way that says: 'I'm here. I care. I'm not going to leave you alone. I'm listening in case you want to tell me anything.'"

- *(If the feeling you were trying to be with was difficult, they might have said:)* "You know how your body feels inside when you care for and love your [teddy bear, favorite stuffed animal, pet, doll, baby sister or brother, etc.], So, see if you can be that same way now with your body carrying this *(…scary, sad, hurting, etc. …)* feeling."

INSIDE QUIET TIME PART ONE: After reading the above, take whatever time you need to go inside yourself and quietly experience in your own body how such an attitude and invitation from your parents might have *felt* inside you as a child—if they had consistently responded to your deeply felt, important feelings in this way. (If you go through the exercise with a friend, take some time afterward to share anything which feels important for you before continuing.)

Now, Let's Go A Bit Further.

INSIDE QUIET TIME PART TWO: What if your family's response of supporting you in noticing and nurturing your important feelings, had then developed into *a habit* of knowing how to notice and take care of your feelings in this more caring way *on your own*, and you had learned to carry that habit into your teen years and young adulthood? Would your life have been any different during those years? Again, allow some time to sense how your body responds now to this question.

INSIDE QUIET TIME PART THREE: What if this habit of noticing and nurturing your hidden story, your emerging, unique self-identity had then been intimately connected by your parents to the presence of God in your life and the body-feel of God's Grace working inside you? What difference might that have made for you? How does it feel in your body now when you ask yourself this Part Three question?

INSIDE QUIET TIME PART FOUR: Finally, what would it feel like now in your life if your own body could become your best friend, companioning you *right now,* burdened as you may be with scars, unhealed wounds and neglect from the past, yet still filled with unexplored hopes, talents and dreams lying dormant and hiding within the untouched treasure of abandoned feelings? Again, allow time to feel your body's response to this question.

ENDING: In closing, give yourself a moment to sense how your body now carries the exercise you have just completed. Allow whatever feelings may have surfaced to be heard and let them know by the quality of your presence that you care for them. Remember, this is all about *establishing a new kind of inside relationship with your own body and its feelings*.

As you bring this exercise to an end for now, you might promise any important feelings still needing more care that you will come back to them with a presence that says: "I'm here with you." "I won't neglect or leave you alone." "I'll try to be with you in an open, listening way if you want to say something to me." "Speak in whatever way you want, with tears, a memory, a felt color, an image, words…whatever feels connected."

■

Over the next few days, you might want to reread the exercise a few times, noticing and nurturing any further feelings that may surface. Be aware of any changes that come in your body as you do the exercise. Give your body's knowing or remembering, along with any gift *(grace)* that may unexpectedly arrive, an opportunity to connect with one another. Your important feelings deserve this respect, care and

'What Would it Have Felt Like if...?'

an opportunity to tell you their stories. After all, you wouldn't even experience them unless they were trying to tell you something important and help you find God in all things.

Allow some time to sit quietly with all this before moving on. If gratitude feels appropriate let that, too, become part of your journey. ■

Personal Notes

*A **Second** Body-Learning*

■

Nurturing

Growing Into an Inside, Physical Presence That Helps You Care For the Burden and Pain Your Body Carries Around Difficult Feelings When You Make Them Into Enemies

Chapter 3

A Story for the Hiding Child in All of Us

"The Kingdom of God is within you." (Luke 17:21)

"Truly, I say to you,
whoever does not receive the Kingdom of God like a child
shall not enter it." (Luke 18:17)

An Introduction to Transformational Knowing

IN A MOMENT, you will have an opportunity to read a charming tale written as much for the child within every adult as for our kids. This metaphor as story helps us develop simple, practical approaches that can encourage even toddlers and youngsters to notice and take care of their important feelings. We must become as diligent in educating young people about their feelings and how they work inside their own bodies as we are in providing them with early preschool skills and information that helps them to succeed during their more formal years of education. Doing this will also lay a more solid, lifelong foundation for developing a healthy spirituality that can include what our bodies know as integral to our experience of God. Yet, not surprisingly, the biggest challenge in all this will be for parents and adults themselves to begin practicing this same caring awareness within their own lives and feelings so they will then know in their bodies what children need to listen for and learn from them.

The number one underlying problem, when attempting to create healthy people, is an imbalance between *informational* knowing and organismic, *transformational* knowing. Societies today seem less able to pass on from generation to generation the development and nurturing throughout life of a vital *balance* between these two very different ways of knowing. By this we mean a balance between conceptual, rational logical, analytical knowing and *felt-sense* knowledge. As Dr. Gendlin reminds us, meaning is not only thought in our minds, but also felt in its own way throughout the entire human organism.

If every cell of the human body has its own intelligence, then we should not restrict our intelligence development to just one aspect of human consciousness. We become physically, emotionally and spiritually sick when we find ourselves disconnected from the felt-sense knowing of the whole body. That disconnection quickly spreads into a blocked awareness of being a living cell within a Larger Living Body, which healthy spirituality must cultivate or it will eventually degenerate into some form of pathology or ideology often expressed in rigid legalisms and compulsive, even superstitious attitudes and practices.

Noticing and nurturing our own body-feelings constitutes an indispensable first step toward experiencing ourselves within this Larger Living Body which St. Paul preached as the Living Body of Christ. Our very foundation for living a physically balanced and healthy emotional and spiritual life depends upon developing this important habit. When you are out of sync with your body's felt-sense knowing and its forward movement, healthy growth rapidly deteriorates.

The simple act of noticing our feelings opens the doorway into our felt-senses so that the *felt* meaning in our lives, our personal, embodied stories can then become an integral part of our developing self-identity. We come to know ourselves from within the relationship we have to our own body's inner environment as well as through our outside environmental connections—our communities, the global family of humanity, living creatures and the earth's ecology—the balance that sustains all of life. Without a sense for such *felt linking-together*, we end up destroying ourselves and everything else that sustains life on this planet.

This habit of noticing and nurturing your important feelings so they can reveal your own story, who you are and how you must live in relationship to everything else, represents *the key* to your own health and the survival of life on the earth. This book shares a simple way of bringing that balanced, transformational knowing back into your everyday living.

Why do people get so sick when they lack this inner balance which their own body's transformational knowing is meant to bring into their lives? Because organic, transformative knowing is the very foundation of our entire *relational* world. It creates in us the *quality of physical presence* we bring into *all our relationships*. If that level of embodied, inner and outer presence never gets developed as a habit in our lives, we then enter into our relationships in a dysfunctional way, usually for the wrong inside reasons, trying to compensate in these relationships for some missing ingredient within ourselves. You have, no doubt, experienced how people whom you know, even love, find themselves often caught up in their relationship to work, to politics, their hobbies, their eating, their exercise, their church, synagogue or mosque or even their atheism for all the wrong inside reasons. We sense this person *has an ax to grind* or a chip on his or her shoulder.

The great American psychologist, Abraham Maslow, called this *deficiency cognition* based on unfulfilled deficiency needs.[1] Gordon Allport, another great American psychologist in his classic study of religion called it, *"security-centered religion"* which he contrasted with *"growth-centered religion."*[2] Anne Wilson Schaef in her studies and writing called such deficiency relationships, *"codependence."*[3] The Irish poet, William Butler Yeats in one of his sonnets, *A Prayer for Old Age*, put it this way:

> God guard me from those thoughts men think
> in the mind alone.
> He that sings a lasting song
> thinks in a marrow bone.[4]

In today's doctors' offices, hospitals, remedial classrooms, prisons, and last-chance-high-schools we find people whose bodies and relationships have broken down because no one has ever helped them to develop the habit of noticing and nurturing their important feelings so their inner felt stories, their real identities can blossom and unfold. The physical relationship which individuals have with themselves forms the firm foundation of those nonviolent, peace-filled, healthy, creative, life-giving capacities found within maturing people. We bring this fundamental relationship into all our interactions with one another and the earth around us.

The unfolding inner process of establishing a new relationship to your own body introduces a rich metamorphosis into human experience, much like the difference between a caterpillar and a butterfly. All our interactions change. In the evolutionary words of St. Paul, each person in Christ becomes, "…a new creation; the old has passed away, behold, the new has come." (2 Cor 5:17) A transformative potential lies waiting within each of us to become more whole, to live a more balanced relationship between informational knowing and our body's capacity for more organic, healing learning.

The point of reading the Little Bird story which you will do in a few moments is, obviously, not just the information of a story that even a three year old child can be pulled into. It puts you in touch with the experience of a universal, timeless metaphor, an inner process at work in your own body around how you relate to your own difficult feelings in a caring way so their hidden meanings can eventually surface and be known by you.

Little Bird has the potential of empowering your self-worth, engendering a hope that difficult feelings are never the walls that block your growth, but from within themselves offer the launching pad toward a transformed future if you can risk the caring relationship they call out for from you. Moving forward involves taking the time to rewire old habits of neglect and active rejection. Transformative body-knowing and an experience that such change is both possible and what the wise old owl guides Little Bird into can plunge you right into the heart of what it means to be fully human.

We hope this tale may act as a personal metaphor for you, bringing missing links from your past back into awareness as something of your own life-journey surfaces within your remembering, allowing the Wise Old Owl in this tale to teach you how to notice and care for whatever hidden or long forgotten felt meaning still waits to unfold from within your important feelings.

So, as you read the story of Little Bird for yourself, try listening *beyond* the story-line for felt-sense doorways within *your own inner story.* Listen for what your body knows and how you might be connecting and feeling about something it wants to tell you. Be attentive to how your body expresses what it experiences through the language of feelings, memories and physical sensations. You're not merely reading a child's story about some Little Bird. You're reading a story *about you*, about your unique journey as you struggle to find your own voice so you, too, may sing your own song. You have been given life not only to discover who you really are, but also to know from within the marrow of your bones who you are in the process of becoming as a living membrane within a loving and even Greater Unfolding Presence.

**The Little Bird Who Found Herself
A Tale for Both Children and Adults**

This story was written for a young girl named Elizabeth, who is very special. But it is also written for you, too, because you are very special.

Once upon a time, a tiny bird's nest sat high in a tree. The beautiful tree was growing in the backyard of a house where three children lived, Elizabeth and her two brothers. There were many trees around the homes in this town so birds loved to live there. In a tiny nest was one gorgeous, violet-blue egg. The mother bird was so very proud of it she showed it to all the other birds around her.

One day, it suddenly burst open and out popped this tiny, naked baby bird. The baby bird couldn't see too well, felt cold, and was kind of scared, so the mother covered it with her wings to keep it safe and warm while the father bird flew off to look for some bugs for dinner.

A few days later, the baby bird began to grow her own downy, baby feathers to keep herself warm. She felt more like opening her eyes and looking around at everything. She noticed a funny feeling inside herself.

"I wonder what this funny feeling inside me is," the little bird said to herself. As the days went by, the funny feeling kept growing and growing, and the little bird wondered and wondered what it was all about.

One day, she heard her mother chirping around the nest as she was tidying up. Suddenly, the little bird knew what the feeling was all about. That was what she wanted to do! She wanted to CHIRP! In fact, the little bird knew that she just HAD to do that to be herself.

Without waiting another moment, she opened her mouth and let out the loudest chirp you have ever heard. Even the children who were playing in the house came outside to see if they could discover what the sound was. The dogs began to bark and the lady next door, who was hanging out her wash, stopped to look around and listen.

The mother bird, who had not been paying any attention to the little bird as she did her morning chores, was so startled she fell over backwards right out of the nest. Since she could fly, she opened her wings and flew right back up to check out what was happening. When the little bird saw her coming back, she felt it was time for another big chirp. So out it came!

A Story for the Hiding Child in All of Us

Seeing all this and feeling all the attention, the little bird said to herself, "Wow I'm really somebody, and this feels so good inside me."

One of the cousins said to the little bird's mother, "You have to stop this!"

Someone else added, "You need to teach her the right way to chirp."

As others nodded their agreement, more and more kept saying things like that to the little Bird's mother and father. The little bird just sat there in the nest quietly feeling very confused and lonely, and sadder and sadder inside as all the birds went on and on with their comments. "My chirp is me and I am my chirp," the little bird said to herself. "But all these birds who are older and bigger and smarter than I am say this is not the way a bird chirps."

This confused the little bird very, very much, so much so that all the happy, good feelings inside began to slip away. The little bird's mother didn't say much because she was also confused and embarrassed that all her friends and family thought she was a bad mother. The father bird tried to pretend that nothing had happened by going off as usual getting very busy finding more worms and bugs. That left the little bird very much alone and not feeling at all like chirping.

In fact, she was scared to even try again. Day after day she got sadder and sadder and lonelier and lonelier. Each day, she sat by herself on the edge of the nest or on a nearby branch because, by now, her feathers had grown and hopping around on the branches felt like the only fun in life.

Sometimes her cousins would come over chirping and playing, asking her to join in. But whenever the little bird would risk trying to chirp as softly as she could, they would say, "That's not the way we chirp. Either you learn to be like us or we won't play with you!" That would make the little bird so mad her chirps would come out anyway, and when the other birds would try to drown her out, feathers would fly.

All the noise would bring the lady next door running out of here house, banging on a pan to scare then away. So the little bird stopped trying to play with the other birds and would sit all alone day after day by the nest.

One day, a wise, old owl flew by and saw the little bird all alone looking sad. The old owl flew down next to the nest. When the little bird looked into the kind face of the big owl, something inside felt safe and right to ask, "What do I do?"

The old owl gently moved over next to the little bird and said, "When you grow quiet inside and listen to your body, what does it tell you needs listening to more than anything else?"

Quietly, the little bird went exploring down into all the feelings in her body under the new feathers that were growing. The old owl said nothing, but the little bird could feel his reassuring presence and that helped her stay inside herself with her feelings. It didn't take long before her body told her, "I'm very, very sad." She shared that with the wise old owl.

The owl moved ever so gently closer to the little bird, saying, "Can you move up closer to that sad place inside yourself like I'm doing with you and let it know that you are there and will listen to it patiently?"

The little bird could feel how to be with her sad place from the way the old owl was with her. Together they were very quiet as she moved even closer to her sad place inside.

After a moment or two, the owl quietly said, "Now let yourself really, really feel in your body what it's like to be next to your sadness like I'm next to you." And then they both grew even more still as the little bird tried to do just that. After awhile, in a whispering, very quiet voice the wise, old owl softly encouraged the little bird to stay inside with the sad place saying, "Take your time and listen to that place inside, because if you can feel it you know it wants to tell you something." As the minutes passed, the little bird became aware that the sad, hurting, scary place didn't feel so bad because it wasn't alone anymore.

The little bird realized, "It feels better not to leave sad, scary, confusing, lonely places inside me all by themselves. I ought to be taking care of them and playing with them."

The old owl smiled and replied, "Take some time now to notice how that feels in your body." So the little bird paid attention inside to what those words felt like in her body.

Almost right away, she noticed the sad place didn't feel as sad now. "I think it wants to tell me something else," she said.

The owl responded, "just stay in there with how it all feels and listen patiently."

A Story for the Hiding Child in All of Us

Suddenly, the little bird looked up at the large grey owl perched next to her and said, "CHIRP! Yes, that's it, I need to chirp and chirp and chirp and chirp!" So the little bird began to chirp, and the smiling wise owl flew off with the promise to come back again if the little bird needed him. But, the more the little bird chirped, the better everything felt inside. On and on she chirped, day after day, week after week, even when the neighbors and the aunts and uncles would fly by and voice their disapproval. The little bird didn't pay any attention to their scowls but just kept on chirping the way it felt right to chirp.

Even though the little bird was still all alone on that branch chirping away, inside there was no sadness or confusion anymore. The sadness and confusion were no longer alone because she had gone inside to be with them and they had become her friends.

In fact, they could tell her what they wanted to and so they didn't feel like she needed to be afraid of them anymore. They could say what they needed to say to her now and that changed the way all the feelings felt in her body. Once again, the little bird felt very special inside; so special and good about herself, in fact, that the funny feeling she had felt so long ago returned again. "I wonder what it is this time," the bird thought to herself. The more the little bird chirped away, the more that funny feeling grew inside her until she felt like it just had to come out.

One beautiful sunny morning, as the little bird woke up and opened her mouth to chirp, out came the most wonderful sound instead. The little bird began to sing! All the other birds stopped their chirping and listened in amazement. The dog stopped barking down the street and the children on their way to school came over to listen. The people in the neighborhood came to sit on the lawn under the tree and listen to the beauty of the little bird's singing. She sang and sang and sang for everyone, but most of all for herself.

The other birds said to each other, "Why can't we sing like that? All we can do is chirp like we are supposed to do. Why is the little bird so different?" When the little bird and the wise, old owl (who came by to listen) heard that, they smiled and winked at one another.

And so, the little bird grew to sing more beautifully everyday because she never again left those special feeling places inside herself alone.

The End (5)

An Exercise After Reading 'The Little Bird Story'

Take some time, now, to grow quiet inside just as Little Bird did. Then, use the following questions to help you notice whether any memories come in a feeling way within your body.

(a) Ask Yourself: "From my body's memory, can I recall any time or times when I felt like Little Bird? For example, embarrassed in front of family or friends by an adult who humiliated me by saying something like: 'You don't know how to chirp the right way.' Do I remember not just the incident or situation, but also notice whether I still carry any of this same feeling in my body now?" Allow quiet time for noticing whatever may come. *(pause)*

(b) Then ask yourself, "If I am able to sense any felt connections with those experiences, can I also notice where I actually carry such feelings in my body right now? Is it in my throat, my chest, my heart, stomach, behind my eyes, etc.? If I'm unable to find a single location, is there some *all-over-my-body kind of feeling* which I can sense inside? Or, is it more like some kind of *background feeling*, such as never having enough time, *always* feeling put-down, *always* needing to please people, never measuring up or not feeling as smart, pretty or successful as others?" Take time to be with whatever comes inside. *(pause)*

(c) Finally, ask yourself, "Can I right now be present in a quiet, caring way to whatever I'm feeling, just like the wise old owl was with Little Bird?" Then ask yourself, "Does my feeling have anything it wants to say to me?" Allow time for waiting until something comes like a word, tears, a memory... anything that feels connected to how this whole thing feels in your body. *(pause) Be as gentle and caring as you can while listening into your own remembering.* ■

Personal Notes

Chapter 4

Journeying into Your Own Inner World of Felt-Sensing

THE METAPHOR you have just read in the format of a child's story invites you to cross boundaries that might otherwise be closed to you. By reading her story, you are invited to explore the same inner process Little Bird discovered, but inside yourself, a story which can carry you from the reading of her unfolding tale into your own unique, personal journey. The process itself then becomes an alive metaphor inside you. It opens up a new kind of relationship with your own physical organism as you enter into and through your own feelings, just as Little Bird did. Developing a sense for this more extended environmental organicity *within yourself* means setting out upon a fresh, even radical kind of *incarnation*, a *new paradigm experience* of being present to yourself in a way that allows your own body to unveil its hidden, inner felt connections. Eventually, this experience can encourage the dawning of a new body-habit, bringing an even Larger, more integrated world into clearer focus.

So let's begin with a brief personal example as a starting point for illustrating how your body knows in a distinctly different way from how your mind thinks. At this point, we just want to crack the door open a little, allowing some light to spill through our stories and illustrations which will begin to illuminate the learnings that yet lie ahead. We can start with a short illustrative story.

Many years ago during one of our Spring workshop tours we were having dinner with a friend at a midwest restaurant. Pete's mother, who lived in San Francisco, had been ill prior to our departure from California and was scheduled for a series of diagnostic tests. Her call came during dinner.

The news was not good. Tests indicated colon cancer. She needed immediate surgery within two or three days. On returning to the dining room Pete laid out the painful situation. He continues his story below:

■

I felt conflicted with a jumble of inner feelings. In the middle of a workshop I couldn't just stop and fly home. Although well cared for, Mother had no other family support except me. At the table I found it nearly impossible to continue following the thread of our dinner conversation.

So, sitting quietly, I allowed my attention to settle inside my body, becoming attentive to the inner whirlwind of concern and troubled feelings surrounding my lack of any practical alternatives that might allow me to be in San Francisco. I felt the utter frustration of being unable to do anything.

At first, this inner attending felt almost useless. It brought no comfort in my body. In fact, as the discomfort grew, I felt terrible inside. No amount of reasoning, arguing, or talking at myself could relieve my inner disquiet.

So I sat still, trying as best I could not to reject, but rather listening into and being present to the swirl of emotion around how my body carried all this internal distress. Knowing I could do nothing, I simply cared for my body bearing such painful feelings. It felt terrible inside and much in need of my caring presence. In the end, this proved sufficient.

Across the room from our table an open door revealed a small corner bar. A pianist had been quietly playing for some time. At one point a young woman walking over to the piano began singing along with the music: "*Que sera, sera,*" she sang, "Whatever will be, will be. The future's not ours to see, *que sera, sera!*"

Just hearing the music and those few soft words in that unlikely setting brought a surprising release in my body. The disturbed feelings I carried inside quietly vaporized and began drifting away, much as an early morning mist will dissipate when warmed by the rising sun. It was so clear. There was absolutely nothing I could do in this situation. But experiencing this from within my body felt so dramatically different from the fevered grappling and analytic chattering in my mind.

I still carried concern for my mother. But I also sensed an incredible *felt-shift* in how my body now bore the situation. I changed from being edgy and anxious to calm, more accepting and in the present moment. I became aware of a complete transformation in the quality of my presence to my surroundings and my friends. In that surprising experience I received clear evidence that while my mind could in no way *think* my difficult feelings away, simply hearing those words from the gratuitous, unplanned song enabled the feelings to mutate inside my body.

The mere fact that I had allowed time to stop, to notice and nurture how my body carried mother's phone call made all the difference. I had deliberately held with caring attention my private inner turmoil, neither stuffing, controlling nor shunting anything aside—not even asking God to take it all away. That simple act of committed, solicitous, caring presence had somehow introduced an inner climate within which gifted, positive change might occur. The experience served as an open disposing of myself for some graced interaction, if that were meant to take place inside me. Upon hearing the gentle words of the song, some *deeper felt meaning* spontaneously moved forward within my body, transforming the inner landscape of my felt inner world.

But what actually happened here? The following diagram and explanation can begin to illustrate the hidden interactions which allowed such transformation to occur.

■

Entering into and Through Your Feelings

Your body's capacity for knowing and being in-touch with your inner world of feelings and felt meanings may be regarded as much like an iceberg floating in the sea, as in the illustration on page 31. Only a small portion of the iceberg sticks out above the waterline. The larger mass lies hidden beneath the surface.

Above the waterline, everyday consciousness makes available some portion of bodily knowledge, such as ordinary feelings or emotions and physical sensations. You know when you're angry, lonely, or sad. You know when you feel tears, a rapid heart beat, or delighted laughter. You are aware of such feelings and may, if you choose, deliberately turn your attention toward them, thinking about, analyzing them or even feeling your way further into them.

Journeying into Your Own Inner World of Felt-Sensing

Now, let's step a little deeper. While listening to a beautiful aria or song, have you ever felt the physical sensation of a chill running up and down your spine, or experienced spontaneous goose bumps raising up on your arm and shoulders? Have you ever deliberately tried to *will* a goose bump to rise up on your arm? Can you see how that makes about as much sense as Pete trying to *think* or reason away his feelings of helplessness? Yet, at the same time, the chill and those goose bumps contain *further hidden felt meaning*, equal in importance to your ordinary feelings or emotions. In other words, *your body talks to you*, directing your attention toward a special inner doorway that makes vital information available, information just as important as what you can think in your mind if only you know where to look and how to listen for this inside your body.

The topmost part of our illustration represents the whirlwind area of inner concern and troubled feelings that Pete felt about his mother's situation. For the most part, he could readily hold this in his awareness. But all the while, beneath the surface of his thinking mind and troubled emotions, another form of knowing lay hidden, waiting to move forward in his body.

Your mind finds this deeper, more *embodied* knowing rather vague and opaque. The intellect's eye cannot easily penetrate this inner world of *felt meaning* in order to figure out, conceptualize, analyze, and organize. Your body expresses a meaning you surely *feel*, but often without your mind being able to formulate or say it with words. As we have indicated earlier, Gendlin calls such felt meaning a *felt-sense*. "Felt," because you feel it in your body. "Sense," not like the five senses but more like, "She makes good sense," where *sense* is a *meaning* word. Felt-senses express your body-awareness of meaning-filled body-connections.

To develop the habit of noticing and nurturing your important feelings, you must first learn how to enter *into and through* your surface feelings, emotions, and physical sensations. That is what Pete was doing when he took time to be caring with and *listening into* his feelings of confusion and frustration around his mother's illness. Feelings, therefore, present themselves as *our doorways* into the felt meanings we seek. They offer a precious opening or entryway into felt-senses which lie deeper within our body's knowing. By establishing a different

Rediscovering the Lost Body-Connection

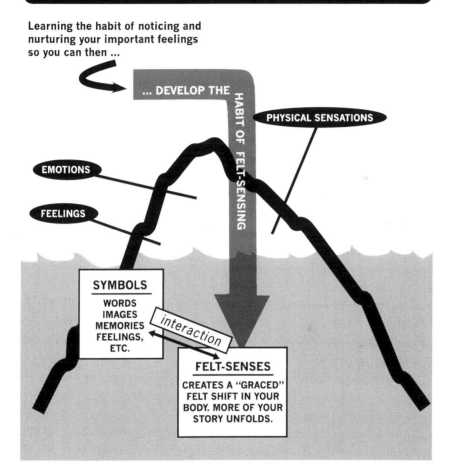

kind of relationship to his feelings (not pushing them away, but being caring, gentle and listening to them), this enabled Pete to begin his inward journey. We need better understanding and knowledge about how to recognize felt-sense knowing because, as we shall soon learn in coming chapters, this experience becomes the gateway into our body's sense for membraneship within some Larger Body.

We all struggle to draw out such dimly felt answers *(felt-senses)* from within our bodies so we can then think and express in a more verbal way the meanings which up until now have lain largely hidden, implicit, unformulated and locked within our body's knowing. At the moment when Pete heard the words, *"Que sera, sera,"* his feelings dramatically changed inside. He could actually *sense* the difference. A felt meaning physically moved forward, unfolding inside his body with a surprising and noticeable shift in how he carried that feeling. What had been *implicit* in a body-way became more *explicit* in both a thinking way as well as in how he felt inside himself. But, once again, what actually happened here?

How Symbols Work

For Pete, the music and words of the song functioned as *a symbol* that could reach into and through his troubled feelings in a way that touched and connected with the deeper felt meanings, or felt-senses he carried about himself in relation to his mother's situation. A symbol may be anything, a word, an image, a memory, or even another feeling or physical sensation.

Symbols that brush up against us can come from outside, as they did in Pete's experience with the song. Or, they may emerge from inside ourselves in the form of spontaneous memories, words, images, or other feelings that touch our felt-senses, allowing them to move forward. But such symbols or metaphors accomplish far more than merely *describing* a felt-sense. Dr. Gendlin realized that something very important occurred when he began digging deeper into the relationship between meaning felt in our bodies, our felt-senses, and the symbols which connect with them, allowing change or some felt *forward movement* to unfold.

He observed that a symbol does not merely equate with or explain a felt-sense, it interacts with it.[1] *(Refer back to the iceberg image on page 31 if you need to.)*

Symbols are not mere mental stand-ins for your mind to think about. They not only help to describe something of the informational *content* of felt meaning in your body. But a symbol *physically interacts* with a felt-sense carried in your body. That describes its *function—interacting not equating*. This *interaction* then allows fresh, perhaps unexpected, and at times even surprising felt, personal meaning to surface into more conscious awareness and viscerally move forward or unfold inside your body. Gendlin's research has provided us with an inside look at just how symbol and felt meaning interact and *function together* within your body's knowing in order to promote some kind of *forward movement* within our inner experiencing, an unfolding of personal individual identity which can then gradually mature into an empathic experience of being part of something greater than oneself. Such felt meaning does not surface simply because you happen to *think* something right inside your head. Your body enters actively into the knowing process as well.

Symbol as Metaphor

But how could the random music and words of the song possibly bring about any change or transformation inside Pete's body and feelings?

Have you ever had a similar spontaneous experience as, for example, when some uncomfortable feeling in your body suddenly dissipates and you immediately feel better about an issue or concern? If so, have you ever stopped to ask yourself, "What happened *just before* my inner world brightened? Where did that bad feeling go?"

Recall, once again, Joseph Campbell's earlier quoted comment on Judaeo-Christian spirituality and metaphor:

> Let me begin by explaining the history of my impulse to place metaphor at the center of our exploration of Western spirituality.[2]
>
> Failure to appreciate the metaphorical nature of religious literature and discourse has led to numerous embarrassing crusades or expeditions to defend the biblical accounts of creation...Men mount expensive expeditions to locate the remains of Noah's ark on Mt. Ararat but, of course, they never find it...The ark, however, can be found easily and without travel by those who understand that it is a mythological vessel in an extraordinary story whose point is not historical documentation but spiritual enlightenment. To appreciate Genesis as myth is not to destroy that book but to discover again its spiritual vitality and relevance.[3]

Also, remember as well Eugene Kennedy's further remark that Joseph Campbell was:

> ...preoccupied with solving the enormous problems that flow from institutional religion's ongoing misinterpretation of spiritual metaphors as

33

historical facts. Metaphor comes from the Greek *meta*, a passing over, or a going from one place to another, and *phorein*, to move or to carry. Metaphors carry us from one place to another, they enable us to cross boundaries that would otherwise be closed to us.[4]

This precisely describes Pete's experience. Alone, his mind was unable to cross the body boundary in order to change his troubled feelings. He simply could neither *think* them right nor analyze his way through them in a manner that compelled them to change. Yet, upon being touched by the inviting call of a metaphoric symbol, "What will be will be," his body quickly became an open bridge for song and words to enter. *Que sera, sera!* Symbol and his body's felt-sense could mutually *interact* with one another, thereby enabling heretofore unrecognized felt meaning to flow forward and his personal inner life to unfold. Pete's feelings changed.

They transformed and his inner landscape brightened. A new paradigm appeared, along with the dawning exclamation, "I didn't make that happen!" Pete had absolutely *no control* over the appearance of such a blessed interaction nor the happy release in his body-feelings which followed. It all came as pure gift. Within such a transformative moment, that was how *grace* felt in his body.

For Pete, the words, *que sera, sera*, offered no *rational explanation* for his troubled feelings nor any logical solution for his dilemma. Rather, the song functioned as symbol, a metaphorical bridge that could interact with his deeper felt sense, thereby opening a door and carrying him across some visceral threshold into a different place and a transformed feeling within himself—*within his own body*. The words of the song, as *explanation* and *information,* in no way could account for the sheer visceral power of this *interacting relationship* between symbol as metaphor, and his own body's unique felt-sensing.

Gendlin suggests that there exists a deeper felt meaning, a *felt-sense* within the body which can be accessed and encouraged to unfold further when interacting with an appropriate symbol or metaphor that lights the fuse, so to speak, allowing further felt-revelation and visceral change to emerge from within.

Scripture can become metaphor when it touches a felt-sense in the reader. A phrase, a word, some passage connects, reaching deep within the body's knowing. Such experience produces a truly *sacramental* moment. The Word of God becomes flesh once more within daily living. Incarnation happens. Faith revives. Hope springs anew.

For now, we will leave this introductory explanation as a brief glimpse forward into what awaits throughout the pages ahead. In the next chapter, you will have an opportunity to dip your toes in the water of body-knowing, so to speak. An easy exercise that brings your attention to some physical sensation, feeling or experience that doesn't overwhelm you in any way, yet somehow stands between you and feeling all OK.

Your real challenge on the journey you undertake here lies not merely in our *explaining* this process more clearly. Rather, it challenges you to learn for yourself an entirely new skill for putting one foot in front of the other on an *inside-body-path* of actually living your life forward as you develop a new habit of being open and attending to what your physical organism knows and not solely to what your mind can think. We all need to learn easy and systematic, yet practical, doable steps which direct attention inside our own bodies in ways that invite us to be caring and present to the deeper stories we carry within—stories which still await our caring, listening presence. Such challenging body-experience provides a key which unlocks the next step of opening yourself to the experience of being an integral membrane of something greater than yourself.

By entering into the simple exercises in this book you begin laying a foundation for learning how to listen inwardly to what your body can tell you about the Larger Body within which we all "…live and move and have our being…" *(Acts 17:28 RSV).* ■

Personal Notes

Chapter 5

Easing into Steps that will Help You Develop A Caring Relationship With Your Body's Ordinary Physical and Emotional Discomforts

YOU MAY HAVE NOTICED that certain steps are already implicit in both the *Little Bird* story, as well as in the exercise, *What Would it Have Felt Like If…?* Later, we will give you further suggested formats for these steps, enabling you more easily to develop the *habit* of noticing and nurturing your important feelings.

Let's now try another short exercise which may open the door a little further into your body's knowing. This exercise will work with your ordinary physical and emotional discomforts that you might be carrying around right now—e.g. tiredness, stress from some situation or relationship, etc. We're not yet turning attention toward any old time *biggie* issues from the past or large-scale worries about the future. At this point, we simply suggest that you go through the following exercise because it offers an easy way to bring a caring presence to your emotional or physical discomforts so you have an opportunity to become more aware of how it feels in your body when you create a caring relationship with these irritations. It also helps you experience that your body carries feelings about everything going on in your life right now, whether significant or insignificant.

An Exercise

Preparation

First, Take a moment to close your eyes, growing quiet inside, and allowing your attention to settle into the center of your body. *(pause)* Then, read through the Noticing Step below.

Noticing

Now notice whether your body is carrying any physical discomfort like tightness, pain, heaviness, or any other sensation such as a slight headache, tiredness, etc.; anything that lets you know there is something between you and feeling all OK. It could be a hard chair, a stuffy room, or emotions like irritation at an annoying person or noise that bothers you, feelings of loneliness, being put down, never having enough time—anything that feels uncomfortable in your body. Notice where you especially feel this in your body right now as well as how you feel about carrying such discomfort at this time. *(Pause to sense whatever might be there before continuing with the Nurturing Step below.)*

Nurturing

(a) Staying inside your body where you most feel the whole of this discomfort, let your body's instinct for compassion and affection guide you in being present to this hurting place inside, creating a caring relationship with it. Be present as you might instinctively pick up and hold a hurting little child in such a way that he or she could feel being cared for, not alone, companioned, and safe in your arms and loving presence.

Take your time, allowing this caring presence to sink in, being absorbed and felt by this needy or hurting place inside. *(pause)*

(b) As you allow time just to be with and in this needing place inside, also notice how it feels to be paying attention to your body in this caring way. How does your body respond and feel as you consciously and deliberately begin treating it in a companioning, respectful, open, and listening way?

(c) Allow your body to speak inside you in whatever way it wants, with words, an image, a memory, perhaps tears, laughter, or just some further feeling. Try to be there in a non-judging way, receiving what comes, honoring and listening to whatever story unfolds. *(pause)*

Ending

(a) When it feels right to stop, take a moment to get a body-feel for where you are inside yourself right now. You should always do this, especially when you run out of time and must stop before something feels finished. The felt sense for any unfinishedness will help you know where to return whenever you might want to continue at a later time. *(pause)*

(b) Take a moment to recall how it felt in your body when you began and how it feels inside now. *(pause)* Whether it feels the same or has changed, if it still feels unfinished inside, then ask this feeling place, "How do you need me to be with you so we can continue our journey together?" *(pause)*

(c) Finally, allow yourself some quiet time to be grateful for the gift of this new relationship to yourself. *(pause)* If more story needs to unfold, promise this feeling place you will come back to go further at another time. Then, whenever you're ready, you can stop.

THE GOAL: To notice in your body how it feels to create a caring relationship with ordinary physical and emotional discomforts.

Why Develop These Steps as a Habit?

Instead of beginning with some old issue, situation or event which you have already carried in your body for years, the above steps begin directly in your body right now. Why? Because many of us have found ways to cut ourselves off from being in touch with how *our body* carries issues or feelings like these. Without introductory steps like those above, our more routine, everyday body knowing can often be just too confusing, painful, or even terrifying to get near to. So, we not only disconnect from how most things feel inside, but eventually even refuse to relate to any of our body's language *(feelings)*. We deliberately choose *not* to answer the ringing phone of our feelings, either because we fear what the message might bring or find ourselves terrified even more by our catastrophic expectations of what might come for us as a future possibility.

Therefore, in this exercise, rather than triggering an old habit of disconnecting from familiar past trauma, events or relationships, you begin by entering directly into your body. Before any connections to the past can surface and trigger your old shutoff valves, notice whatever might feel uncomfortable *right now* without all this baggage from an earlier time. You begin by establishing a caring relationship with what first identifies itself as feeling annoying, uncomfortable, ill at ease, anxious, or not quite right in your body.

You begin developing a new habit of *relating with care* to any unwanted feeling or sensation that may surface in your body, and then start to get an inner sense that *you can actually do this.* Your already familiar instinct for being gentle and caring with a hurting child or pet can enable you to relate to your own body in this way. Of course, the more you practice this, the easier it gets. Just performing this simple act represents a huge step forward toward eventually living with a more balanced whole-body knowing, instead of only allowing inside whatever limited data your bottled-up fear will allow through the gate.

Right now, concentrate your attention upon a new way of relating to whatever physical or emotional discomfort is there, and turn your affection and caring toward how your body carries this. If there is some message waiting here, you will be available to listen as well as learn how to treat *all* your feelings that your body carries each day with attentive openness and respect. It takes time to develop such a new habit. But even if your uncomfortableness has little if any meaning or story within it, this simple exercise still offers you the opportunity to begin companioning your hurting body in a felt way that says, "I'm here with you just so you won't be alone, and to let you know that I care. If you want to share anything, I'm available to listen. If not, that's OK, too." Remember, it also takes time to develop mutual trust.

At this early stage in developing a new habit of noticing and nurturing your body's language, also try to become aware of how it actually feels inside to be caring with something difficult for your body to carry. For example, chronic pain, physical handicaps, difficulty breathing, etc. You will learn in time that no matter how severe or minor the ailment, this always has something important to teach you about situations and experiences that are *not* part of your script or list of how things *should be.* First, though, you develop a new habit in your body in order to change your relationship away from one of simply *enduring* or regarding it as an *annoyance* or even an *enemy.* Your goal is to grow in caring for how your body carries its discomfort, not as a nuisance or even an enemy but as a teacher of vital information about who you are, as well as *a friend* trying to tell you something you need to know. So, try to listen in an attentive, open and caring way.

The world of unsought or initially unwanted feelings all have an important role to play in your emotional and spiritual growth. If you can allow them to be your teachers and not turn them into nuisances or enemies, then they will offer an invitation and opportunity, a gift in fact, to bring love into your relationship to your own aching and needy body.

Relevance for Christian Faith

This workbook is all about laying a new foundation within your body's knowing for finding God in all things. But the hard work of growing into such faith experience will not arise solely because you acquire copious amounts of new information. Rather, this experience matures almost entirely within your growing capacity for presence (or *Presencing* as Otto Scharmer, Peter Senge and others have attempted to describe it earlier within the context of conflict-resolution and peacemaking). Furthermore, your primary foundation for learning and expressing presence in the world and in your relations with others lies in the quality of loving presence you learn to bring to your own body and feelings. If you cannot be kind, caring and supportive inside yourself, then how can you possibly presume that this capacity will magically appear in your dealings with others and the world around you? How our body carries the feelings we have about ourselves is the primary factor influencing all our relationships.

Throughout coming chapters you will learn how *congruence*, as a capacity for caring self-presence, relates to the quality of presence Jesus preached in his New Commandment when he said, "Love one another just as I have loved you." (Jn 13:34–35 JB) Over and over again, we will come back to this quality of *relationship* as the rich, interactive matrix within which the Presence of God in Christ appears. All the practical steps we teach in this book feed back into loving presence and into the human body as the source of our most intimate connection with one another *within* God. God is love, is *agápe*! Congruence, presence, *agápe*, the Larger Body, all represent bright, colorful strands woven together within a gifted garment of Greater Wholeness. Yet, when becoming aware of such unfolding wholeness, we first begin with baby-steps into a new, often unfamiliar language and experience that flows from our body's knowing. That's what the introductory exercises in this book are all about.

If as a Christian you believe that St. John's teaching in his First Epistle reveals a precious truth from God, then whenever you bring love into your relationship with any hurting place in your body you bring God into the relationship. For John writes, "God is Love. A person who dwells in love is dwelling in God, and God in that person." (1 Jn 4:16) The more we bring love into our all relationships, then John tells us that God's presence, *(agápe),* "...is brought to perfection within us." (1 Jn 4:12)

At its very core, therefore, Christian spirituality is meant to be a lifelong, organic, developmental process of noticing and nurturing your body's feelings as a doorway allowing the gift of God's *agápe* love to open your pores of loving presence toward all things. This includes the burden your own body often bears when carrying difficult feelings. As this develops into a habit in your body, the hidden depths and breadth of God's Presence can then break through in renewed and often surprising ways.

Living within this more *organic* way of habitually bringing love (God) into your relationship to difficult body-feelings does not mean you neglect consulting your doctor when necessary, nor do you omit using helpful medicinal support for some problem when this would facilitate healing.

What this new habit of noticing and nurturing feelings helps change is the attitude you carry around inside about pain. You learn a new respect and care, a listening to how your body tries to communicate with you in and through pain. Your loving presence offers an opportunity to bring God's healing Presence into your hurting body-relationship in and through your own loving presence.

All feelings, even when their origin is primarily from physical pain, such as in an accident or viral infection, will eventually include some emotional component, even if it's only how you feel *about* getting sick or enduring an accident. For example, you may become fearful about what this pain could develop into. You might feel annoyed or angry that a cold or headache has struck at an inconvenient time, given your busy schedule.

By acquiring the habit of noticing and nurturing your body's language, you begin learning how to move your awareness *inward* to help you hold *any* feelings around how you carry situations in your body. Developing the habit of bringing a caring presence to every uncomfortable feeling helps your body begin to trust that you will care for *all* feelings not just in good times but in tough times as well. Building such an attentive, trusting relationship will positively impact your body's natural healing process in many physical ways, reducing fear and providing a sense of being companioned and not alone. You become your body's most intimate friend and companion when you stop rejecting it by turning away from its language—feelings—whenever it hurts or is scared.

It is so important for parents to empower their children in this way, enabling them to realize that if they learn to take care of their bodies whenever they ache and their feelings whenever they hurt, they then invite God's love into their hurting body through and within their own loving presence. God can then become an integral felt body-experience within the healing process because, "A person who dwells in Love is dwelling in God and God in that person." (1 Jn 4:16) What an awesome gift to pass on to young children for the rest of their lives. Nothing could be more practical. Nothing will have more of an impact on them than falling in love with God in the very process of discovering themselves. This needs never to end.

Later on, during our senior years, this will pay off with extraordinary benefits within the life of faith. As the aches and pains of aging become integral to our daily routines, this habit of a loving, *caring presence* can bring a profound sense of peace as one of the deepest satisfactions in elder years when you feel your aging body being filled with the presence of God's love. You need never age alone! ■

Personal Notes

Chapter 6

The Master Key for Opening Up a Potential You Already Possess for Taking Care of Your Difficult Feelings

WITHIN THE DIFFERENT CULTURES and countries where we have worked, the two of us find, with rare exception, that people have developed *a habit* of treating their so-called negative feelings as though they were some sort of enemy, a threat to their well-being. As a result of this common perception, they have also evolved internal and external rituals, myths, art forms, initiation rites and even religious practices to help them somehow cope with or exorcize these enemies out of their lives. This common perception of our negative feelings invariably creates low self-esteem, guilt and knee-jerk reactions of helplessness and fear whenever such emotions surface.

Deciding to make a deliberate U-turn to embrace your body with *all* its important feelings, whatever these may be, does not happen overnight. It means developing a new habit of caring love for your own body bearing the burden of such stress-filled feelings. This involves learning and practicing a different *body-way* of relating to feelings we often label as *bad* or *negative* so that such old fears and helplessness no longer enslave us. Any religions we have ever come across, including our own Christianity, have totally neglected this most fundamental obstacle to human wholeness (and holiness) in their educational and formation programs—not to mention the development of their spirituality.

Until marriage preparation courses, parenting classes, formal schooling and formation for ministry programs can help free people from this pathologizing habit in their bodies, we can only talk the talk instead of putting our bodies where our good intentions may be by walking the walk toward greater inner freedom and human wholeness.

So, when trying to bring emotional health into Christianity, it is common to find patterns of deep inner conflict between stuck feelings in a person's body and *the ideal* being held up to them as a teaching of Jesus Christ. For example, Jesus is quoted as teaching: "I say to you, love your enemies." (Mt 5:43) Why does this raise such a problem? Because there is hardly a person alive who does not carry stuck feelings about some handicap, limitations, a debilitating disease or deep feelings about being verbally, emotionally, physically or sexually abused at some time in their lives.

Given the stuck or often even life-threatening feelings which inevitably arise from such traumas and humiliations, there can be little wonder that such a teaching feels hopelessly frustrating and impossible—especially after one carries around years of anger, hatred and a desire for revenge, along with the additional pain or suffering from problems which these unprocessed feelings then create within all their other relationships, most especially the relationship to their own physical body. Usually, such unhelpful responses are even more difficult and deeply patterned in their body-behavior because a person feels justified in their anger since the abuse, especially from another, when measured by any system of values, remains terribly wrong.

As a psychotherapist working primarily with Christians for decades, I (Ed) must have heard this plea hundreds of times:

> How can I ever change this habit of carrying anger and hate toward so and so…? How can I ever be a good Christian with these feelings in my heart? I've asked God to take away these feelings for years. I've tried to think it out of my body, forget all about it, etc., etc. … All to no avail.

We have not come across any Christian communities nor people from other religious traditions who do not need help in developing an inner body-process for internalizing their religious teachings on love. For Christians, the very heart of Christ's new commandment, along with development of a healthy prayer life that nourishes wholeness (holiness) in people, builds upon just such an embodied, personal integration.

The following pages in this chapter describe a shift, not only in perception but in the body-habit which all Christians, even young children, need to be companioned into developing so they can grow into the practice of an emotionally and, therefore, physically healthy Christian spirituality.

Nobody likes pain! We run from and avoid it, pushing away, trying to numb or distract ourselves from difficult feelings. This is especially true of the chronic pain we create in our bodies when we carry unprocessed hurts and fear around inside us. For many, a burdensome feeling is viewed as some sort of malevolent, alien force running wild inside our bodies. We want to control and subdue it, forever flushing it out of our systems. What, then, can help us to turn upside-down all these old perceptions and habits around how we treat our painful feelings? A few simple reminders may help you begin learning a new perspective.

Don't Throw the Baby Out With the Dirty Bath Water

Imagine, for a moment, that you find yourself standing with arms stretched out before you, pushing away whatever feeling you find inside that you don't like. Then, ask yourself, "What precisely is pressing against the palms of my hands that I'm so vehemently rejecting? What is the *abhorrent something* I'm straining to wring out of my system? Is it not my very own body itself expressing the burden of painful feelings from my past, the difficulty of present circumstances or some anxiety about what the future may hold for me? All such feelings express the language of my own body's consciousness. They represent a vital ingredient of my organic system of communication, yet I continually refuse to let this operate as it is meant to function."

Here are four learnings that may help you develop a new perspective.

- Every difficult feeling is really my own body responding in pain to the burden it carries. This is not some outside thing. It's really me! When I push away my feelings, I am rejecting my own flesh and blood.

- The question is not, "Can I be caring with a difficult feeling that I don't like?" Rather, I need to recognize the simple fact that my own body expresses discomfort and pain around some issue or circumstance in my life, past or present. The question, then, needs to be turned around and asked anew: "Can I be caring with *my own body hurting*, scared, lonely, confused, angry, jealous, put down...etc.?"

The Master Key for Opening Up a Potential

- Can I be gentle with my body suffering beneath this heavy load? Can I be a caring companion, walking a journey with my own body in its pain, inviting it to tell me its story? Can I begin sensing the possibility of an entirely different perspective and relationship that might emerge by trying something so simple as this? I'm being challenged *to create a new bond* right here and now with myself, with my own body bearing this emotional baggage. Would I neglect or abandon someone I love who is enduring such pain? How about giving some of this same caring attention to my own body?

- My painful feelings are really me, my own body crying out just as surely as it yells when I accidentally hit my thumb with a hammer. It does no good for me to yell back, *"Bad finger,"* just because it hurts. The issue for healing is never blaming myself or someone else for the accident. Blaming always misses the point. It skips around what actually needs to happen for healing to unfold or for wholeness to be restored *inside my own body*. My body hurts and needs me to companion it in these painful feelings with a physical presence that says, "I'm here. I care. I'm not going to abandon you. I'm listening when you are ready to tell me something."

The more relevant question here is not only, "How can I get rid of this?" but "What deeper message is my body trying to bring into my life today?" "Can I listen and be caring with the hidden story that waits to unfold from within my body's knowing?" But most of all, "Can I be caring with *the difficult feeling* that offers my most effective *doorway* into that felt inner meaning which calls out to be heard?"

The approach we teach in this book helps you to begin establishing a new kind of relationship to your painful feelings. However, entering fully into this relationship may mean dropping some misguided strategies which are *not* on-target.

The Paradox Hidden Within a New Perspective

Jesus taught a strange paradox to his disciples, as we read in the gospel of Matthew. Yet, one can only wonder how many among them were able to catch the full significance of what he shared that day in Capernaum when they asked:

> 'Who is the greatest in the kingdom of Heaven?' He called a child, set him in front of them, and said, 'I tell you this: unless you turn round and become like children, you will never enter the kingdom of Heaven. Let

a man humble himself till he is like this child, and he will be the greatest in the kingdom of Heaven. Whoever receives one such child in my name receives me. *(Mt 18:3–5 NEB)*

The Body-Learnings and exercises you experience in this book support you in an *inside turnaround*—much as Christ sought to generate a change in the perspective of his disciples and followers. The body-learnings invite you to own, to receive the vulnerable child who you really are within your relationships inside yourself as well as to the Loving Presence of God "in Christ," receiving Christ (*agápe*) in the very act of finding a new kind of strength and inner wholeness within the acknowledgment of your own weaknesses.

This hidden paradox, with its power to transform lives, is accurately portrayed in the tableaux of the Christmas creche with its vulnerable infant, if one has the eyes to see and ears to hear. It reflects the same paradox that Paul attempted to convey to us in his, "when I am weak then I am strong" metaphor—just as Christ teaches us through the inner knowing of metaphoric meaning within the Paschal Mystery of his own Crucifixion, Death and Resurrection. Such experience tells us something about an essential component in our own human journey into wholeness—our passage into becoming more fully who we are as very finite and limited, yet inspired, gifted, living membranes within the mystery of this Larger Body. We are meant to become a living paradox so that organic, creative change may occur within the experience of who we really are in our *agápe* presence *within one another* as well as *within ourselves*. Then our problems can be solved in new and previously unknown ways.

Psychologically and spiritually, such experience lies at the heart of what we are all called to become—more fully human in the Larger Body—especially if you call yourself a Christian. This radical conversion matures and nurtures your body-sense for the common good within your every relationship to all that sustains life on this gifting planet that we have been given.

Approaches That Get Us Off Track

- We are not suggesting that you must relive painful past incidents and experiences, acting out or purging your old feelings about them so you can change and grow beyond their influence. Cathartic release and tension reduction are never the same as learning to *process* the inner stories in your feelings.

- We are not saying that you must learn to like some person who has hurt you in the past as a way to make the residue of feelings they may have raised up inside you go away. The first step in restoring any broken relationship starts with *owning the real feelings inside yourself*. When such feelings can unfold and tell their stories, the resulting inner change in how your body carries them will then often come up with far better guidance toward a resolution around some situation or relationship than can any external moral or religious ideals imposed from outside on your unique relationship and feelings.

- We are not here suggesting that you must somehow force yourself to be kind to painful feelings as though they were unwanted, uninvited guests needing to be treated in a polite, hospitable, and friendly way.

- We are not embracing any form of the Mind-Cure Movement which in one way or another exhorts us to think positively by imagining everything as right or originally perfect, and then all will be well.

- Nor, finally, are we suggesting that you must put your arms around a difficult anger which you feel is justified. The issue here has nothing to do with whether your anger is well-founded or biased. It is simply asking yourself, "Can I notice how it feels in my body to be carrying the burden of this anger that so often repeats itself over and over again? Am I able to notice where I most feel this heavy weight in my body, and can I be *physically* present to it in a caring, listening and empathic way?"

The off-track approaches above try to *control* feelings, or *substitute* better feelings in place of those that are painful. They temporarily distract us from whatever hurts inside through activities that divert our attention away from what we need to care for in our bodies. However, such diversions never invite our hurt feelings to unfold their deeper felt meaning, their hidden inner stories.

Your resource for an inner change in your feeling lies right within the present moment, not in the past. As you began to learn earlier in this book, your real feelings *right here and now* are the doorway into what your body carries from the past or anticipates about the future. The outside triggering event or circumstance has either already occurred or not yet happened. Learning to care for your body here and now, developing a habit of noticing and nurturing your important feelings within the present moment, offers a healthy starting point from which you can then begin a journey into greater personal wholeness and integration. ■

Personal Notes

Chapter 7

A New BioSpiritual Way of Loving, Guided by Your Affection Teacher Through, '...the Eyes of Your Heart' (Ephesians 1:18)

THROUGHOUT THE HUNDREDS OF PROGRAMS we have given since the 1970's, we have faced an unmitigated challenge when setting out to help people grow beyond their stuck and difficult feelings. How could we help them discover a rich resource right inside their own bodies which would nurture an alternative habit to replace the unhealthy approaches they had learned as children from their parents or religion for escaping from difficult feelings? How could we develop a simple process and way of companioning young children that ordinary adults could easily learn and pass on to others?

What could we do to help parents, teachers and child caregivers set children on the right foot early in life so they might avoid developing habits of disconnecting from their important feelings? How could we help parents to develop healthy emotional habits different from the more problematic ways they may have been taught to deal with their own difficult feelings? And, more to the point, could emotional and spiritual health become a single, unified process, taught in the home and through religious education programs within the churches?

Remembering back to the days when we first started asking each other such questions as young Jesuits, the problems certainly felt like impenetrable walls. But once we stopped trying to figure everything out with our minds and, instead, learned to balance our headbrain thinking with listening to our own bodies from the inside as well, we realized that the answer to these questions lay in our entering into a new relationship with our own body's feelings. We found when doing this, that an even more surprising side-effect of such transforming interaction could reveal itself. An unexpected doorway opened into a spiritual universe one might never have imagined lay hidden there. Truly, the kingdom of heaven does lie within.

We found a barely yet explored universe of human feelings that offered a whole new frontier for spiritual exploration in our time. Also, as we shall soon see, especially within under-examined evidence about the human body hidden away within the Christian spiritual tradition, there lay even greater potential for expanding investigation. Evidence, which can create a fresh experience for Christians of our humanity *in Christ,* lies waiting to be explored within the *embodied* experience of noticing and nurturing our own inner world of felt-sensing.

Exploring Untapped Potential within Your Capacity for Affection

Working toward a transforming relationship to your feelings, the first body-learning we explored in this book was, *"Changing the Relationship to Your Own Body by Noticing Your Feelings and How You Treat Them."* Developing a new habit around this changed relationship means setting aside a few minutes each day to practice. For example, when you first wake in the morning, ask yourself, "What in my body right now most needs my loving presence?" Where do I most feel my body telling me to pay attention? Does anything stand out in my stomach, behind my eyes, neck muscles, tight shoulders, etc.? Can I say, "Hi," and let it know that I really feel this and am prepared to take a few moments just to own and be caring with how my body carries whatever is there? Can I respect and be present in an open enough way so if it wants to tell me something I need to know, I'll actually hear it?

Maybe I need to turn off the computer, TV, Twitter, Facebook, Ipods or music, put aside the magazine or phone so I can pay attention to the ways my body tries to tell me (through my feelings) how I really am inside.

Developing such a necessary noticing and nurturing routine will involve disciplining yourself enough that *a new habit* can gradually form. This means setting aside specific times to do this, perhaps even putting a sticky note on your desk or bedside lamp shade to remind you. It takes time to change an old habit of neglect. But the more you do this and your body begins to trust your sincerity and commitment, the more you will notice how good it feels to take care of your body and your feelings. It will become easier to practice these learnings regularly with routine daily care and deliberate connecting.

Rediscovering the Lost Body-Connection

In this chapter, we want to introduce a few practical suggestions for *nurturing* your important feelings. By *important* we simply mean whatever feelings you notice your body asking you to care for because they upset, worry, frustrate or scare you. This can also include experiences of physical pain and how you carry feelings *about* having such pain, as well as feelings about a life's call, a creative project, a dear friend's illness, a long-awaited vacation, etc.

Important feelings always carry some mostly hidden sense of information, story or hidden meaning that tries to attract your attention. You get a headache, a backache, diarrhea, difficulty breathing, stomach ache, unbidden tears. All such physiological signs call out through your body's language, demanding that you notice, *listen to and take care of* how your body carries some hidden messages. Feelings like this alert you through symptoms which we all try to numb or run away from before their story and message can get through to us.

After years of neglect and a deliberate deadening through all manner of often addictive habits that defensively push your more difficult feelings out of sight, all of us need more than just *a good intention* in our minds to develop this new habit of taking care of our own body and its feelings. Developing a mental attitude in your head of being kind, caring, gentle and open expresses only a small part of what these feelings need. In order to develop a new habit of being *physically* and not merely mentally present to feelings, you need to discover an additional resource within your own body that will enable you, gradually, to replace an old habit of disregarding or pushing your feelings out of the way with something new and different. For this reason, we now introduce the memory and experience of what we call, "your Affection Teacher."

An Affection Teacher Exercise

Let's begin by creating a situation that will invite you to better notice where and how your body responds with an empathic and more caring presence.

■

Imagine the following: You are attending a group meeting. A nurse from a nearby hospital phones. A few hours earlier the police have brought an abandoned newborn to the emergency room The nurses and doctors have stabilized the infant's condition. But the nurse has a feeling that if the baby is not held with the physical presence of loving care during the next few hours he may not survive. Short-staffed, the emergency room cannot spare anyone to do this.

The nurse inquires whether a couple of people at the meeting can each spend an hour or so after the meeting to give the newborn this care. You decide to volunteer.

Now, imagine that you arrive at the hospital and a nurse hands you the baby. How would you communicate without words through your body holding the infant that:

"You're not alone. I'm here. I care. Please live.

You're precious. You're safe in my arms."

Remember, the rational understanding of words you might say matter little. The *body-feel* of your caring presence behind the words must say to his little body:

"Live. Keep breathing. You're wanted."

This little infant desperately calls out for the physical body-feel of a loving, life-giving, life-desiring, and enhancing presence coming from some person, like yourself; a person capable of physically communicating with him in his scary, lonely, abandoned, first experience outside the womb. This newborn needs to feel wanted enough in this frightening new world to make an effort to live.

(Take some time to sense how your body responds to the baby's need before continuing.)

Allow yourself a moment now to close your eyes, growing quiet inside, and letting your attention notice that your body already knows how to communicate a caring presence through your hands, arms, fingers, open chest, quality of your voice, muscles and breathing.

Can you imagine being with your own hurting feelings just like you were inside when holding the infant? The feelings you push away and deny, or treat like enemies need to experience your caring touch and *physical* presence, just as much as the abandoned baby does in order to trust and begin sharing their stories with you. Your own Affection Teacher can guide you in learning how to do this.

(Allow time to do this before continuing.)

Extending the Exercise

For a moment, simply notice whether your body might be feeling anything about the exercise you just did. If a particular emotion or sensation inside calls out to be heard, then pay attention to where you most feel this in your body.

In a caring way, imagine yourself physically holding your own body, along with whatever feeling most needs listening to, just as you would hold the abandoned infant. Let this feeling place inside know that you are available and listening. Carefully pay attention in case your body wants to tell you something of its story or meaning through words, tears, a memory, an image, whatever. Notice whether any feelings arise around your experience of just taking the time to be more open with whatever surfaces inside you. Allow a moment to do this before continuing with your reading below. ∎

Most people have more of this caring body-potential than they might ever imagine. This is important for all of us because our capacity for caring presence can also teach us how to love the scared, lonely, abandoned, or confused feelings inside ourselves which we so often run away from. When you bring this same *physical presence* of caring love to your own body in distress, you actually bring the gift of God's healing, life-giving-love-*agápe* into your needy feelings as they cry out for some loving care. Caring body-presence can bring a frozen feeling back to life when good intentions in your mind just sound like more talking heads. Learning how to re-ignite this inner physical spark of caring presence opens your body so you can begin to discover who you really are becoming in God's love through the gift of this interaction with your own body's feelings.

As you work your way through this book, routinely allow your feelings an opportunity to be heard, respected and balanced in with your reading and reflecting. In this way, you invite your body's responses to become an integral part of your reading experience.

Learning from Your Affection Teacher

In the preceding exercise with the abandoned baby, you began turning your attention toward the physical language of how your body communicates a willingness to connect, to care, to be open, participating, available, vulnerable, and bringing a loving presence. Your body says, "I want you to live, eat, breathe, grow strong. You are precious and lovable."

In much the same fashion you can bring a body-way of respecting and caring for a hurting, lonely feeling inside yourself. "You're precious and lovable. I want to hear your story. I'm listening and won't abandon you. I care enough to go inside and wait with you." Hopefully, with practice you will sense an entirely new potential for being present to your own feelings in so simple an exercise.

For example, when lovingly holding a baby, your skin and the baby's becomes porous, so to speak, allowing some special quality of *felt presence* to flow back and forth between the two of you. You don't just physically hold the baby as you might carry an inert sack of potatoes from your car into the kitchen. You connect in a totally different way from *inside your body*—expressing a quality of caring, felt presence that somehow involves far more than just a simple intention in your mind.

Consider another example. Have you ever been caught out in the open during a sudden thundershower or downpour? Do you notice how you often pull your coat or sweater around your neck, perhaps even trying to tighten up your skin in an effort to stay dry? When holding a hurting child or frightened little animal, however, the tone of your body and skin softens. This stark contrast may be physically felt. Your quality of *body-presence* becomes more open and engaged—like when you're walking in the rain without an umbrella and eventually get so soaked that you *give up* holding your skin tight and trying to stay dry. You feel your tight body relax and just enjoy walking in the rain, maybe even deliberately stomping in a puddle or two.

Looking at all this from another perspective, have you ever paused to consider that you can never simply grunt up a feeling of affection whenever you choose to do so? It takes some immediate here-and-now interaction or a strong memory to surface your Affection Teacher into awareness. You may think about affection abstractly, but you can never command your body's felt awareness to appear on demand any more than you can deliberately *will* or force a goose bump to rise up on your arm or a chill run up and down your spine. You need the cute, cuddly puppy chewing away on your shoelace, your sweet child hugging your leg, or the embrace of a loving spouse, parent, or friend. Affection arrives quietly, more like a wandering breeze or a gentle grace blessing you on your journey through life.

When visiting someone in the hospital, too ill, weak or medicated for verbal talk, recall how you instinctively reach out with your arms and hands, letting *your body* express your caring presence as you share a warm caress or embrace. In much the same manner, your own body and feelings often reveal a precious part of yourself calling out like a baby or an aging loved one, pleading with you to take care of them by noticing and nurturing their increasingly muted attempts to catch your attention. Your own Affection Teacher can guide you in learning how to do this.

Lessons from My Grandmother's Lap

For Ed, many different Affection Teachers have come into his life just when he needed their help in order to become more whole and find God in this process. Here are two examples.

> When I began my church supervised training for the priesthood I entered a Jesuit novitiate after graduating from University and one year of graduate school. My relationship with God had always been important to me from childhood. I welcomed going from public schools onto a Catholic university campus because I hoped I would learn more about my faith as well as find an atmosphere there that would make it easier for me to grow closer to God. It did. But not in the way I had anticipated.
>
> In the heady schedule of endless lectures, religion turned out to be more of the same, except for some off-campus ministries and daily Mass. But in the convenient, centrally located, usually deserted chapel or along the many garden paths, I found an opportunity to rest my weary mind. This helped me bring balance into my life. There I could notice and nurture whatever felt important for me to be with in God's Presence. Only when I experienced very difficult feelings did I find it hard to stay with them, or heard myself asking God to fix or take them away. I knew of no other way to connect God with these so-called *negative* feelings.
>
> Then one day, while sitting in the chapel during one of these struggles with difficult feelings, out of the blue I remembered how much easier it

had been *not to push away* my scary feelings as a child when I was snuggled up on either of my grandmothers' laps. So, I tried right there in the chapel to hold my confused and painful feelings as best I could with that same warm, open, available, loving presence my grandmas had created within and around me as a little boy.

What really surprised me was discovering that it didn't seem hard to do, even though my grandmas were no longer around. Once I turned my attention back to how I had felt on their laps years earlier, my body remembered it all very clearly. To my amazement, it felt so much better to be with my feelings, even those I didn't like, in this more caring way. Everything seemed to loosen up inside, and I felt more whole and connected. I must have remained there for quite some time, just enjoying being present to my difficult feelings in this new and unusual way.

While I was doing this, something my mother had said to me as a child then popped in and it, too, felt somehow connected with my troubled feelings. Her words from the past felt like a fresh direction to follow at that time. The entire situation I was struggling with then changed and felt entirely different inside my body than it had just a half hour earlier. I went back to the dorm fascinated and grateful for what just happened.

From that time on, what I had labeled for myself as *the feel of my grandmas' laps* became my Affection Teacher, a teacher to whom I would return many times in order to hold in a loving way any difficult feelings I didn't want to listen to or found myself pushing away.

My experience over the years has been that when the going gets more difficult than usual, often a new Affection Teacher arrives on the scene to help me over the difficult bumps. I have learned to welcome these new teachers as an integral part of my prayer life. I reverence them as sacred gifts, unique, personal metaphors from my own lived experience, inviting and teaching me how to love my body carrying feelings I don't want to approach.

One such occasion surfaced years later around a stroke I had experienced while giving a series of workshops across the U.S. and Canada. I didn't realize at the time how serious this had been. The event was misdiagnosed while on the trip, and not fully recognized until I returned home for further medical exams in California. I kept thinking that once I was finally home and rested, that my multiple vision,

Rediscovering the Lost Body-Connection

dizziness, and inability to walk without help would improve and return to normal.

After resting a few days when I got home, a beautiful sunny morning invited me to venture out into the garden. But no sooner would I begin to weed or prune than I would lose my balance, falling over into the garden and decorative rocks. Gardening, planting, or redesigning a new area of the yard was a long-awaited project I had been looking forward to for weeks. Now, it not only felt dangerous, but as though I had just lost one of the healthiest, most creative links I had to beauty and spiritual growth with my body. I felt devastated and hopeless inside. Then, when I went into the house and sat down at my typewriter, I couldn't even focus my eyes on the notes when moving my head from the typed page in the machine to the notes on the desk. The whole experience felt like life was falling apart for me. All I could do was just sit there and weep.

After awhile, I got up and went into the bedroom to finish unpacking. While hanging up some clothes in the closet, suddenly a large plastic bag on a high shelf filled with childhood stuffed animals came loose and fell open on the floor. Out spilled a bundle of childhood memories, like a handful of cards thrown on the table before me. And, right there on the floor, face up was the most special one himself, the most beloved, most esteemed of all my assorted menagerie of favorite childhood animals—my teddy bear. Along with Raggedy Anne and Andy, there was Teddy looking straight into my eyes as he always did when I talked to him and told him my troubles as a little boy. Why, I wondered, had my frail, aging mother months before cleaned out the family attic and given me this circus of stuffed animals I once had loved so much? I recalled telling her, reluctantly, "I don't have any storage space for them." Her response was immediate, simple and direct. "You'll need them some day. Too much love has gone into them to throw them away."

As I stood there looking at Teddy and then picking him up, I could sense throughout my body how it once had felt to put my arms around him, holding and loving him so intensely that I wore all his fur off and Mom had to make little trousers and shirts to protect his stuffing from my vigorous affection. The memory oozed out so intimately that it felt like only yesterday when he lay on the pillow beside me with my arm around him, drifting off to sleep together. And then, of course, I knew what was happening. Teddy was again coming back into my life, teaching me how to love the pain and despair I then carried in my body. Mom was right. I did need him, and so would many other adults who once upon a time loved a special doll or teddy bear and now needed to know this teacher was also still alive and well in their bodies, waiting to be called upon.

These beloved dolls and pets recall such a treasure chest of lost jewels, often at the very center of our undiscovered, personal metaphors which draw us into our own body *in Christ* as we discover the biology of Christian prayer and faith.

So you, too, can bring back your dormant Affection Teachers to help you learn how to love, just as Teddy did for me. Not with the love we had as children for our stuffed animals, but with our bodies now as they can learn to use this great inner gift of affection—so essential to physical, emotional and spiritual health—to teach us how to love and respect ourselves bearing the burdens around a lifetime of hurts, uncertainties, fears, and losses. All the groaning and growing that brings our love to fulness and completion in the Body of Christ, our bodies, is meant to nurture our self-awareness as living cells of His Body.

The Christ we learn to love and never abandon or betray is the Christ in ourselves and in others—betrayed, on the cross, in the garden's agony, forsaken by his friends, stripped, humiliated, and beaten. This *Christ-in-ourselves,* inside all those inside feelings we run from and avoid, is the Christ that our habit of noticing and nurturing such feelings in our own bodies reveals to us today—the Christ-within-us.

Learning the practical, physical details of how to love ourselves carrying the burden of all these feelings in our bodies is the basic curriculum in the school of Christian love. We are meant to feel this Loving Presence as a child in our families, and this childhood pain, lovingly companioned by our caregivers, offers a graced invitation to continue such learning for the rest of our lives. Such experience helps to make so much more sense out of the many questions we have about pain and suffering, and their relationship to God in our lives. God has already given, and will continue to provide you with Affection Teachers that can help you learn how to love your own hurting body because God is that loving relationship and your suffering body already is a living cell within the Body of the Whole Christ.

So, what I did was to take Teddy back to my desk, where looking at him helped me remember the feel I had in my body when I hugged him.

Then, closing my eyes, I would put my arms around my chest, holding my scared, helpless hurting and dizzy body just like I once held Teddy. Not trying to fix anything or ask God to heal me, I just brought love to my body carrying all my burden of discouragement, loss and pain.

It wasn't long before the words came, "Try a new way of using the typewriter to finish your book." So, I picked up the first page of my notes next to the typewriter and put them directly in front of me on the typewriter where I wouldn't need to turn my head to read them. Then, I quietly and thoughtfully read through them, putting them back on the desk when finished. Afterwards, I closed my eyes, typing what felt like it was the right way to express my notes.

It worked. The book, *Beyond the Myth of Dominance: An Alternative to a Violent Society*,[1] which I had been trying to complete for about five years was done in four months, and my body also healed very quickly.

Every time we try to love our hurting selves burdened with difficult feelings, God dwells within us. As St. John wrote: "God is *agápe* (love) and a person who dwells in love dwells in God and God in that person." (1 Jn 4:16) This, then, is how we find God in all things. Again, John writes in his first letter, the more we grow in love within all our relationships, "His *agápe* presence *is brought to perfection within us.*" (Jn 1, 4:12).

So, a first step in the radical reformation that Christian spirituality so desperately needs, requires that each of us return to our body's memories of this gift of affection, discovering there the embodied relationships that your physical organism still carries as potential Affection Teachers.

Why is it so important to discover your own personal Affection Teacher? Because your major stumbling block to spiritual growth, as well as developing your own continuing creativity, self renewal and growth in self-esteem throughout all your relationships, including both emotional and physical health, happens to be *fear.* Fear can become so deeply lodged in your body that only another equally powerful body-habit will eventually melt and invite it to change. Discovering your Affection Teacher greatly assists your body in learning the nurturing response to how it carries feelings of fear.

In the language of psychology, the body-experience of your Affection Teacher draws you into the world of relationships — even if in the beginning it's just wanting to hold, pet, and hug a little bunny rabbit, puppy, or doll because it feels like your body needs to care and love. We must learn to recognize such ordinary, everyday experiences as part of *a developmental process in your body*, a process eventually maturing into a quality of presence named *agápe,* in the Scriptures, in its more fully matured expression. Affection, then, becomes your body's doorway, an early developmental, physical point of entry into the greater mystery of *agápe*. And *agápe*, even in its very limited, yet tangible, accessible Presence of God *as a relationship of love*, felt and expressed in the Body of Christ, through, with and in our own bodies, becomes integral to *rediscovering the lost body-connection in Christian prayer and faith.*

Eventually, this early body-sense can develop into an experience of entering more consciously within another person, companioning them in how they feel inside. Dr. Carl Rogers discovered that this experience generates *an empathic presence* and *unconditional acceptance* which others can sense in a bodily-felt way. They feel themselves *no longer alone* in your presence. They experience *being fully received*. They sense that you care for and are truly present *with/in* them. You do not remain so absorbed within your own world of concerns or preoccupied inside your head with personal issues that you cannot really be physically present and available to them.

Empathic presence and unconditional acceptance say non-verbally, "You are lovable." This experience becomes the powerful gift you bring to your own neglected body and often rejected feelings. No wonder such body-knowing became the very description of God which St. John uses in his First Letter quoted above. In the body-knowing of your own lovableness, self-identity grows, along with a capacity for sharing this same gift with others. You learn to love your own abandoned, lonely, scared, often hurting feelings. You find yourself plunged into the pastoral missing link in Christianity—an experience of the *raw biology* of Christian faith. And such *body-connecting* experience, finally, makes it possible to travel the path of Christ's teaching—"I say to you, love your enemies."

Ed's Story of Yet Another Affection Teacher that may Call Forth the Body-Feel of One in Your Own Life

A powerful Affection Teacher surfaced for me from an incident at a summer camp for grade school children that was owned and run by my family. One day we received a call from a first grade teacher, asking whether we could include a little girl from her class. The teacher went on to explain that earlier in the year this child had come home from school, opened the front door and called out, "Mommy, I'm home." As she closed the door and looked up the steep stairs to the second floor, she saw her mother, still in her bathrobe, hair uncombed, who had just slashed her wrists in a suicide attempt. She was on her way from the bathroom to her bedroom when the little girl had come in as she passed the top of the stairs. Turning toward the sound of her daughter's voice she fainted and tumbled down the stairs, landing at the little girl's feet, blood all over her and her robe. The child ran screaming into the street as neighbors rushed over to help.

Her mother recovered. But the child had not spoken a word since that terrible experience. Seven or eight months had passed before we received the call, during which time every child healing resource had been made available, but to no avail. Nothing had brought forth a single word from this little girl. Her family's finances were at rock bottom, the teacher told us, so we would have to cover the costs ourselves if we took her, hopefully for the usual two weeks on our ranch in the Sierra Nevada mountains of California.

My mother was a former elementary teacher, Dad, a rancher with only a high school education, my sister was in high school and I, only 20, in college with no experience as a therapist, not even a course in psychology at the time. But we agreed to take the child, making it clear that we, our staff, and the camp were not trained in recovery from this type of trauma. The teacher agreed personally to come and get her if it didn't work out. But she emphasized her belief that getting the girl out of her home and away from so many helpers into a loving family in a fun atmosphere with other kids might help.

Every evening, we made sure she was tucked into bed, kissed, and hugged goodnight by my sister, cuddled into Dad's lap every night at the campfire, and taken by the hand from his lap afterwards along with another little girl who was her *buddy* back to her tent so she would never be alone in the dark. There was always someone with her on any walks away from the main buildings. My Mom in the craft room saw to it there was a lot of tactile contact with her while reading stories, playing games, and during times when there was discussion and sharing together.

After about a week of such constant loving presence and care, I had her by the hand on a hike with a dozen or so other kids. We were collecting wild flowers, cones, and pine needles to weave when all of a sudden without any warning she started to sob and screamed out, "I want my mommy!" It somewhat frightened the other kids, who thought she had been quiet simply because she was shy. By now, however, they were familiar with the *homesick* thing and over most of it, so they were beginning to wonder about her silence. I told the children and other counselors to continue on their walk. I would stop for a while with her, and we would either catch up with them or meet later back at the camp.

Instinctively I knew how important those first words and her crying were. She had done neither since that terrible afternoon so many months before. So, I gently led her over to a big pine tree and sat down, leaning up against the tree and inviting her to sit on my lap if she wanted. She did, and I put my arms around her as she lay her little head against my heart. Then I said, "Let's be quiet together so we can take care of that place inside you that wants your Mommy. It's a very precious place and needs us to be kind to it and love it." As I was directing her attention inside her body, I noticed that the sobbing began to diminish. I could feel her attention going inward, so I asked her where in her body she most felt, "I want my Mommy?"

She moved her tiny hand over and placed it on her heart. I said, "If it's OK with you, I'll put my hand there too, and we can both be with that special, precious place where you feel, 'I want my Mommy.' Let's just be quiet together and let it know that we are listening to it and taking care of it."

By now, the crying had completely stopped and we were both inside with that scared and hurting little heart. I don't remember how long we both sat silently leaning against that tree, nor which one gifted the other the most. I do know that almost 60 years later, when I need to be with scary and hurting places inside myself, the physical feel of holding that child against my heart with my arms around her so my loving heart could touch her wounded little body in its pain went to the top of my list of Affection Teachers. It's always ready to serve at a moment's notice as though the experience happened only yesterday.

Rediscovering the Lost Body-Connection

After a bit, I felt her grow a little restless, like something was finished. So, I said, "What does that place in your body want you to do now? Shall we go back to camp or catch up with the rest of the kids?" Before I hardly had the words out of my mouth, she spoke her first words in months without any hesitation, "I want to go on the walk with the rest of the kids." From that point on she continued to talk at camp and calls from her teacher at school that Fall reported that she was again fitting into class very well, and continuing to grow and learn like the rest of the children.

For me, what happened that day set my life on a journey to understand more fully what it means to be *wholly present* in a loving way both to ourselves and one another. I became fascinated with the gifting power of healing love in our bodies. How was this connected with some Greater Living Presence and Power expressed through our caring for ourselves, each other, and all living things? From this remarkable incident I felt drawn like a magnet to better understand and experience more fully St. Paul's understanding of our embodiment as living cells within the groaning Larger Body of Christ. St. John's description of God as *agápe* love was obviously a quality of presence in relationship. I came to realize that what I am now calling, your Affection Teacher, is your body's doorway for finding answers to the mystery of what it means to be human and how to grow more whole in Christ from within our bodies as they are felt from inside.

Decades Later an Affection Teacher Returns

As a result of degenerative osteoarthritis of the spine and several surgeries, I often get intense muscle spasms in my legs whenever I suddenly roll over in my sleep. If that occurs in the middle of the night, I may have an intention in my mind to be caring and present to my leg in it's agonizing pain, because I really believe in this approach. But when the pain becomes so intense and gripping that I can only be there to fix and not to companion it, that narrowed perspective then takes over and my pain usually gets worse.

After a few of these episodes I realized this scenario was likely to repeat itself for the rest of my life. So, I turned my problem into an opportunity for further learning. Fortunately, I could draw upon the Affection Teacher experience I just told you about because it was so real to me. I was easily able to recall the inside body-feel of holding the little girl against my heart, and instinctively knew physically how to companion my body suffering these spasms with a quality of felt presence that said, "I'm here. I'm not going to leave you. I really care about how badly you hurt."

Such experiences taught me that I have an empathic, compassionate teacher inside me, a physical sense of caring presence which could then be called upon not only to help others, but as a support to help guide me with my own inside hurting places—both emotional and physical. Over time I came to realize that this process of healing would occur only when I was able to bring my own physically-felt caring presence to these muscle spasms, with no hidden agenda to control, fix anything or ask God for relief. From that point on in my prayer, I have never again used God to make things work the way I want them to work. It feels so dishonest and disrespectful of what I experience as God's intimate presence in everything that goes on in my life as long as I am present to companion with love, and not to fix or use God in order to get my own agenda accomplished.

I already knew how to be this way with my so-called *negative feelings*. But the sudden, overwhelming *physical pain* in my legs at night would catch me off-guard, triggering my old knee-jerk reaction of turning the muscle cramps into an enemy that must immediately be pushed away or fixed. Eventually, I discovered for myself a novel approach to this dilemma of the sudden, intense spasms.

Every night before going to sleep, I repeat several times a little mantra-like prayer that helps remind me that if I suddenly feel the spasms, this is just like the pain in that little girl, and all parts of me need to come together to care for one another. So I say, "May the Lord (meaning God's Loving Presence in Christ's Body) be with us as we try to take care of each other." I must confess that this is a prayer I now routinely say not only before bed but at times during the day as more of the aches and pains of aging come into my life. I no longer believe in misusing prayer in order to badger God into fixing all the things *I think* need fixing, including my aging body. Instead, I only ask that I, or the person for whom I am praying, may find and grow closer to God in all things.

Now, whenever the muscle spasms suddenly hit or any other pain arises, I imagine my leg (or wherever the pain may be) as that little girl,

Rediscovering the Lost Body-Connection

while I move my presence where it may be needed in the same physically loving way that I was with her. I have found, often within seconds or perhaps a minute at most, that the muscle spasms begin to release and my leg relaxes. Using this same approach with either physical pain or feelings, or even post-surgical wounds, I can sense an increase in circulation, warmth, and an enhanced sense of well-being in the area where I simply bring this quality of loving presence into the wounded part of my body several times a day. Clearly, this has assisted my physical healing process and brought greater emotional integration and wholeness into my life.

My sense for God in the experience of such caring presence continues to grow, whether or not any kind of healing I might prefer takes place. The way I carry physical pain certainly has been changing with the help of various Affection Teachers. Sometimes, even if physical healing occurs, this seems less important than the growth of my experience of Christ's presence and the change in attitude toward suffering that is unfolding within me. It feels like the whole of my humanity is being set free and will never again feel alone.

From my living experience I would say, for someone beginning to learn this process, that what has helped me the most is just learning to be with a hurting inside place in a physical, caring way rather than one of always trying to fix it or ask God to fix it. With a quiet inner presence, you can talk to your body in pain, taking responsibility for your part in this, expressing to your body how sorry you are that it hurts so much. Allow your pain-filled place to know you won't neglect or abandon it. Promise to be a good friend, remaining as long as it needs you. All this lets you stay with your hurting places in a new way. The pain in your body acts like a tangible *handle* that your capacity for loving can hang on to in order to keep you there with it. Period.

I have found, over time, that the most important lesson I have learned through nurturing both pain and painful feelings by using my Affection Teachers is that the relationship to all my feelings has changed and grown into one of caring and respect. Trust has grown from this quality of presence. It becomes the vital ingredient helping me to mature beyond old habits of learned responses about always relating to almost everything, including my own feelings, in order to gain new skills of control. It was so easy to sprinkle holy water, so to speak, over the entire control-game in order to make it Christian and convince myself that it was God's will that I lobby Him to fix me according to my script.

In summary, then, two important learnings have emerged for me from the experiences that I have been graced with in finding "Affection Teachers" in my body's relationships:

(1) Your Affection Teacher can become the practical, physically felt, Loving Presence of God in your own body that will help you replace old *fix-it-and-control-it-habits* which were often the way we were taught to pray.

(2) Your Affection Teacher also brings God (*agápe-love*) through your loving relationship to your own body into the Body of God-with-us, Christ. This is something you can tangibly *feel* right within the heart of everyday experiences without always needing to *think* God into them. You bodily-feel the process of change into more wholeness (holiness) as this happens.

   This gift of Affection-Teacher-presence has brought me to the practical, daily contemplative prayer life for which I have always yearned. It unveiled what had consistently drawn me to Christianity. Here, finally, was the missing link in my own spiritual life, an *embodied keystone* always left out of the Christian spirituality I had been taught.

A Brief Summary: Why are We Asking You to go into Your Own Experience of 'Affection Teachers?'

Memories invariably lead into your own body's knowing. Their roots thrust deep within your physical organism. Your Affection Teacher pulls you out of your head thinking and into your body's memory of physically being loving, caring and affectionate. With this felt memory of empathic presence experienced from inside your own body, you can then *physically* try to bring that same caring presence to how your body now carries your current hurting experience of fear, loneliness, sadness, anger, pain or whatever. Such memories of affection can rise up as cogent teachers and metaphors for you. Affection thrives in your body. It drinks from the wellspring of your own life experience, your embodied interconnections.

Exercise: Time to Recall an Affection Teacher of Your Own

What memories of affection stand out for you right now? Can you recall special moments when you expressed such nurturing. These experiences began to lay down a pattern in your body, a design that can now stand as a marker, a living reminder that you already know what affection feels like and how to do it. But how far back must you travel in order to discover your mentor? Some recent incident? A warm and tender moment? Was it only yesterday, or must you dig way back into the past, perhaps loving a favorite pet, a doll, your mom, dad or one of your own children as a baby or in school—or even the kitten or puppy you recently adopted as you hold and care for it in a loving way?

Allow yourself a few moments, now, for remembering. As you do this, note carefully how the memory felt in your body then, and how it feels in your body now. Ask yourself, "Do any memories feel like they could be an Affection Teacher for me the next time I need to hold a feeling I want to push away?"

Take time to sit with this question in your own way, spending a quiet moment in gratitude for the gift of whatever teachers your memory may bring. And if none should arrive, then be especially gentle and caring with how you feel about that. This realization, too, will have an unheard tale to tell, a story still needing to feel the embrace of some further caring presence before finally being able to unfold from within and begin sharing the felt meaning it contains. The more you practice noticing important feelings, trying to hold them in a caring way, Affection Teachers have a way of showing up to help unexpectedly. ■

Personal Notes

Chapter 8

Daily Check-In Exercises for Noticing and Nurturing Your Important Feelings and Helping Others to Do the Same

Some Helpful Guides for Companioning Yourself and Others

IN CHAPTER 5 you began easing into steps through a caring relationship with ordinary, everyday physical and emotional discomforts in your body. At this point in the workbook, we make available various formats of these same steps in order to familiarize you with additional options so you can choose which one feels the most helpful, either when working with yourself alone or when companioning another person or a group. We also include in this chapter a page titled, *Suggestions for Developing in Very Young Children the Habit of a Caring Presence for Their Important Feelings*. A second format for older children and teens is called, *Helping Children to Develop the Habit of Noticing and Nurturing Their Important Feelings*.

Both children and adults will generally find it easier to bring a caring presence first to their own bodies when they experience hurting or scary feelings before they can then bring a nurturing, listening presence to the actual feelings themselves. So, it becomes easier in the beginning to let our Affection Teachers guide us in being gentle with and kind to our own bodies carrying those feelings. After all, the feeling is really my own body trying to talk to me. So, can I listen in a way that allows some deeper story to unfold? How is my body trying to talk to me through this feeling? What is it trying to tell me? Can I be present inside my body in a way that allows it to tell me its story through my feelings—and, ultimately, through my deeper felt-sensing of more visceral felt meanings which arise from this caring, *agápe* relationship?

In the next few pages you will find various card formats outlining steps that support this process of noticing and nurturing. A master for printing these cards in a smaller size may be downloaded and printed from our website at *http://www.biospiritual.org* without charge. You might think of these cards as starters which support you in getting a feel for the road, so to speak, as you begin establishing a new kind of relationship with your own body and feelings or help others to do the same with theirs. Once you develop a sense for how to companion yourself and others you will gradually find your own words for doing this and won't need the cards any more. The simplest way for this to happen is to use some format daily, regularly setting aside time for noticing and nurturing what your body tells you most needs listening to. The teacher waits inside you. All you need do is to just start listening, caring and learning until you no longer need a card because the habit of noticing and nurturing is now in your body.

In order to develop a more environmental sense for ourselves as being integral membranes of something greater than ourselves—for many of us an entirely radical, new kind of personal identity—then we need to learn simple, entry-level steps for gaining access to such experience. For example, most of us at sometime in our lives fall into the dead-ended trap of blaming outside circumstances or other people for our difficult feelings. But in the final analysis we alone can assume personal responsibility for growing beyond stuck feelings. Blaming does not facilitate your personal wholeness. That sobering realization can mark the beginning of a dramatic change in how we relate to our own bodies and our feelings.

As already mentioned earlier, it helps to learn this process together with another person or with a small group. The mutual support for one another and building of community which can occur offers a steady support setting within which it becomes easier to begin learning a new habit in your body and building a new kind of relationship both to yourself and with others.

Our first card, *The Basics of a Personal Check-In (facing page)*, gives you the essential wording needed by those becoming more familiar with the process through regular practice and for whom too many words are unnecessary and distracting. The page titled, *If You Get Stuck* (page 77), suggests questions you can direct toward your own body in order to help pull your attention into how your body actually carries a particular feeling—not just what you may think about it.

These questions sometimes sharpen the body-sense of how you are carrying a particular feeling so you can then, in a caring way, hold how it feels using your Affection Teacher as an internal guide for encouraging a more caring relationship.

N.B. This card may be used by you alone, or for companioning another. *Italicized texts in ( ) are added directions you speak when companioning another.* **Be sure to end your companioning directions with:** *("Let me know if anything further comes along ...')* like another word, image, memory or feeling that fits the way this all feels in your body right now. Bracketed texts [ ] are instructions for you that don't need to be spoken.]

The Basics of A Personal Check-In

1. GROWING QUIET AND GOING INSIDE

Take a moment to close your eyes, growing quiet inside, and allowing your attention to settle into the center of your body. [If companioning someone, add:] *"Say OK when you're ready to go further."* **[pause]**

2. NOTICING & NURTURING

Now ask yourself: "What in my body right now needs my loving presence?" *(Let me know if something identifies itself.)* **[pause]**

Take time now to notice where you feel it the most in your body. *(Let me know ...)* **[pause]**

As you stay with whatever has identified itself, try to hold and be present to it in a way that says, "I'm here ... I care ... I'm not going to leave you alone ... I'm listening if you want to say anything." Let your Affection Teacher guide you in creating a loving presence.

If it helps, put your hand on the place where you carry this feeling, especially if it hurts, letting your hand also say, "I'm here. I really am trying to be with you."

(If something comes that feels connected inside, like a word, an image, a memory, tears or another feeling—then let me know.) **[pause]**

4. RECYCLING

[When a bodily-felt link, like a memory, word, tears, etc. comes, then if companioning another, and they share it, respond by reflecting back their word or symbol saying:] "Stay with how you now carry the whole thing inside. Allow time to hold it with care, noticing if it feels any different. Sense whether any further symbols might want to come and bring more links." *(Let me know if anything comes ...)* **[pause]**

(1)

Keep nurturing & recycling as long as your inner story still wants to unfold and you have time to be with it. *(Let Me know ...)*

[If you or the person you are companioning gets stuck—read the next section. If you want to stop, go to 4. ENDING]

IF YOU OR THE ONE YOU COMPANION GETS STUCK

Sometimes, asking your body questions like the following may help:

1) "How does the worst of this feel in my body?"
2) "What needs to happen inside me for this whole thing to move forward and feel better?"

If these questions don't help, then try the following: "Ask your body, "How does it feel to be stuck?" [pause] "Does this feel familiar, or is it something new?" [pause] "Try to hold your stuck feeling place like you would hold a little child, or someone you love who was feeling the same way. Take your time and sense whether your stuck place wants to say anything about how it feels. Try to be present in a caring way with your feeling of being stuck." *(Let me know ...)*

4. ENDING

Ask yourself: "Does this feel like it still wants to unfold a little further, or would this be a good place to rest and stop—at least for now." [If it's the right place to stop, then continue with the brief ending exercise below:]

Allow yourself a moment to recall how it felt in your body when you began and how it feels inside now. [pause] Does it still feel the same or is there a difference?" [pause]

Whether it feels the same or has changed, if it still feels unfinished inside, then ask this place, "How do you need me to be with you so we can continue our journey together?" [pause]

Finally, allow yourself time to be grateful for being able to companion your feelings and for the gift of any forward steps you may have been given Then, whenever you're ready, you can stop."

*** *** ***

*For further information visit our website at: **http://www.biospiritual.org**. The Institute and its members do not teach the habit of noticing and nurturing important feelings as a substitute for professional psycho-therapeutic or psychiatric care for those who need it, nor as a substitute for training and licensing in the above health fields. (© Card written by Edwin M. McMahon, Ph.D. & Peter A. Campbell, Ph.D.)*

(2)

If You Get Stuck
Asking Your Body Questions Like the Following May Help
(Be sure to keep your attention inside your body while listening for an answer!)

❀❀❀❀

"How does the worst of this feel in my body?"

Ask Your Body, "What needs to happen inside me for this whole thing to move forward and feel better?"

"Does this feel familiar, or is it something new?"

"What would feel like a small step forward with this?"

"Can I be with this feeling or issue without trying to fix it? Or, do I first need to spend time caring for my felt need to fix it?

"How does it feel in my body not to hear the message these feelings are trying to tell me?"

"How does it feel in my body to have these same feelings return over & over again?"

(Ask your stuck place inside:) **"How do you need me to be with you so you can tell me your story?"**

(When Companioning someone who is really stuck, you might ask:) **"Would it help to stop for a moment and just talk about what's going on inside you right now? We can return to noticing and nurturing feelings again later—if this feels right."**

For further information visit our website at: http://www.biospiritual.org.
The Institute and its members do not teach the habit of noticing and nurturing important feelings as a substitute for professional psychotherapeutic or psychiatric care for those who need it, nor as a substitute for training and licensing in the above health fields.)

Helping Children Develop the Habit of "Noticing" and "Nurturing" Their Important Feelings

(A companion's role is to be a caring presence that helps a child attend to how their body feels inside, so their inner story can break through and be heard. Your role is not to judge, give advice, analyze, or comment upon what they find.)

"Bold text in quotes ..." *is what you say to the child whom you are companioning. (Italic texts in brackets ...) are instructions for you.*

NOTICING

1. Responding to a Child's Important Feeling

"Those tears, (or that excitement, challenge, etc.) feels like there's a story inside your body, asking you to listen to it."

"Would you like me to sit with you while you close your eyes and hold the feeling inside you right now, just like you hold your... *(teddy bear, doll, puppy, etc.)***?"...** *(pause)* **...** *(Older Children:)* **"... like you used to hold ...etc..."**

NURTURING

2. Helping a Child to Nurture an Important Feeling

"Notice WHERE you carry this feeling in your body and HOW it feels inside you." *(This helps a child to hold their attention inside.)*

"You might want to put your hand on the place where your body feels this the most, just letting it know that you care, and that you're going to be with it for awhile." *(pause)*
"I'll wait here with you while you quietly sit with how your body feels inside. Take your time and let me know if it wants to say anything to you—with a word, a picture, a memory or some other feeling that seems to fit the way it feels." *(pause)*

Going Further with "Noticing" and "Nurturing"

3. Reflection

(Say back whatever the child shares. Use his or her words--not yours! If they say a lot, reflect back just the most feeling part.)

4. Recycling

(Whenever something fresh or new, unexpected or surprising comes inside, and your child shares this, say it back so they know you heard it. Then, help them to notice and stay with the body-feel of that. e.g.:)

"... ('scary') seems to say how it feels. So, now notice how saying ('scary') feels in your body, and try to be with that like you would hold your...(...teddy bear, doll, etc.)."

"Let me know if anything further comes that fits the way this feels inside you right now." *(pause)*

(1)

Rediscovering the Lost Body-Connection

(Keep inviting them to go forward by repeating #s 3 & 4 as needed, until they seem ready to stop.)

Ending a Session

(a) Checking to See whether it's OK to Stop

1) "Does this feel like it wants to unfold a little further at this time, or would this be a good place to rest and stop—at least for now?" *(If they want to stop, then say:)*

2) "Take a few moments before stopping to remember how it felt a little while ago when you began being with your feelings. *(pause)* ...Now notice how it feels inside. *(pause)*...Does it feel the same, or is there any difference?" *(If it feels the same, go to (b) below. Otherwise, close with (3) below.)*

3) "Stay with your body's feel of this difference in a way that says, 'Thank you.' Then, when you're ready, you can stop."

(b) Stopping in an Unfinished Place

1) "We need to stop in a few moments. So, ask this feeling place that still has more to say: 'How do you need me to take care of you so you can be my friend and teacher?'" *(Wait, and give the child time to listen for direction.)*

2) "Also, promise this place that you'll come back to see how it feels when you have more time to be with it again, so it can continue to tell you more of it's story." *(pause)*

3) "Then, when you're ready, you can stop."

After a Session

1) "Is there anything you want to say about what we just did together, or would you rather just be quiet?"

2) *(If your child wants to talk, don't just respond to "what" they say. Respond, instead, to how they feel inside "as they say it." Perhaps another important feeling will surface as you respond in this way, and they may need you to companion them further.)*

(Remember, this unfolding journey of awareness at the body-level of knowing does not often happen according to our schedule or convenience. You need to be flexibile enough when your child shares important feelings so you can take advantage of this learning opportunity.)

Institute for BioSpiritual Research
Visit our website at: http://www.biospiritual.org.

The Institute and its members do not teach the habit of noticing and nurturing important feelings as a substitute for professional psychotherapeutic or psychiatric care for those who need it, nor as a substitute for training and licensing in the above health fields.)

(Card written by Edwin M. McMahon, Ph.D.)

Suggestions For Developing in Very Young Children the Habit of a "Caring Presence" for Their Important Feelings

Edwin M. McMahon, Ph.D.

DURING CALM, non-trauma, relaxed, and fun situations when you notice a child loving a doll or pet, snuggling with it, petting it, etc., you might ask: "What does it feel like in your body when you hug and love your (teddy bear, doll, puppy, kitten, etc.)?" Or, you might ask: "Do you have a warm, huggy, good feeling place inside here (pointing to heart, tummy area) when you love your (bear, kitty, etc.)?" "I remember when I was little like you, I had a warm, huggy place inside me when I hugged my puppy."

"You have other feeling places inside you, too. Remember when you fell down and skinned your knee and your hurty place inside made you cry? So, you sometimes have a hurty place inside, too. Remember the time when .... (describe a situation where the child got angry). So, you sometimes have a mad place inside you." Perhaps recall one or two more emotional/feeling instances--scary, lost, sad.

"So, you have a happy place, a sad place, a huggy place, a hurty place inside you. All these places are part of you—and very, very precious. And they all need you to pay attention to them when something happens to make them mad or sad, happy or hurty. These places don't like to be alone, so they let you know when they need you to notice that you are scared or hurty, excited or mad. Sometimes, they even want you to be very quiet inside and listen to them, because they want to tell you something."

"I'll help you to do that, and we can take care of those feeling places together until you know how to do this by yourself when I'm busy or not with you."

*((You need to play by ear when to introduce the above for the first time. **The most important learning, however, will come from consistent responses to a child's feelings using simple phrases like those below:**))*

Entry Phrases That Help Young Children Go Inside To Notice and Nurture Their Important Feelings

1. "That sounds like those feelings are really important and trying to get your attention so they can tell you something."

2. "Is there some place in your body where you especially feel this .... (mad, scary, teary, curious, excited) .... feeling? "If it helps, you can put your hand there to let it know it's not alone."

3. "Would you like me to sit with you while you hold those feelings in a gentle, caring way like you hold your .... (teddy bear, doll, kitty, dog, favorite stuffed animal, etc.) .... so it can tell you something if it wants to?"

Closing: *If you sense that the child is finished, you can close by saying:* "Is it OK now to say goodbye to this place."

Afterwards, when you feel it's appropriate to support development of the habit of going inside, you might ask: "How does your (mad, scary, teary, etc.) place feel now **because you were kind to it and didn't leave it alone**?"

Finally, this chapter closes with some common sense observations titled, *Suggestions for Companioning,* which can be useful to read through every now and then as a reminder and guide helping you to remain clear about your role when accompanying another person on their inward journey. Little tips and suggestions like, *What do I do if...,* will be useful in certain situations, summarizing a few of the basics which, over time, become second nature—common sense learnings which your own body will reveal as you commit to building a new kind of relationship inside yourself.

Some Suggestions for Companioning

YOU DON'T HAVE ANSWERS: Remember that you really don't have any answers for the person whom you are companioning. Rather, your role is simply to companion that person, responding in a special way which supports them in discovering their own answers! The answer that a person discovers for himself or herself is always far more satisfactory than any answer from someone else.

TRUST THE PROCESS IN THEIR BODY: Your primary role for companioning another in their inner process is twofold, (1) to help that person remain in the body-feel of their issue, and at the same time (2) to help create a more open, accepting, caring relationship to whatever feelings they are carrying so it becomes easier for that person to risk being inside and "owning" how it feels.

THE QUALITY OF YOUR PRESENCE: As a companion, you help another to create a safe and supportive environment by the quality of your presence in the relationship, one which is not hampered by your own need to provide answers, to control their unique journey, or succeed as a helper! Such a non-interfering, non ego-centered attitude creates an atmosphere that encourages and disposes the one you are companioning to create the same kind of relationship with their scary, lonely or hurting inner places. This simple act of yours is, in itself, a great blessing that can heal and open a person for a whole new kind of "graced" relationship to themselves.

VERBAL RESPONSES: Your verbal responses as a companion are not to comment upon nor analyze what a person shares, but to support a forward movement of felt meaning within their body. This means your interventions are meant to support a body-process as it unfolds. You're not there to talk or inquire about an issue, but to help the person stay in touch with their body-feel of that issue so it can gradually unfold and tell its story.

NOT ORDERS BUT "OPTIONS": Your role as companion is not to "direct" or "order" a person to do something. Rather, you "invite" and offer "options." The person whom you are companioning makes the "choices!" For example, if someone comes to a fork in the road and doesn't know which way to turn, your task is not to say, "Go Right," or "Go left." Instead, you lay out the OPTIONS. For example: "Sense whether one of those paths or issues draws you in some feeling way in your body more than the other. Ask yourself, 'Toward which side is my body drawing me? Is it one or the other, OR is it toward putting both of them together and holding that in a caring way? Or, maybe the real issue is my sense of being unsure about what to do in this situation right now? Can I sense deeper into what my body is actually feeling the most around all these possible choices?'"

CARING PRESENCE: Caring presence, especially when directed toward a hurt or difficult feeling in our body, is especially important for creating a bond with alienated or rejected places inside ourselves. Remind the one whom you are companioning to find their own unique body-way of being present in a caring way to how their body carries whatever is difficult inside. (Their Affection Teacher). This is what makes it possible for them to "own" what they actually feel. Then, a symbol may eventually interact with it and a felt shift occur in how their body carries these feelings. Caring presence is the key that brings God (*Agápe*) into the relationship.

With beginners who are struggling with an obviously difficult issue, first have them ask their body whether it is OK to be with these feelings in a caring way. If they say, "No, it's too much to do that," then help them to be with the feeling that, "It's just too much to be with this right now." (cf also: www.biospiritual.org and check the links at the bottom of each page about: "Caring Presence," "Your Affection Teacher," "Caring for Enemies Inside Yourself" and "Turning Old Perceptions Upside-Down.")

BRIEF RESPONSES: Remember, the person whom you are companioning cannot fully turn their attention inward while you (the companion) are talking or giving directions. Be mindful, therefore, of brevity and clarity. Say what you need to say in order to support their process and provide direction. Then get out of their way and be quiet so they can go inside and continue on their own.

CLEAR GROUND RULES: Always provide clear ground rules so the one being companioned knows what to do next, and how to let you know when they have done what you asked. For example, after inviting someone to stay inside with a feeling or issue you might add, "Take whatever time you need to be inside with that, and then let me know if anything further comes that feels connected, a word, an image, a memory—or whether it feels stuck." Clear ground rules free the person going inside to concentrate on their feelings and felt senses without worrying about how or when they are to respond to you. At the same time, such ground rules also free you from worrying about whether it's clear how you are to be called upon. It helps right at the beginning to set up this ground rule: "If at any time you feel stuck or not sure about what to do next, just let me know and I'll try to help."

WHAT STANDS OUT IN THE BODY?: Remember to remind the one going inside themselves to notice, nurture, and take time with how an issue feels in their body, not what they may "think" about it. Felt meanings unfold in the body, not in the mind analyzing.

HELPING A BEGINNER: If a person who is new to this process remains quiet for an overly long time, and you're not sure whether they're lost or, perhaps, don't know how to proceed or respond to you, gently come into a prolonged silence by quietly saying, "Ask yourself, 'How does it feel now inside me? Does this still feel the same as when I began, or has there been some movement or change in all that?' Let me know what you find."

WHEN YOU DON'T KNOW WHAT TO DO NEXT: If at any point you become unsure yourself about what to do next, simply ask the person whom you are companioning: "Check inside and ask yourself, 'What does it feel right to do now?' " If they say: "I don't know", then inquire whether it would be OK for a moment just to sit with that feeling of being unsure and sense whether any further direction comes from that. It can often help to ask: "Does this feeling seem familiar, or is it something new?" Whether familiar or new, invite the person to be with whatever edge of feeling surfaces in their body, and sense further into what that might have to say.

YOU'RE NOT IN CHARGE: The person whom you are companioning is always the one in charge! If someone wants to stop because it feels too scary to go further, then as their companion you might suggest: "Would it be all right for a moment just to turn your attention toward being caring and gentle with the feeling in your body of how scary this is now becoming and your wanting to back away from it?" Help the person stay with whatever comes as the felt meaning. After pausing, if appropriate, you might ask: "What does it feel right to do now?"

RUNNING OUT OF TIME: If you are running out of time you might ask, upon arriving at a natural resting place, "Check inside to sense whether what you're working with still needs to go further at this time, or would it be OK to stop and rest here—at least for now?" Generally, we find it better to weigh the option in favor of proceeding further rather than abruptly injecting a stop sign. What you regard as a natural stopping place may NOT be such for the person you are companioning. It can also help to set up a ground rule beforehand: "I'll let you know five minutes before we need to stop."

ENDING A SESSION: If the person you are companioning wants to stop, then move into the closing phase of the session. If they want to continue a little further, and you have the time, then invite them to be with the feeling inside of whatever still needs to go further. It also helps in advance to have an agreement that you will let the one you are companioning know when it is five or ten minutes before you need to stop. You are the timekeeper.

STOPPING IN AN UNFINISHED PLACE: Whenever you need to stop in an unfinished place, have the one whom you are companioning ask their feeling that still has more to say: "How do you need me to be with you so we can continue our journey together at another time?" Support them in building some kind of bond with their unfinished feeling.

Rediscovering the Lost Body-Connection

Help them promise to come back at another time to go further with any feeling that still has some further story to tell.

AFTER A SESSION: After a session it can be helpful to allow some extra time in which to ask the person whom you've just been companioning: "Is there anything you would like to share about this experience, or would you rather just be quiet for now?" Offering this "option" allows a person some space in which to reflect upon and share what has just happened if that would be helpful for them. Your responses as a companion during any time of sharing will be more supportive of process if they are "reflective" or "active listening" responses rather than analysis or information sharing, unless there is some call for the latter. Often, with the support of reflective listening, further feelings and felt senses will surface during this sharing time which can then be followed up on in a later sessions, or right at that moment if there is time and it's appropriate.

PRIVACY ISSUES: It can be very helpful for the person whom you are companioning to realize that you don't need to know the details of whatever feelings they may be working with. They are free to guard their privacy. You can still effectively companion them without knowing any of their private content. What you do need to know is how they are feeling in their body right now. It is possible to go through an entire session of noticing and nurturing feelings without you, the companion, having any idea about private content. Your job is to support an inner body-process, not to get content out on the table. If a person wants to share what is private, that is their choice.

WORKING WITH STUCK, BLOCKED PLACES: Sometimes, when a person seems completely blocked or unable to find a feeling or felt sense, it can be useful to ask something like this: "Would it be alright just to talk a little about what is going on inside you right now. You can go back to noticing and nurturing your feelings after talking a bit, if that seems OK."

Then, you listen and reflect with "healing" or "active listening." You respond not only to the content being shared, but to how you sense the person must feel inside in their sharing this content. It can help to ask yourself: "How is this other person *IN* what he or she is saying?

Let the person know that you hear not just *what* they are saying, but *how they are in what they are saying*—e.g. angry, lonely, sad, excited, confused." If during the course of this dialogue other feelings or felt-senses appear, you can invite the focuser to check whether he or she might want to be with any of these in a Noticing and Nurturing way.

STAYING IN TOUCH WITH YOURSELF: Be aware as much as possible of how you are in your relationship with the person whom you companion. Do you have subtle needs for control, or a happy outcome? Are you threatened or defensive around anything that emerges in the process? Be sure to *notice* anything like this and after the session find some quiet time in which *to nurture* whatever needs listening to inside yourself.

Finally, remember that your role as a companion is not one of being someone's therapist, unless you are professionally trained and licensed to do so. Although the process of noticing and nurturing feelings is invariably therapeutic, suggest professional psychotherapy when that is called for. ∎

Personal Notes

*A **Third** Body-Learning*

■

Balancing the Difference Between What Your Head Knows About the Body of the Whole Christ and How Your Body Feels It

**Developing the Habit of Noticing
and Nurturing Your Felt-Senses Builds
This Missing Body Connection.**

**Christians Need to Build a Felt Bridge
Between What Their Minds Can Grasp
Intellectually About a Teaching, Like St. Paul's
Meaning of 'in Christ,' and How Their Body
Actually Experiences This Same Teaching
Through the Gift of Their Living Faith**

**This Habit Opens the Door of Christian Awareness
into the Wider, Gifting World of Grace and Spirit
in the Body of the Whole Christ, so that
Even Difficult Feelings Become an Integral Part,
not an Obstacle on Your Journey into God**

Chapter 9

Ancient and Modern Intimations of a Larger Body— But How Do We Connect?

Children Teach Us to Decipher the Hidden Language of God

ONE DAY while in the nursery school classroom, I (Pete) had a fascinating experience. I had been talking with one of the mothers when her four year old son came running over crying because he'd been hurt. His mom then sat on the floor holding him in her arms but he wouldn't be comforted nor stop crying. At that point, she turned to me and said, "Well, here's a real life situation. What do we do now?"

I then sat down on the floor beside him and asked where in his body he could feel the hurt. He pointed toward his ankle. I reached over and gently held his ankle. Then I asked him: "Do you think you could go down inside your body into your ankle and tell it how sorry you are that it hurts, and ask if it needs you to help it in any way?" As soon as I asked him to go inside his body, his mom and I both noticed that he immediately stopped crying. The little boy was quiet for a time, and I then suggested he be nice to his hurting ankle, holding it in a caring way like he held his puppy, and listen further in case it had anything it wanted to tell him.

While all this was going on, I happened to glance up and notice that the boy's two and a half year old little brother was watching us, quietly taking it all in. He had been fifteen or twenty feet away when the incident began, and since then had moved in closer to observe what was going on. As his older brother's crying died down, his younger brother could sense the three of us interacting with one another in a loving, caring way with the hurting ankle. Then, this little fellow responded without any words, by toddling over and leaning first against his mother. Then he moved around her and sort of rolled against the back of his brother. After that, he came around behind me and rolled his little body against mine before quietly leaning against my back and then resting there. He never said a word. But it was clear he had been touched by what was happening among the three of us and wanted to be part of it. So, not having words to express what he felt, he instinctively rubbed his body against all of us in order to be connected with what was going on.

During this entire episode, no one said anything. But a world of learning and communication was alive and vibrant in our presence to one another. Throughout the rest of my morning the two and a half year old, whom I had not previously met, would occasionally toddle over behind me while I was seated on the floor taking photos of the class, and then just lean against me as if asking for more of what we had all brought into his little world earlier that morning.

A profound human longing surfaced that morning, something hungered for within the human body, whether in a toddler or an adult. This same message came through in ancient times when non-Christians exclaimed about the early Christian community, "See how they love one another."

This world of our human body together with its feelings and felt-senses offers a whole new frontier for spiritual exploration. Under-examined evidence about the human body hidden away within the Judaeo-Christian spiritual tradition still offers even greater opportunity for the Christian community today. Evidence that can create a fresh experience of our humanity *in Christ* lies waiting to be discovered—within the *embodied* experience of relating and interacting through *agápe* within ourselves, with one another, and the world around us.

We need an entirely new understanding and experience of the human organism—no longer viewed as a self-contained object examined from the outside, but as an awareness known and felt on the inside. This deliberate step inward toward *a new kind of interiority* brings with it a momentous transformation in our understanding and experience of the human body.

Even more, it opens a breathtaking vista for future developments in consciousness, along with an evolution in spirituality which offers exciting potential for generating immense social and personal benefits, unveiling a beckoning new horizon and paradigm for Christian faith. The transforming experience of *your-body-as-it-is-felt-from-inside*, under the guidance of your own Affection Teacher, can gradually change the relationship you have to your own body as you learn to take care of the pain you create inside yourself when you turn negative feelings into your enemies.

Building the Body-Bridge of Christian Faith

The lost body-connection examined in this book is not about conceptually articulated truths of biblical revelation or teachings, but in failing to identify the missing bridge in a Christian's experience of *living out* and effectively *incorporating* a Scriptural message into their own body's knowing. We're not addressing the *information* side of human knowing, but opening up how the physical process of *embodying and internalizing* can transform one's everyday living—and faith.

This pedagogical challenge is not informational but *transformational*. How does a conceptual truth, for example, "God is love," actually enter into and become expressed within your own body's knowing and relationships? The missing link in religious education lies in developing *new habits in our bodies,* not just acquiring more information in our minds. Most people seem totally unaware of this critical missing piece in our religious and spiritual development.

Earlier we emphasized that knowing and learning something intellectually is not the same as experiencing a process of genuine change in how your body carries an issue or truth. We talked earlier about driver-training classes and then getting into a car so your body can give you an actual *feel for the road*. The educational gap, especially within religious formation and instruction, lies in knowing how to take that balancing step beyond abstract information into acquiring a new habit of knowing how to be in your body as it is felt from inside.

This more *balanced* body-way of internalizing an important teaching within everyday living has either been lost or never adequately explored, owing to historical misunderstandings and prejudices about our bodies and their feelings, which have hindered any educational priority being given to this crucial ingredient in the development of Christian faith.

Growing into and practicing the habit of noticing and nurturing important feelings opens up and disposes your body's knowing ability to receive the gift of symbols, such as words from the

Gospels—symbols that can then interact with felt-senses, often seemingly out of the blue. Acquiring this new habit teaches you how to carry felt-senses around inside in a nurturing, caring way until the right symbol connects and interacts, then allowing them to reveal their felt meaning. This entire experience embodies a living, forward moving, internalizing process of personal, organic wholeness.

When experiencing such wholeness in our bodies, we then *physically* feel and find ourselves blessed with a gifted influx of energy, inspiration and empowering creativity—which can touch and move us far more profoundly than any rational understanding or analysis of abstract teachings can ever generate in our minds alone. Felt meaning and the forward movement of a felt-sense changes the way our bodies carry this new understanding. We and others then feel the depth of meaning this can have for us in our excitement, conviction, awe, surprise, wonder and gratitude. Dana Ganihar, a Focusing Coordinator in Israel, illustrates this point in a touching way through a charming interaction with her son:

> …my ten year old son came to me excited, trying to explain something he had suddenly realized. It was something about how a fantasy movie he saw and liked very much was actually happening in our own world, we just don't notice that. After several sentences he said, a bit in despair, "I can tell you but you won't…" and I couldn't help saying "feel it." "How did you know I was going to say that?" he exclaimed. Young as he is, he sensed the difference between understanding the words, and experiencing their meaning.[1]

Experiencing a *felt* meaning impacts our entire organism in an entirely different way from how an abstract piece of information enters our mind. When symbol and felt-sense come together, physically interacting within us in a living, changing relationship—this experience changes our body, our feelings and our relationship to everything.

The habit of being in touch with what your body knows takes you through the doorway of your feelings into a larger world of gift or *grace*. When Christians can bring their faith awareness to such experience, they then recognize that this experience within their own bodies *in Christ* opens up what Saint Paul tried to describe in words, inadequate though they may have been, "…It is no longer I who live, but Christ who lives in me..." (Gal 2:20 RSV)—the bodily-felt sense for a Larger, Loving, Living Presence then comes alive within everyday life.

The more Christians can develop an awareness of the language spoken within their own bodies, the more they will then, through faith, grow into an openness and availability for sensing grace when it unfolds inside them. In addition, by developing a deliberate commitment to the habit of bringing the gift of a listening, loving presence *(agápe)* into how their body is carrying difficult feelings such as fear, anger, pain, loneliness or loss, this loving presence can then help them to mature in their body's experience that God dwells in them because, as St. John reminds us, "...God is love." (1Jn 4:8 RSV)

Moreover, for those who believe we are all integral, living cells within the Resurrected Body of the Whole Christ, every important feeling comes to be seen as a loving gift, not an obstacle on our journey into God. Christians learn from personal experience inside their own bodies that feelings are inherent to the profound transformation in our awareness of who each of us really is, "in Christ."

A Curious Parallel Within the Structure of Scientific Revolutions

To explore this parallel we must take ourselves back to the mid-twentieth century. The Times Literary Supplement lauded Thomas S. Kuhn's classic book, *The Structure of Scientific Revolutions*, first published in 1962, as "one of the hundred most influential books since the Second World War." Kuhn put his finger on an essential inner dynamic at work within every scientific revolution which introduces a major transformation in our world view and experience of ourselves. He called such innovative breakthroughs—*paradigm shifts*. Without downplaying the role of an inquiring, analytic mind, Kuhn demonstrated how such significant advances in human awareness all flow out of *some physical process moving forward in your body* and your body's unique way of knowing.

While Kuhn found himself unable to explain in concrete detail the inner psychological dynamic that occurred during such scientific discovery moments, he nonetheless recognized that major revolutions in science cannot in any way be reduced to a simple *reinterpretation* of already existing and familiar data. In other words, the breakthrough was not thought-driven by some logical, rational enterprise through careful analysis of cause and effect. Putting this in his own words Kuhn wrote:

> What occurs during a scientific revolution is not fully reducible to a reinterpretation of individual and stable data...(The) interpretative enterprise can only articulate a paradigm, not correct it. Paradigms are not corrigible by normal science at all. Instead...normal science ultimately leads only to the recognition of anomalies and to crises. And these are terminated, not by deliberation and interpretation, but by a relatively sudden and unstructured event like the gestalt switch. Scientists then often speak of the "scales falling from the eyes" or of the "lightning flash" that "inundates" a previously obscure puzzle, enabling its components to be seen in a new way that for the first time permits its solution. On other occasions the relevant illumination comes in sleep. No ordinary sense of the term "interpretation" fits these flashes of intuition through which a new paradigm is born.[2]

Such transformative moments not only animate the emergence of new scientific advances, they also contain a profound seed potential for the continual renewing of Christian spirituality as well. But until the body's contribution to spiritual development can consciously be recognized and deliberately incorporated in its vital role within Christian pastoral care, we will never unearth the personal inner resources to grow beyond our current, often outdated, monarchical, mechanical and Newtonian models of both ourselves and of God. As Alan Watts reminded us over forty years ago,

> "We do not need a new religion or a new bible. We need a new experience—a new feeling of what it is to be 'I'."[3]

For far too long, Christianity has experienced itself in crisis and needing some fresh paradigm-experience of itself in order to heal the debilitating disconnection from our human organism's inner process of wholeness, a severance which throughout history has resulted in endless scandals and largely impotent attempts at self-renewal and peacemaking.

From today's vantage point in our understanding of what it means to be human, we can now better understand that the origin of such resurfacing crises within Christian spirituality became locked into the institutional structure and expression of Christianity at the moment when the emperor Constantine absorbed the nascent and struggling fourth century Christian communities into the political structures and legal paradigm of the powerful Roman empire. While this move admittedly provided sanctuary, legal rights and a social status to the fledgling religion it also burdened it with structures that in its early growth set it on a very different path from the one which St. Paul had envisioned and prayed for in his foundational pastoral letters.

As a learned Jewish rabbi, Paul personally experienced throughout his mission to the Gentiles that Jesus was, indeed, the longed-for Messiah, the *Christos*—but not under the umbrella of an older, more powerful and anticipated warrior king paradigm. For Paul, Jesus Christ was the new paradigm, but in a form breaking all the old divisions, class structures, and social conventions that rigidly determined who's in and who's out in the Roman way of doing things. Within Paul's crisply stated new paradigm formula:

> There is neither Jew nor Greek, there is neither slave nor free,
> there is neither male nor female; for you are all one in Christ Jesus.
> *(Gal 3:28 RSV)*

From Paul's experience, the unfolding Body of the Whole Christ within us reveals the appearance of a radical new paradigm experience—the enduring, living Presence of God on this earth mediated through, with, and in a quality of *agápe* presence we bring into all our relationships, including the relationship we have to our own bodies and feelings. This gift of a new sense of "I," revealed in the life, death and resurrection of Jesus Christ and through the pioneering efforts of the Apostle Paul, reveals the Presence of God with/in us.

The writings of Sts. Paul and John unveil this embodied experience for the Christian community, as well as for other interested persons because, as we shall see in this and the next chapter, one discovers an entire lexicon of words describing this *new feeling of what it is to be "I"* throughout their letters and teachings. In addition, they also identify a concrete direction and actual steps Christians may take in order to move forward into such new awareness. Yet, while we can mentally grasp the cognitive meaning of their words—the information they impart—somehow most Christians have yet to *experience* the deep impact of this message *in their bodies*, sufficiently motivating them to pass on this same organic, creative experience to others.

Reading Through the Eyes of Your Body-Knowing

As a reminder that our bodies recognize significant felt meanings which touch our lives, we suggest, once again, that in the coming pages when a word or phrase, some idea or description stands out for you with a felt edge that piques your interest, curiosity or recalls some significant past experience, we encourage you to stop and allow a moment to notice and nurture whatever jumps out and touches you *in a bodily-felt way* around your reading the words on these pages. Allow your own body's knowing some space to be heard. Allow it, too, to read along with your eyes the printed information before you. Try to imagine the words on the page as symbols reaching deep inside you to touch and call forth some movement in a felt-sense that may have lain dormant and unnoticed, perhaps for a very long time. Realize that you yourself are an integral part of any felt meaning that rises up out of your reading in this book. Try not to read solely for information alone, but allow any story that spontaneously seeks to unfold from within your own body's knowing to be heard as well.

Body, Flesh and Spirit in the Writings of St. Paul

Both Paul and John wrote their original letters and gospel in the language of ancient Greece, and one can easily identify several Greek words which contain the seeds of an emerging new sense of what it means to be "I"—"in Christ." We will briefly introduce a few of those words here, and then explore further in the next chapter how St. Paul weaves them together in ways which point toward an inner body-experience that can guide us into a new sense of "I," integral to being part of something greater than ourselves.

Three meaning-filled words of Paul highlight the body's vital role in spiritual development and Christian salvation history—*soma* (σῶμα) *body*, *sarx* (σάρξ) *flesh* and *pneuma* (πνεῦμα) *breath, wind, or spirit*. Paul mixes these words together in ways which make it amply clear when preaching or using them in his letters that he referred to an actual experience within our bodies, a physical, visceral way of knowing in contrast to some form of thinking or truth pondered as conceptual information in the mind alone. These original Greek words have a profound relevance for us today because they direct attention toward our own personal body-links into some deeper, felt meaning in our interactions with ourselves, one another and both the Hebrew and New Testament writings, together with their symbolic invitation to grow further into the experience of what it means to be human "in Christ."

Paul opened a door for the educated Hebrew and Gentile communities of his day when unveiling a new perspective upon the human body, *soma* (σῶμα), as distinguished from the flesh, *sarx* (σάρξ) in his preaching and letter writing. He also introduces *a powerful evolutionary sense of Salvation History* in his understanding and experience of the biblical Adam and the Body of Christ—the *New* Adam—when referring to the body of flesh as *soma sarkikon* (σῶμα σάρκικον or ψυχικόν), and the body of spirit as *soma pneumatikon* (σῶμα πνευματικόν) (1 Cor 15:44).

The point Paul makes with these words is that the seed must fall into the ground and die before a plant can germinate, grow and mature. The *body-of-flesh* provides the seed context, the fertile soil within which the *Body-of-Spirit* within each person germinates and matures into the Larger Body of the Whole Christ—"And the Word became flesh and dwelt among us..." (Jn 1:14 RSV) Salvation history becomes the historical legend or metaphor chronicling the transition from an old to a new order within the evolving consciousness of humankind.

In an earlier work, *BioSpirituality—Focusing as a Way to Grow*,[4] we introduced a rediscovered Christian Biospirituality which opens an inward path for growing into the developmental body-sense that we are part of something Greater than ourselves.

> The unified *soma* of humanity in *sarx* is the biblical *Adam*! For Christian believers, all of humankind is the body of Adam, the corporate personality of our fleshly origin. But because we can evolve, because the primary axis of consciousness evolution still courses through our human unfolding, we are opened in this gifted advance to perceive and to participate in the birth of a New Adam, a new corporate personality and *Soma* called *Christ*.[5]

Within the framework of a Christian faith tradition one rediscovers a physical sense for being part of something greater than ourselves by reaching all the way back into our Hebrew roots to recall, both in mind and body, a long-forgotten, *visceral environmentalism*. The One and the Many, the Whole and the Parts all blend together organically but with individual identities left fully in place. It's rather like the gestalt image displayed here, where two black faces or the white goblet as ever-changing figure or background are different, yet at one and the same time inseparable from one another within the larger picture because each forms the visual background without which the other foreground image would not be visible. From a Hebrew point of view, *everything is a gestalt*, never reduced to a mere dualism. The Christian challenge, therefore, would be to remember our Hebrew body-roots, consciously bringing this experience back into an excessively unbalanced and heady spirituality.

In every gestalt your attention shuttles back and forth between figure and ground as one or the other draws your conscious awareness. On closer examination, however, you may gradually come to recognize *a third something* at work within the dynamism of any gestalt.

In addition to white and black visual objects, your attention finds itself drawn into a constant *interaction* between the two. Just as one image cannot exist without the other and they *go together* like two sides of one and the same coin, so too, your own body's perceiving enters into the total gestalt-experience by becoming an integral participant or membrane within this experience. An ongoing, interacting connection bonds the images, *the-gestalt-and yourself-together* in a continuing back and forth movement in awareness of the shifting between two images, just as there is a back-and-forth between your head knowing and body felt-sensing. A balancing. As your body-perception shifts between the two images, the shape of one figure becomes a background for the other and a new figure appears, but with a decided twist. Within such experience *your own body has now become an integral piece of the entire interacting whole*.

The gestalt, of course, offers only a limited illustration. It cannot fully demonstrate an unfolding, forward movement which may better be imaged through the descending layers of an onion. As you peel one layer open and cut it away, another appears beneath it. As one felt-sense unfolds to reveal the connected other side of the gestalt, this new image or story then becomes a new gestalt in itself, awaiting some further felt forward shift in the fresh edge of story that promises still further unfolding yet ahead.

Keeping this in mind, remember that in your reading right now, you yourself have been drawn into becoming part of an interacting gestalt. Words and symbols on the pages before you speak inside and your body replies. There is interaction. Back-and forth movement and shifting. Felt-senses respond, come alive and begin to move forward. Everything in life expresses itself in some form of relationship, interacting—some expression of a larger gestalt, an ever-expanding, Greater Whole.

The body-feel for a new sense of "I," which arises from within through a step-by-step, developing awareness of being part of some ever-enlarging, interacting Whole, has become lost in our so-called Age of Information with its emphasis on *objective* analysis. A more ancient body-sense for some maturing solidarity, unity, wholeness, the common good and, ultimately, human communion all struggle to be reborn once again in some new way within our own time. The goal is never to replace the mind's objective analysis but rather to include the body's felt-sensing along with it. Not *either-or* but *both-and*. Everything in this book stands as a support for allowing this more holistic sense for a returning environmental sense to emerge even more vividly from within our body's awareness.

Noticing and nurturing your important feelings, your Affection Teacher and, just ahead, our beginning to examine the Christian roots of some emerging Greater Wholeness—all reflect and become part of *reseeding* a new sense of "I." We struggle to find our way back into a body-consciousness of this Larger Gestalt in which each of us plays out our individual role as an integral, interacting membrane from within. Paul encourages this habit in the Christian community when he writes that they should,

> ...seek, reach out for, and perhaps find the One who is really not far from any of us—the One in whom we live and move and have our very being...*(Acts 17:27–28 TIB)*

In our view, all religions, including Christianity, have a vital, integral and urgent role to play in bringing this universal sense and need for wholeness back into human awareness. At this critical point in history, as mentioned earlier, Christian spirituality is being called upon to witness, in a clear and recognizable way that for believers, the Body of the Whole Christ, ourselves, can reveal the living, hope-filled, peace-making new paradigm which masses of serious seekers the world over hunger to discover.

Paul's Creative Efforts to Show His Experience of Living Within the Body of the Whole Christ

It is rare in today's spiritual literature to find a clear acknowledgment of the body's integral role in spiritual development. It is rarer still to discover a deliberate, detailed attempt on the part of spiritual authors to probe into and describe the actual inner unfolding of how the body itself expresses our human incorporation into some Larger, Somatic, Greater Living Organism. But it is almost unheard of for a writer creatively to go so far as attempting to reach deep within the body-knowing of his or her readers and *experientially awaken* some sleeping gestalt, so to speak, that can display in the reader's awareness a dim but actual body-sense for being an integral participant or membrane within some Larger Body.

Yet, St. Paul tried to implement just such a new transformational pedagogy by creatively stretching and twisting the very Greek language in which he wrote to get his point across. He physically shaped, twisted and deliberately reformed the actual words he used in order for them to feel just strange and unfamiliar enough for both eye and ear that the bodily-felt possibility of a new perspective, a different and refreshing body-sense might be drawn forth from within his listeners' and readers' awareness.

As part of our goal in this book, we once again remind you while reading these pages that you remember to listen inwardly to your own body as you absorb the written material. Whenever a passage, phrase or idea stands out in some bodily-felt way, be sure to pause for a moment, noticing and nurturing how that experience feels inside and whether it wants to tell you anything. Allow your Affection Teacher to guide you in your noticing and nurturing so that more than information alone can enter into your awareness.

Christians and non-Christians alike may well marvel at St. Paul's creative struggle to tinker with language in order to describe and perhaps have it become a metaphor in calling forth the believer's experience of being a membrane, a living cell within the Body of Christ. In his book, *The Body—A Study in Pauline Theology*,[6] the late Bishop John A.T. Robinson, Fellow and Dean of Chapel, Trinity College, Cambridge, provides a sense for the extreme lengths to which Paul went as he deliberately twisted the Greek language itself, attempting now one approach, now another in his effort to open the experience of a dramatically transformed world view for the early Christian communities. Robinson wrote:

> As Fr. Thornton well puts it, 'We are in Christ, not as a pebble in a box, but as a branch in a tree'...for there is a real sense in which the tree is in the branch. We are in Christ in so far as His life is in us.
>
> ...To us, the idea of being 'with' Christ conveys something more external than that of being 'in' Him. But almost certainly it did not to Paul. In Gal. 2.20 he combines it with what is perhaps the closest of all his expressions of identification with Christ: 'I have been crucified with Christ' (Χριστῷ συνεσταύρωμαι)...Professor Mersch's translation, 'I am **"con**crucified-with*"* Christ...' perhaps gets the force of the verb Paul has invented.[7] *(**bold** emphasis ours)*

Paul introduces some creative alchemy into the Greek language in this example. The preposition **συν** *(syn)—with*, can stand alone, as it does in English. But in the classical Greek it may also be added as a prefix in order to incorporate a sense of *with-ness* or **within-ness** into the meaning of a word. In the above text, "I have been crucified with," (συνεσταύρωμαι), the prefix **συν–** has been added on to the front of the verb. Often, however, Paul will intentionally add this same prefix to other words where it would normally not have been used. Robinson offers several striking examples:

> Time and time again...(Paul) coins strange new words with the prefix συν—rather than use the plain preposition. He clearly feels the painful

inadequacy of language to convey the unique 'withness' that Christians have in Christ. We are 'joint-heirs with Christ (literally, of: **συν**κληρονόμοι Χριστοῦ);...we suffer with him (**συν**πάσχομεν), that we may be also glorified with him (**συν**δοξασθῶμεν)' *(Rom.8.17)*[8] *(**bold** emphasis ours)*

In his own, very deliberate way, Paul went about creating a new *language structure* and a whole new *felt*-world-view or *paradigm* by moving the lines on the tennis court, so to speak, consciously changing the rules of the game in order to catch the attention of his readers and listeners. The Greek words he carefully crafted would have *felt unfamiliar*. The possibility of some fresh meaning and an experience of some new sense of "I" might then begin to spill forth and be highlighted inside this unusual experience.

Going even further, when employing this same literary device Paul again used **συν–**, in order to express a transformed level of Christian theology by incorporating the entire Gentile (non-Christian) community into the Body of Christ. His graphic twisting of the very *anatomy* of the Greek language itself emphasized the depth of his moral, personal and visceral faith-conviction that Gentiles, too, had been fully integrated into Christ's Body *as* God's new paradigm.

> ...The Gentiles are fellow-heirs (**συν**κληρονόμα), and fellow-members of the body (**σύν**σωμα; Mersch: 'concorporate'), and fellow-partakers (**συν**μέτοξα) of the promise in Christ Jesus' *(Eph. 3.6).*[9] *(**bold** emphasis ours).*

Here again, Paul relies not merely upon the common conceptual content or defined meaning of individual words to get his point across. He also adds a structural, linguistic twist in order to convey his own body-sense that the deeper meaning of Christ embraced *a far more inclusive bio-theology* for experiencing the New Adam, the Body of the Whole and Risen Christ. This Larger Body, quite literally extends to the limits of what exists, and for Christian believers, this sense of "being bodily alive in a vast system" represents the Body of the Whole Christ as this can be *felt from inside our own bodies*.

Robinson's treasure of biblical research brings into clear focus the strange new vocabulary which Paul struggled to create. By literally *welding* the preposition συν–, *(with)*, to the front end of words where it generally was not used, he forcefully contorted the Greek language to more closely express the *embodied* meaning and personal felt-sense of experiencing a maturing Christian world view and experience of "I" from inside his own body.

The effect may be compared to the photographer, Ansel Adams, deliberately using a red filter to dramatize his black and white photography of Yosemite Valley by sharpening the contrast between light and dark within clouds, rocks, and trees. When viewed through a red filter, the whites become whiter and the darks, darker. This striking effect presents not only an artistic impression of Yosemite, but of what Yosemite stirred within the eye, heart, and perspective of the artist. By employing this device, Ansel Adams became as integral to the photographs he created as was the subject matter before the lens of his camera.

Moreover, Robinson further identifies and highlights, not only the sheer physical unity of the believer's *membraneship* within Christ's Body, but also the *developmental* nature of this ongoing process of unification:

> It is surely clear that for Paul to do or suffer anything 'with' Christ speaks of no external concomitance, like the P.T. instructor who says, 'Now do this with me,' but of a common organic functioning, as the new tissues take on the rhythms and metabolism of the body into which they have been grafted.[10]

The implications are staggering. Paul used every means at his disposal to wrench his readers' attention in a new direction, trying to get both readers and listeners to experience a new perspective. He attempted to raise a more expanded awareness of *with-ness*, or *within-ness* in those to whom he wrote or preached. Bending language was not only an attempt to reach into the mind. It involved a creative outreach, or perhaps better—*inreach* within their bodies as well. Paul's effort, of course, was lost and ineffective with non-fluent Greek listeners or readers—as happened with the rapid spread of Christianity beyond the Greek-speaking world. So, today we must find a new doorway into such experience—one not dependent upon a particular language, as was Paul's attempt to draw attention to his message through his use of the Greek language.

That new doorway—our own body and its feelings—is the pathway, we believe, through which human evolution (and this workbook) invite us forward as a first step in *"Rediscovering the Lost Body-Connection Within Christian Spirituality."*

Contemporary science for the most part acknowledges that every cell of the human body has its own intelligence and is in communication with every other cell. They all *talk* to one another, so to speak. Therefore, the human body needs to be regarded as a complex communication system, an organic, interacting bundle of relationships.

Many educated Christians feel strongly that they are not being nourished by the spirituality they so often receive in church—and they suspect that it has something to do with their churches' inability to help them connect with what their bodies know. They feel a lack of support for their own feelings and don't yet know how to be congruent with those feelings in a way that invites grace to touch and heal them from the inside.

Well-meaning Christians often become disaffected and walk away from their traditional churches because they feel in their bones that something important is still lacking in their experience of Christian spirituality—even though they can't quite put their finger on what causes their disquiet, let alone come up with a solution for how to remedy it. The missing piece lies in their not knowing how to include vital processes within the human body and its knowing, bringing these into their spiritual experience as well. Weaving that synthesis is the purpose of this book.

On all too many occasions, church leaders attempt soothing or pious words as a way to fix or change feelings. But all such verbal talk doesn't bring about *visceral* change in how our bodies actually carry hurting feelings.

It reminds us of a story Pete's mother once told him about the time when she was a young violin student at the Royal College of Music in London. While winning full scholarships for her entire six years at the College, she would invariably dissolve into paralyzing bouts of fear when waiting offstage before a recital. Her professor would stand next to her and run through all *the reasons* why she should not be afraid.

She knew the piece she would play backward and forward; she had performed on this stage many times before; she knew the people in the audience and how supportive they were of her career, etc., etc. Peter's mother would say, "Yes...Yes...Yes," to each of his arguments, and then at the end quickly add, "...But I'm still afraid."

No rational explanation or information offered by her professors included any inside body-process that might have enabled Pete's mother to cross boundaries and barriers that otherwise remained closed to her. She could neither think her fear away on her own, nor could her professor accomplish this impossible task for her with his well-intentioned and reasoned arguments.

Simply acknowledging the cognitive *truth* of answers and explanations in your mind can never bring about a changed experience of feelings in your body. In order for this to occur, you must first develop the habit of an entirely new relationship with your own body and feelings.

Going Shopping for Inside Metaphors
Within The Mystery of Your Body's Knowing

The psychologist, Abraham Maslow, once shared a heartwarming tale about his two daughters when they were little girls. In the Springtime it was customary for the family to go marketing together when the first fresh strawberries arrived. Upon returning home, Maslow and his wife, Bertha, would prepare the strawberries. Then, together with their children, they sat down to enjoy their annual Springtime ritual. The two little girls would immediately begin gobbling up their berries while their mother and father dawdled over theirs. Scarcely eating any, the two parents would toy with the strawberries in their bowls, occasionally looking up to glance knowingly at one another—and then waiting. Eventually, the girls would finish their strawberries and immediately begin looking hungrily at those still remaining in their parents' bowls.

Then, Maslow said, "One by one we would each feed our own strawberries to our little girls—and you know, those last strawberries always tasted better in my child's mouth than they did in my own. The line between us had somehow disappeared. Our separateness from one another had been transcended."

Is such a deeply touching message from the world of our feelings just another endearing tale from a loving father's memory, or does more lie hidden within these words than at first meets the eye? Does an entirely new viewpoint for understanding human self-awareness patiently wait to be born from within just such ordinary, everyday experience in each of our lives?

Karl Rahner has described the Holy Trinity as, "...the fundamental mystery of Christianity...,"[11] and the very inner unfolding and interaction within Trinitarian life has historically been expressed through the ancient Greek word, (περιχώρησις) *perichoresis*, which translates as, *being-in-one-another* or *having-one's-being-within*. In simple terms, therefore, the central mystery of Christian life includes something to do with a developing capacity for growing into *a maturing body-sense* for experiencing yourself not solely as some exclusive, separated, distinct object set apart from everything and everyone else, but as an integral organ or living membrane, somehow distinct yet bound into a Greater Living Body. *Unique identity,* along with *interdependence* are both preserved in *perichoresis*. It has been suggested that the intertwining ribbons of the Celtic knot graphically portray this doctrine of *perichoresis*—the mutual interpenetration and yet distinctness of Persons, Father, Son and Holy Spirit within the Triune God.

Maslow's charming example invites us to realize that we're challenged to inspect more carefully such experiences within human awareness. They reflect this *having-one's-being-within* experiencing which matures in *a developmental* manner within human evolving. Trinitarian awareness cannot possibly spring full-blown out of a person's calculating, theological analysis. Not surprisingly, the lifeblood which brings this sensitivity into full awareness, may be recognized within ordinary, everyday experiences of *agápe* love as these can be experienced within the body's knowing.

"The strawberries tasted better in my child's mouth than they did in my own." What can we possibly learn from this intimately human, yet equally mysterious capacity so filled with veiled potential? What can our bodies teach us about a truly Christian Bio-Spirituality?

> Philip said to him, "Lord, show us the Father, and we shall be satisfied." Jesus said to him, "Have I been with you so long, and yet

you do not know me, Philip? He who has seen me has seen the Father; how can you say, 'Show us the Father'? Do you not believe that I am in the Father and the Father in me?" *(Jn 14:8–10 RSV)*

The ability, even though dimly perceived, to discern our linking and connecting within some Larger Body or Greater Whole thrusts roots deep within our human felt-sense knowing. It signals a gradual reaching out for or being drawn forward from within our own seemingly isolated and separated body of flesh on the way toward penetrating, being invited into an ever-enlarging world and environment of felt meaning wherein the lifeblood of this new kind of knowing carries us through the experience of *agápe* and into an unfolding Body of Spirit— the New Adam, the Christ. That is our developing, embodied sensitivity to an unfolding process of, περιχώρησις *(perichoresis)* insofar as all humans are made in the image and likeness of God.

From an evolutionary standpoint, expressed within our Christian tradition through the unfolding mystery of Salvation History, yet another Greek New Testament word surfaces in the growing lexicon of terms reflecting humankind's incorporation into the Body of Christ. (πλήρωμα) *pleroma, fullness, that which makes full or complete*, a rare word of obscure meaning appearing within the New Testament carries the developmental sense of an unfolding manifestation of the *fullness of God,* (πλήρωμα τοῦ θεοῦ), appearing through Christ and His Body within human history and the evolution of the cosmos. "For it is in Christ that the complete being of the Godhead dwells embodied, and in him you have been brought to completion (πεπληρωμένοι)." (Col 2:9 NEB).

Paul prays:

Out of his infinite glory, may he give you the power through
his Spirit for your hidden self to grow strong, so that Christ may
live in your hearts through faith, and then, planted in love and
built on love, you will with all the saints have strength to grasp
the breadth and the length, the height and the depth; until,
knowing the love of Christ, which is beyond all knowledge,
you are filled with the utter fulness of God (πλήρωμα τοῦ θεοῦ).
(Eph 3:14–19 JB) (Greek language insert ours)

Ancient and Modern Intimations of a Larger Body

In his Foreword to our earlier book, *Bio-Spirituality—Focusing as a Way to Grow,* Robert T. Sears, S.J., a professor at Loyola University of Chicago wrote the following:

> ...faith is grounded not in formulated beliefs but in the experience of the unfolding process itself. The very process of believing gives us an analogous way of understanding its deepest ground, the triune God. "I" focus on a "felt sense" which "unfolds" into who I am in the process of becoming. Analogously, the Father (I) forms his perfect Image (felt sense) which gives rise to an unfolding process of integration and self-transcendence (Holy Spirit). Focusing is a doorway beyond formulations of belief to faith or believing itself. As one moves more deeply into it, every event, every "felt-meaning," can become a religious event opening one to incarnate Spirit unfolding in evolution.[12]

In his own charming, diminutive way, the toddler who leaned against Pete expressed his own little *perichoresis* as he found himself drawn to become a more involved participant within the Larger Dance of *agápe,* discovering a new sense of "I" within something greater than himself.

Membranes Within the Body of Christ

The undiscovered missing link for developing Christian faith in our time lies right within our own bodies. Here, though, the revelation and links no longer arrive written upon dried old parchment. The journey before each of us opens an unexpected path for *believing in and being-in yourself as you discover anew more of who you are from within the Body of the Whole Christ,* "...it is no longer I who live, but Christ who lives in me..." (Gal 2:20 RSV).

Bishop Robinson surprises us with the following biblical perspective:

> The force of Paul's words can today perhaps be got only by paraphrasing: 'Ye are the body of Christ and severally *membranes* thereof' *(I Cor. 12.27).* The body that he has in mind is as concrete and as singular as the body of the Incarnation. His underlying conception is not of a supra-personal collective, but of a specific personal

organism...its unity is that of a single physical entity: disunion is dismemberment. For it is in fact no other than the glorified body of the risen and ascended Christ.[13]

We catch glimpses of Robinson's emphasis on the *physical* changes in experience that a renewed Christian paradigm shift might offer and what this must have meant for Robinson as he reached beyond the concept of distinct separation implied in *members* to embrace the more blended or fused term, *membranes*, thereby breaking through the autonomous billiard balls or peas in a pod order implied in the former word. The body-sense for this new paradigm of *blending together, having one's being within* represents a clear step beyond the classical autonomous order of a Newtonian universe.

Unfortunately, we have never really been taught how to search for the *embodied* human roots of Christian faith and revelation right within our own maturing experience of self-esteem, the ripening quality of our personal presence to self and one another, or within our experience of a growing capacity for ongoing self-renewal and development.

The telescope may offer a helpful metaphor for your journey which lies ahead. Through the lens of the telescope's eye you are enabled to see new things because the lens gives you *a new eye* through which to see. The contemporary challenge for both faith and personal growth calls out for each of us to find our way through the lens of our own body's feelings and on into the deeper meanings which lie within our even more compelling felt-senses. Throughout such a challenging journey of exploration one finds that discovering God and finding oneself are cut from one and the same dance.

The Miracle of Yet-To-Be-Discovered Blessings

After a month's visit to Turkey in 1992 a strong, unfinished felt-sense never left me. I (Ed) knew it wanted me to return. So, in the Spring of 1997, I finally had an opportunity to let it tell its story. Once again, I returned for a month with no agenda, other than to care for it, assisted by a rental car and this compelling felt-sense as my guide.

It took me to strange out of the way places on its own schedule, as if to say, "Well, for five years I've been trying to tell you something and you have avoided me. Now, you just be patient and let me enjoy your TLC for a while, and in good time you will know what I want to say."

Then, one beautiful May morning in the Taurus mountains of southern Turkey, not too far from the valley region of Tarsus where St. Paul was born and raised, I was resting in the ruins of an ancient monastery chapel built in the 5th century. No one else but Pete was around. We were high up on a mountainside, looking out upon a spectacular view of valleys and lower mountain ranges stretching as far away as the eye could see. Leaning against a pillar, now supporting only the open sky, I listened to the gentle breeze as it stirred the pines of the surrounding forest and sensed the warm patterns of sunlight dancing on the honey colored limestone walls that enclosed me.

This spot felt sacred and so connected to the earth with its gifts of silence, stone, light, sweet clean air, wild spring flowers and singing forests. Every morning here on this spot for well over a thousand years, century after century, Christians had gathered around an altar to commemorate what they called, *the Last Supper of Christ*—and, perhaps, have revealed to them the connection between their own bodies and the Body of God in this precious earth.

My eyes closed as my mind began to wonder how many of the monks and pilgrims who gathered here for Mass ever journeyed beyond external ritual into their own habit-protected inner fears by entering into the Body of God on earth through the consciousness of their own bodies? I sat with my body-sense of that question for a long time.

When I opened my eyes, the sun had climbed higher above the surrounding trees and walls of the ruins to shine through the open ceiling like a spotlight upon an overturned altar that had lain unnoticed in the early morning shadows. I was stunned by what appeared before me as if flood-lit on the center of a stage. And at the same time, an understanding came that might be put in words like these:

The altar where we are meant to find the living God is not made of wood or stone, nor anything else which can be destroyed or desecrated. Rather, it resides within the inner process of connecting, itself. The interacting experience of my own spirit and The Spirit IS this connection, found within daily living, by choosing to hold in my body with *agápe* love whatever happens to me as a yet-to-be-discovered blessing.

This is the holy altar, this 'yes' I can say to such hope—a hope which need not be neglected nor desecrated. All I need do is enter into this Mystery through the sacred ritual of simply welcoming whatever my body tells me is real. What a wonder, even miracle, is this encounter of body finding Body as it births our own spirit in Spirit. And, this is the sacred ritual all human beings are meant to pass on to each other—whatever name they give to it. Paul called this birthing, "Christ."

Throughout the ages, altars within many temples and churches have and will continue to be overturned, left to crumble before the ravages of time and the raging pain of those who find themselves blocked from this sacred passage through a blind quest for wealth or power and often in the very name of religion and enlightenment itself. "What will a person gain by winning the whole world, at the cost of their true self?" (Lk 9:25)

Ed's Suggestion for a Simple Morning Exercise that can Gradually Transform Your Relationship to Everything.

Early in this chapter you have already read the following statement:

> The habit of being in touch with what your body knows
> takes you through the doorway of your feelings into a
> larger world of gift or grace.

Within the very active and busy world which I have always known, nothing has been more helpful for my developing both the habit of noticing and nurturing what my body knows, while at the same time growing in the body-feel of my Christian faith, than to experience walking through the doorway of my own feelings by using the following suggestion—which you might want to try for yourself.

When awakening in the morning and before rising and beginning to plan and think about the day's work, I ask myself: "What in my body right now most needs my loving presence?" Then, I pause long enough before getting up in order to notice whether I can pick up any felt clue in my body, like physical pain, lingering excitement or curiosity around something I was reading or saw on TV.

Perhaps I'm carrying someone's self-revelation in my companioning group that still wants to say more to me. Whatever comes might be an edge of frustration around pages I thought would be easy to write but now feel stuck, or a serious health issue concerning a close friend.

When something finally identifies itself I move my awareness into that place in my body where I feel this the most, bringing a loving presence to how my body carries it. I may look at my watch to judge how much time I can spend with this inside place when I know I'm facing a busy morning. If still drowsy and I might fall back to sleep again I'll sit on the edge of my bed or in a chair in order to stay alert and present. My morning's schedule determines how long I can stay with whatever I may feel inside. If I have to stop, I notice the body-feel of this unfinishedness and promise it I will return.

But quite often routine grooming and bathroom chores that require little direct attention make it relatively easy, (with practice), to complete these morning chores while still carrying my felt-senses with a lot of nurturing, loving presence once I have taken time to do the earlier *noticing* and have a concrete feel for what came and where it is present in my body.

One soon learns the rhythm of this kind of easygoing body-companioning and not to force any connections with the mind. Simply be present in a loving, caring way with no strings attached. What makes such presence a powerful way to practice and strengthen Christian faith arises because the results generally surprise, enlighten and nourish our body's capacity to sense the Larger Loving Presence within Whom, "…we live and move and have our very existence." (Acts 17:27–28) The presence is always there. We simply need to learn how to open our body's consciousness to pick up the body-feel of it.

Often, the hidden meaning in our felt-sensing will more easily connect with random symbols scattered throughout daily life when our felt-senses are deliberately noticed and brought into awareness as we begin our day. Then, when you least expect it while at work, eating lunch, showering, getting some exercise or brushing your teeth, something can then connect and you feel a *shift* in how your body carries your issues and feelings. Something in their hidden story has surfaced. Through this little exercise you begin to learn a habit of active contemplation, active felt-connecting within the Larger Body.

Whenever you invite the hidden or unrecognized felt meanings in your life into daily awareness, the effect can begin to transform your entire body's consciousness. It tones and reenforces an openness to change and surprise when your feelings and felt-senses no longer feel imprisoned and crowded into a repressive silence. Instead, they remain open to every passing symbol that might touch and bring a welcomed release or resolution in how they are carried in your body. When felt-senses can move forward and feelings unfold, one finds more avenues within which to experience an awareness of God's Grace and Presence in all things. Aging does not become boring but deeply freeing, satisfying and fulfilling, because your body's felt-senses are not still hemmed in by the prison of earlier mindsets. We have greatly underestimated our body's capacity to reveal the Presence of God at the very core of life's meaning within our own inner experience of ourselves.

This simple morning habit, which I have described above, can teach you *the art of allowing* along with an inner freedom not to fear the change that greater wholeness always necessitates as it creates a conscious, physical posture which senses and learns through, "the eyes of your body in Christ's Body," the felt presence of God in all things. (Eph 1:18–19; 3:14–19)

So, as you read through the remaining chapters in this workbook, evolve your own format for devising steps that best take you through the process of noticing and nurturing and then set a regular time each day when you are alert enough to listen to whatever feelings your body asks you to notice and nurture. Deliberately use these chapters to start noticing whatever felt-senses seem to jump out from your reading— perhaps an idea, illustration or example, maybe a story or memory that returns. Something in a conversation, an image on TV, a problem at work, a random remark in a movie, play or novel, experiences of travel, a wedding, family graduation, new baby in the family—all these and more represent the usual fertile soil of symbol and metaphor within which felt-sensed stories yearn to bloom into the light of ever-more clear awareness and awakening.

Ancient and Modern Intimations of a Larger Body

Let your reading of this workbook, as well as everything else in all your daily relationships be included and checked out regularly with this new habit. They unveil largely unrecognized doorways into your body's rich inner world of grace and love. "Do you not know that your body is a shrine of the indwelling Holy Spirit, and the Spirit is God's gift to you." (1 Cor 6:19–20 NEB) ∎

Personal Notes

Chapter 10

Clues Unearthed During the Last Century by Scientists From Various Fields Who Discerned the Larger Body Within Which We Live

Your physically felt body is, in fact, part of a gigantic system of here and other places, now and other times, you and other people—in fact the whole universe. This sense of being bodily alive in a vast system is the body as it is felt from inside.[1]

Some Outstanding 20th Century Explorers

EUGENE GENDLIN'S challenging paradigm shift, in the quote above, balloons the lines on the tennis court, embracing the entire universe, while the physical instrument for actually experiencing such a "gigantic system" rests within our own bodies "...as they are felt from inside." In like manner, from within this same perspective and experience, we introduce in this workbook a new sense of "I" for the Christian community, one offering a potential to bring greater awareness of the body's contribution to our more consciously *embodied* faith-sense of *having one's being within* the Larger Body of the Whole Christ.

In our programs for Christians, we repeat but then rephrase the last sentence in the quotation above, changing it to read: "This sense of being bodily alive in a vast system is the Body of the Whole Christ as it can be felt from inside your own body." The deliberate inclusion of what the body knows into our more traditional faith and prayer tradition has had an interesting history during the last century, both within and outside the Christian community. In order to appreciate the dramatic expanding of our sense for what it means to be human, let's broaden our perspective on this emerging new horizon within ourselves.

Gendlin's challenging comment offers but one among many attempts throughout the twentieth century to express a rising new tide of awareness regarding the human body. Thirteen years before Gendlin's book on *Focusing* first appeared in 1978, the French Jesuit priest and paleontologist, Pierre Teilhard de Chardin's posthumously published work, *Science et Christ*, had come virtually to the same conclusion. Père Teilhard expressed his own *felt-sense* about the human organism in a way remarkably similar to that of Gendlin:

> ...the limited, tangible fragments that in common usage we call monads, molecules, bodies, are not complete beings. They are only the nucleus of such beings, their organizational centre. In each case, the real extension of these bodies coincide with the full dimensions of the universe.[2]

Père Teilhard also outlined his dissatisfaction with traditional philosophical attempts to explain the meaning of the term, *body*:

> The subtle distinctions and individual explanations we pile up in an attempt to retain in philosophy the empirical notion of 'Body' are simply patches sewn into a worn-out fabric. The very basis of our speculations about matter is defective. We must understand bodies in some other way than that we have hitherto accepted. The problem is how.[3]

Following the trail of footprints even further back in time, one cannot help but observe the felt edge of some new sense for the human body as this has slowly emerged into the light of day.

One finds virtually the same searching quest presented by William James in his conclusion to the Gifford Lectures delivered at Edinburgh in 1901–1902. James closed his lectures on *The Varieties of Religious Experience* by deliberately excluding the details of diverse belief systems from his analysis (*over-beliefs* was his term), while at the same time making sure to include the more *embodied* and common aspect of *felt inner experience* shared by people of every religious persuasion—or none at all:

> Disregarding the over-beliefs, and confining ourselves to what is common and generic, we have in *the fact that the conscious person is continuous with a wider self through which saving experiences come,* a positive content of religious experience which, it seems to me, *is literally and objectively true as far as it goes.*[4]

James extended the sense of *continuity* beyond that of an exclusively *physical* widening to incorporate into it the very heart of human consciousness itself. Moreover, he reasoned that if there is continuity, if there is "a wider sense of self," then at some quite certain and precise points within everyday human experiencing *there must be some sort of interface.*

> The whole drift of my education goes to persuade me that the world of our present consciousness is only one out of many worlds of consciousness that exist, and that those other worlds must contain experiences which have a meaning for our life also; and that although in the main their experiences and those of this world keep discrete, yet the two become continuous at certain points and higher energies filter in.[5]

Wherever sea meets the land, there is continuity—some form of interacting connection. It may be broad and wide as in a delta, or narrow and razor sharp where waves shatter themselves against newly formed lava outcroppings. But wherever and under whatever circumstances this happens, there exists an actual *physical interface*. James' words imply physical points or zones of *continuity* with some wider sense of self inside our everyday awareness, paralleling Paul's remarkable faith-realization, "...it is no longer I who live, but Christ who lives in me..." (Gal 2:20 RSV).

Modern day cell biology adds yet another dimension to the examination of our human interface. This discipline lies along the leading edge of a quiet revolution that ultimately holds the potential to unveil an entirely new understanding and experience of God. Many cell biologists have come to wonder whether each cell's physiology and behavior is governed more by *an interaction with its environment* than by its *genetic content*. In laymen's terms, this means we learn at least as much or perhaps even more from how cells *relate* to the various worlds within and around them, than we do from an analysis of the diverse *components* which we find inside them.

Since ours has become an age of *environmentalism* where survival and human evolving depend upon studying outside interacting as much as one examines the inside contents, then probing the *interactions* themselves, at least as much as we analyze the *contents,* makes a lot of sense. And would it not make equal sense to apply this same realization to our study of religion and spirituality as well? The delicate dance of actual *interacting,* the back-and-forth between each organism or cell and its environment can provide unexamined clues about who we are, why we are here and where we are going. Within this largely overlooked, under-examined world of our connecting interface, the human body itself holds a tantalizing key to unlocking a new paradigm for Christian faith and experience.

The physical organ which mediates a cell's interaction with its environment is what cell biologist Bruce Lipton has referred to as *"the Magical Membrane."* [6] This thin outer cell layer or envelope has been identified by some cell biologists as being the real cell brain. For our purposes here, the parallel we present in this book suggests that your body already knows far more about your actual *experience* of God than your mind can ever begin to think.

Why? Because your physical organism, like the magical membrane, ties you into a much larger *environment*, some ever-expanding, greater whole. For example, think of lungs, air and breathing. These three function not as discrete, separate entities but as the blending together into a single vibrant union. We may examine, analyze or think about each piece *in abstract isolation* from the others, but the reality of *their togetherness* forms an integrated living system—impossible to break apart into totally separate ingredients. Organism and environment merge into a vital interacting whole. Your body knows and lives the intimate details of all the relationships taking place within these unified and unifying larger structures.

But how do you experience all this from within your own physical organism as this can be felt from the inside? With study and experience it eventually becomes evident that you don't simply, *live.* Incredibly, *something is living you.* To grow into such awareness from the inside, however, generally involves a huge paradigm shift, a dawning consciousness which can then emerge as you begin to perceive, think about and sense yourself from within such a dramatic new perspective.

Perhaps Alan Watts, the philosopher, theologian and writer on comparative religion may have come closer to describing the actual truth and experience of *interfaced reality* when realizing that:

Today, scientists are more and more aware that what things are, and what they are doing, depends on where and when they are doing it. If, then, the definition of a thing or event must include definition of its environment, we realize that any given thing *goes with* a given environment so intimately and inseparably that it is more and more difficult to draw a clear boundary between the thing and its surroundings.

...It is essential to understand this point thoroughly: that the thing-in-itself (Kant's *ding an sich*), whether animal, vegetable, or mineral, is not only unknowable—it does not exist...Sharp and clear as the crest of the wave may be, it necessarily "goes with" the smooth and less featured curve of the trough.[7]

Within this workbook, we focus attention upon the kind of *"goes with"* consciousness that can better integrate bodily-felt experience into Christian faith by incorporating the body's knowing within spiritual awareness. For this reason, when opening our programs for Christians, we introduce Gendlin's earlier quotation and then rephrase the last sentence to read: "This sense of being bodily alive in a vast system is the Body of the Whole Christ as this can be felt from inside your own body." Merely stating this revealed truth, however, will never develop a new habit in the body of actually living it. Moving beyond that obstacle was Paul's major pedagogical challenge in his day and, obviously, the challenge still remains in our own time as well.

A New Kind of Interiority for Human Beings

From a totally different perspective, for Einstein, his bodily-felt sense for something which *goes with* another is precisely what enabled him to arrive at the core experience behind his *theory of relativity*. Relativity is all about discovering *new relationships*—heretofore *unrecognized interactions*. And, what is even more important, Einstein openly acknowledged that he knew this as a gut instinct in his body long before he could ever begin formulating it as a theory in his mind. He was *led*, or better, *guided* by a certain feltness in his body, *a felt-sense* that drew him forward on a deeply meaningful and personal quest. For Einstein, space *went together with* time. But how do you become aware of such a guiding linkage from within your own body? Where do you look? How do you feel the inner edges of this *something* that as yet has no name, but for sure *goes with* something else?

Within the human family today, not only the Einsteins are paying increased attention to their *felt-senses*. Christians, too, find themselves being drawn more and more into their bodies' sense for God. In this book, therefore, we add-in *the dimension of what your body knows* to the process of *exploration into God*. We bring the human organism, together with its unique manner of knowing, directly into the religious quest in simple ways that invite children, youth and adults to discover for themselves how their own bodies can become integral to their spiritual journey.

When Gendlin narrowed the scope of his investigation to "your physically felt body" as "part of a gigantic system," he added the further qualifying phrase: "This sense of being bodily alive in a vast system is the body as it is felt from inside."

Here, finally, in those last few words, *"the body as it is felt from inside,"* we stumbled upon a vital clue in our own search for the potential key which might unlock an entirely new awareness of the "wider sense of self through which saving experience comes." When you move beyond looking upon your body solely as *object* and deliberately connect with your body as it is felt from inside, you immediately open for exploration an inner world of *interacting experience* that the human body might actually unveil to Christians about themselves and their faith experience of incorporation into the Body of Christ. As Karl Rahner, one of the most influential Roman Catholic theologians of the twentieth century wrote, "This new situation in the Church...is the situation of a new kind of interiority for human beings."[8] A new sense of "I."

Many years ago, as young priests when we began researching the body as it is felt from inside, we immediately ran into a brick wall. The experience of learning from our bodies "...as they are felt from inside..." was precisely what had been *left out* of the development of Christian theology and spirituality.

Even today, in place of being offered a healthy, life-giving *process* for entering into and experiencing the *embodied* relationship of "living *in Christ*," Christians still find themselves presented with an endless stream of someone else's words, interpretations, and feelings in the form of prayers, rituals, and teachings that don't necessarily connect in any way with each person's unique inner felt-senses which daily call out to be noticed and nurtured in Christ.

Little in traditional Christian spirituality encourages or in any practical way helps us to answer the ringing phone of our inner feelings and felt-senses—let alone their potential contribution to a life of faith. No practical framework exists for seeking out the presence of Christ within this more intimate, personal world of our own body's knowing.

All too often what one finds, instead, are dogmas, teachings, and ideas for the mind, along with numerous moral warnings *about* the body. Yet, merely knowing something in your mind can in no way enable *a process of wholeness* to mature and grow forward within your living organism itself. Knowing in your mind is not the process of changing in your body. Any life-sustaining, peacemaking, Christian spirituality lives within *embodied* human experience.

Growing Into a New Habit Within Your Own Body's Knowing

The information in this book, for most readers, has yet to become *a habit* in their bodies. What does this mean?

Can you remember back to when you first learned how to type or play a musical instrument? Your attention was totally focused upon the keyboard, the violin's strings or the piano's keys, the written musical notes before you or the words you wanted to type. You first had to think every movement, each keystroke or physical movement so your fingers would produce the right word on the typewriter or sound on the musical instrument. Nothing was automatic. You had no habit yet developed in your body. Your teacher made you do little finger exercises on the keyboard to limber up your fingers. You needed to memorize where all the letters or notes were and which fingers pressed what letters or keys. You first had to *think* typing each letter or playing every note.

If you still type, or play a musical instrument today, what happens when typing out some handwritten letter or reading a sheet of music? The musical notes now flow smoothly in through your eyes and out through your fingertips into the melodious instrument. No thought process impedes a seamless flow from a handwritten page before you to the neatly typed text on your computer screen.

In much the same manner, the habit of noticing and nurturing your important feelings seems destined to mature into a new habit of finding yourself as an integral participant within something greater than yourself—if only we can learn how to develop the eyes to see and ears to hear the wondrous spiritual symphony within and around us. Where, one often wonders, can we discover the mother or father hawks in our time to guide us into those grace-filled updrafts? For most, such development unfolds in a rather slow, often jerky fashion through continual learning how to readjust our relationships, much as we now find ourselves becoming more environmentally sensitive and accountable in the interactions with our global body—Mother Earth.

So, the first step toward growing into this sense of being part of something greater than yourself means developing a new habit in your body. And the cultivation of that habit means learning to notice and nurture your important feelings and felt-senses, identifying your Affection Teachers and, as a Christian, experiencing yourself as a living cell in this Larger Body that Paul calls, the Christ.

> (Father)...the glory that you have given me I have given them,
> so that they may be one, as we are one, I in them and you in me,
> that they may become completely one... *(1 Jn 17:22–23 NRSV)*

> For we are God's handiwork, created in Christ Jesus to devote
> ourselves to the good deeds for which Christ has designed us.
> *(Eph 2:10 NEB)*

> Now you are Christ's body, and each of you a limb or organ of it.
> *(1 Cor 12:27 NEB)*

The lesson to be drawn from this experience applies equally to the task of beginning to explore your own important inner feelings, to *touch and feel* your way through your own body rather than always trying to think or figure everything out in your head. You *balance* your thinking by turning to *a different kind of habit* for guidance, a habit which involves putting your analyzing, and problem-solving mind on the shelf periodically in order more attentively to notice, nurture and hold in a caring way the felt-senses within your body. You make space each day for regular check-in time, discovering what stories might lie waiting in your feelings and felt-senses. This more physical task also includes noticing *where* you carry a problem or issue in your body and how this actually feels.

Clues Unearthed During the Last Century

An Old-Fashioned Lesson From a Pre-Digital Darkroom

Pete offers an illustration from his experience as a photographer that may provide a kind of metaphor for how to set out upon your own development of this new habit of noticing and nurturing your felt-senses.

> On many occasions before the advent of digital photography, I've caught myself acting in a somewhat puzzling way when working alone in an old-fashioned photographer's darkroom. The act of physically unrolling and removing already exposed film from its little cassette cartridge before placing it in a liquid bath for chemical development can be a somewhat complex task—largely, because the exercise requires one to work in total darkness.
>
> First, the film must be rolled onto a specially designed plastic spool, an operation difficult enough in a well-lit room where you can actually see what you are doing. But the procedure becomes even more exasperating when the lights are out and you quite literally cannot see your hand in front of your face.
>
> In the past, when I have used this illustration during workshop retreats, a question I routinely ask participants has been: "Can any of you guess the very first thing I do once I turn off the lights and prepare to pull the film from its cassette before winding it into the slotted plastic spool and immersing it in the chemical developing bath?"
>
> Answers have ranged from, "I'd just sit down and cry," to "Maybe I'd pray." But where at first there have been puzzled looks, these are soon followed by smiles of understanding when I share that, "The very first thing I spontaneously do upon turning off the lights—is *to close my eyes*."
>
> Here I am in a totally dark room, unable to see anything. I'm faced with an intricate manual task, and without any thought or deliberation my instinctive first reaction is to shut my eyes. Then I ask, "And what do you suppose happens when I do that?" It has always amazed me how so many of them instinctively knew why I closed my eyes in the dark room before beginning this procedure. They quickly realized how all my inner attention and capacity for *presence* would drain away from my eyes physically straining to visualize the film and plastic spool in the dark. This then allowed my full attention to flow down my arms, out

through my hands and into my finger tips. Once there, I could then *feel my way* through this intricate procedure rather than attempting to think and physically see my way through it. Without any mental reflecting, I spontaneously fell back upon a totally different capacity for sensory presence to the task at hand, letting my finger tips sense their way and guide me through the procedure.

In a similar way, something of this same *more embodied sensing your way inward* illustrates what each of us needs to develop as a familiar body-habit in order to build the missing body-link between religious teachings which our minds can grasp intellectually and the experience for which St. Paul so often prayed that his Christian followers would discover within their own body-knowing— "…it is no longer I who live, but Christ who lives in me…" (Gal 2:20 RSV). "For to me life is Christ…" (Phil 1:21 NEB).

We must learn to bring a loving, caring presence (*agápe*) to the feelings and burdens we bear within our own bodies. They, too, have a story to tell. A healthy self-love, congruent with and owning the reality of one's experience acknowledges and works with the obstacles we all carry in our efforts to love both ourselves and one another. One might attempt to express such healthy self-love by paraphrasing St. John's First Epistle as follows:

> God is love *(agápe)*; anyone who dwells in love is dwelling in God and God in that person… Everyone who has *agápe* love is a child of God and knows God, but those without *agápe* love know nothing of God… Though God has never been seen by any person, God dwells in us if we have *agápe* love for ourselves and each other. Thus, his *agápe* love is brought to perfection within us. *(1 Jn 4:12–16* passim*)*

Learning the Body-Language of *Agápe*

Christian spirituality finds itself challenged to approach the above foundational statement not solely from the vantage point of further historical analysis and interpretation of scriptural texts and other sources, but from inside the development of a more sensitive habit of noticing and nurturing important feelings within the human body itself as these can be felt from inside. This means becoming more aware of and learning *the body-language of agápe*. The data resource for theological and pastoral investigation widens and expands to include what the body knows. Just as we learn how our bodies speak through the language of our feelings, so too, Christians find themselves challenged to learn how the revelations of Sacred Scripture have also been written within our own body-language of *agápe*. The sacred message lies hidden within an experiential process felt inside our own bodies and feelings, unfolding under the influence of deeper, felt personal meanings and the life of faith.

Christian spirituality is meant to be a lifelong, organic, developmental process of noticing and nurturing your important feelings as a very special doorway which allows your body's Affection Teacher—the gift of God's love *in Christ*—to open your pores of *presence*. Then from within, as this develops into a habit in your body, the hidden depth and breadth of God's Presence in all things may begin to break through inside you in a more experiential way.

Some may wonder about the appropriateness of using the word, *agápe*, when it is directed toward oneself. But a moment's reflection on the psychology of this approach can easily clarify its important function.

Ample research, along with commonsense experience show that people *have not* been taught a simple, effective way to process their negative feelings. Whenever they themselves, or their environment, saddles them with a sense of low self-esteem, self-doubt or a negative self-image, they invariably tend to treat other people in exactly the same way they feel about and treat themselves.

We can finally appreciate today that at the time when the Scriptures were written, if the authors had developed a better sense for the above connection, they would have expanded their injunction about "love your neighbor as yourself." (Mk 12:31) The way people feel about themselves influences their treatment of other people. Love your neighbor as yourself makes absolutely no sense psychologically when a person carries feelings of self-hatred or low self-esteem within themselves.

Furthermore, something terribly important becomes lost in the midst of all this confusion. Our fears and tears, our feelings of low self-esteem, sadness, and anger which we so often perceive and label as enemies are trying to tell us *something very important about ourselves*.

They are *not* our enemies. The perennial challenge remains—learning to notice, nurture and listen to the untold stories and felt-senses rising up from within the very feelings we seek to banish from our awareness. Yet, such experience falls directly within the added teaching of Christ, "You have heard that it was said, 'You shall love your neighbor and hate your enemy.' But I say to you, Love your enemies and pray for those who persecute you." (Mt 5:43–44 RSV)

In a paper prepared for a symposium on "Behaviorism and Phenomenology: Contrasting Bases for Modern Psychology" and given at Rice University in Texas, March 1963, Dr. Carl Rogers summarized much of Eugene Gendlin's early contribution to the field by saying:

> "His thinking constitutes one step in transcending the subject-object dichotomy which plagues our thinking today." [9]

Rogers also added a further precision when commenting on Gendlin's work by including a comment to support his own position for advancing the possibility of an authentic *science of the person* by praising Gendlin for:

> ...his careful delineation of the preconceptual process of experiencing and the manner in which it functions in the creation of personal meaning. Here is a concept rooted in naturalistic observation, purely phenomenological in origin, of a process nature, which helps to bridge the gap between the subjective and objective in the way in which it lends itself to objective research. [10]

So long as our perceptual systems, our modes of interpretation and theory-making remain mired *exclusively* in a separated, subject-object, dichotomized universe, our ability to explore experiencing that extends beyond this narrowed framework will remain frustrated, under-explored and little appreciated. The new paradigm, however, to which both Gendlin and Rogers have made a more than substantial contribution over the last 50 years, has been to introduce the inner workings found in the creation of personal meaning into the scope of valid scientific investigation—in short, opening the possibility of an effective and cogent science of the subjective.

This monumental step forward then unfolds a sweeping panorama of inner experience for additional understanding. There now exists *a point of entry* into a vast, largely unexplored world of human awareness. It opens for further exploration that realm of *"going together with"* or *"having one's being within,"* which expresses our embodied selves no longer as individual, separated billiard balls—disparate peas rattling about in a pod against one another in competitive survival mode—but now with a refreshing alternative, a challenging new paradigm perspective on ourselves, one another and the world around us. Moreover, this possibility then opens up the world of personal experience within religion and spiritual awareness for new investigation because the human body itself plays such an intimate role within the unfolding of such awareness.

The implications, both for the Christian community as well as other spiritual communions who value their own traditions and sense for being part of something greater than themselves, could not be more compelling. By deepening our capacity for inviting congruence and inner wholeness to mature within our own individual bodies and feelings we thereby build a far more solid foundation for greater communion with one another in the social order. In addition, there is much within our own Judaeo-Christian spiritual tradition which can support just such a unifying movement forward in human awareness, along with the building of a healthy social order and world peace, if only simple, practical and effective ways for communicating such experience and values can become fully supported and employed.

It can, for example, leave Christian believers genuinely awe-struck when recognizing the significance of the word, *glory*, within the Sacred Scriptures. The passage recently quoted from John 17:20–23 earlier in this chapter is a case in point:

> "Father...the glory which you gave me I have given to them
> that they may be one, as we are one; I in them and you in me,
> may they be perfectly one."

"Glory," for Christians, is not some commodity to be acquired and hoarded for personal gain but a maturing awareness of ourselves *in Christ—the sense of being within a Larger Body*. Gendlin and Rogers provide a new lens through which we may now have better eyes to see and a clearer perspective or vantage point from which to feel our way into such revelation and experience of ourselves which, at present, we can only barely begin to understand. "We see now as through a glass darkly, but then face to face." (1 Cor 13:12)

Moreover, the same word, "glory" appears in Paul's letter to the Ephesians 3:14–19, when he prays, "...out of his infinite glory may he give you the power through his Spirit for your *hidden self* to grow strong..." Paul sheds light upon the gift of a body-sense for knowing or presencing wherein, through faith, you find yourself as a living cell within a Larger Body. "Hidden self," (τὸν ἔσω ἄνθρωπον), literally *the inner human*, or in the language we use, "...a felt-sense of being bodily alive in a vast system is the body as it is felt from inside;" and again, "...this sense of being bodily alive in a vast system is the Body of the Whole Christ as it can be felt from inside my own body." Such experience when embraced with Christian faith represents an awareness of the *communio sanctorum*, the communion of saints as this can be known in our bodies—as they are felt from inside.

Within the context of Christian faith, *glory* has little, if anything to do with honors, position or power. Rather it represents a language from within and about human interiority. It includes a body-sense for *having one's being within* which connotes an ever-maturing inner awareness of tied-in-ness, oneness—a maturing sense of some greater cosmic congruence. The halo on saints connotes neither prominence nor set-apartness, but a grace-filled and harmonious body-sense for unification, integration, amalgamation as well as unity in diversity.

Glory represents an experience which draws our attention toward the world of human presencing, interacting, linking and connecting—sharpening our sensitivity to the *reality* of relationships. Where Christian revelation and spirituality have something substantive to offer science, in this regard, lies in what they unveil about the quality of human presence *in relationships* and the profound revelation which such experience signifies for our sense of both God and ourselves. We will touch upon this further in much greater detail throughout our reflections on *agápe* in the next three chapters.

Paul continually falls back upon his own *inside body-language* while attempting to convey the unique world of unifying with-ness or within-ness which carries the quality of felt presence he struggles to describe. "I pray that *your inward eyes* may be illumined, so that you may know what is the hope to which he calls you, what the wealth and glory of the share he offers you..." (Eph 1:18 NEB) "Inward eyes" is a modern-day translation of the ancient Greek which literally means, *eyes of the heart*, (ὀφθαλμοὺς τῆς καρδίας), emphasizing an inner body-knowing with roots deep in a felt-sense that we live within the embrace of some Larger Body and Power greater than ourselves.

From within this experiential heritage, Paul prays not only for the Christian community but for the entire Gentile world as well, that they may discover the vast resources of energy beyond the power of humans or of this world. As we shall soon see, this is the power of *agápe* love, emerging from a person who truly lives, "in Christ," so the energy of God lives and grows inside that person, penetrating even the mitochrondria of our body's cellular behavior until, "...knowing (in your body) the love of Christ, which is beyond all knowledge (i.e. mental, conceptual knowledge) you are filled with the utter fulness of God." (Eph 4:19)

The pioneering research of Eugene Gendlin and Carl Rogers has opened a welcoming path for new explorers of human consciousness within the twenty first century. A significant part of their generation's task and challenge will be to translate the fruits of their new research into practical, pastoral applications for solving the immense problems which human societies and individual lives must face in this demanding new age.

We close this chapter with a prayer written by Ed for those learning to bring God *(agápe)* into all their relationships, beginning with their own body and its feelings. This prayer is modeled on the Jerusalem Bible translation of St. Paul's Letter to the Ephesians (3:14–19). Ed has woven in Paul's teachings from other letters as well, also incorporating psychological terms which we use to explain the steps of this inner process in order that Christians may more easily begin to experience what we believe Paul was trying to call forth from within our own bodies.

A Prayer Based on *Ephesians 3:14–19*

O God, from out of the wealth of Your *agápe* love, I pray that You bless me with an open and available body through the power of Your Spirit, so my hidden identity in Christ may become more real for me with each passing day.

Rediscovering the Lost Body-Connection

May the Body of Christ in Whom I live and move and have my very existence be so intimately sensed within my own body that I discover a faith in Christ transforming my tears and pain into teachers and friends.

With your *agápe* love planted in my body, and building upon this foundation as I grow in the habit of Noticing and Nurturing how my body carries my feelings, instead of treating some as enemies, help me to share this love with the burden my body often carries.

Finally, through this gift of Your Presence when I can become more loving and companion my body burdened by difficult feelings, may I with all the saints grasp the breadth and the length, the height and the depth of the love of Christ within me, a love beyond all the understanding that reason and thinking could ever bring me.

With these deep roots and a firm foundation in *agápe* love, I continue to thank You, God, for my journey in the Body of the Whole Christ so that I may be filled to overflowing with Your wholeness, Your goodness, and Your life. Amen. ∎

Personal Notes

Chapter 11

Agápe in the Light of Carl Rogers' Research

Ed's Reflection on Experiencing Dr. Carl Rogers

MANY YEARS AGO, when I was studying with Carl Rogers, what fascinated and touched me most deeply was his quality of presence in the relationship both to himself as well as with the person whom he was companioning. The experience was a powerful teacher. At the time, I had already read just about everything he had written, but never did I expect to learn so much from the physical presence of the writer himself.

Studying with Carl in the graduate seminars I attended, meant being with him as he companioned a volunteer from the group. One learned the most from him simply by being with and observing him as he journeyed with another. Within this setting, Carl would often informally describe his approach as an effort to discover the necessary and sufficient qualities of relational presence that could support the development of congruence (inner wholeness) within his client. Many, many times throughout such discussions and presentations I have seen hardened, skeptical psychotherapists, social workers or psychiatrists in the group simply melt into tears as they experienced the transformative power of his personal presence.

Rachel Remen, M.D., who for many years was a clinical professor at the University of California, San Francisco Medical School wrote of her first experience of Carl when she was on the Stanford faculty as follows:

■

While I was still part of the Stanford faculty, I was one of a small group of traditional physicians and psychologists invited to a day long master's class with Dr. Carl Rogers, a pioneering humanistic psychotherapist. I was young and proud of being an expert, sought after for my opinions and judgments. Rogers' approach to therapy, called Unconditional Positive Regard, seemed to me to be a deplorable lowering of standards. Yet it was rumored that his therapeutic outcomes were little short of magical. I was curious and so I went.

Rogers was a deeply intuitive man, and as he spoke to us about how he worked with his patients, he paused often to put into words what he did instinctively and naturally. Very different from the articulate and authoritative style of presentations I was accustomed to at the medical center. Could someone so seemingly hesitant have any expertise at all? I doubted it. From what I could gather, Unconditional Positive Regard came down to sitting in silence and accepting everything the patient said without judgment or interpretation. I could not imagine how this might prove helpful.

Finally, Dr. Rogers offered us a demonstration of his approach. One of the doctors in the class volunteered to act as his client and they rearranged their chairs to sit opposite one another. As Rogers turned toward him and was about to begin the demonstration session he stopped and looked thoughtfully at his little audience, I shifted impatiently in my chair. Then Rogers began to speak. "Before every session I take a moment to remember my humanity," he told us. "There is no experience that this man has that I cannot share with him, no fear that I cannot understand, no suffering that I cannot care about, because I too am human. No matter how deep his wound, he does not need to be ashamed in front of me. I too am vulnerable. And because of this, I am enough. Whatever his story, he no longer needs to be alone with it. This is what will allow his healing to begin."

The session that followed was profound. Rogers conducted it without saying a single word, conveying to his client simply by the quality of his attention a total acceptance of him exactly as he was. The doctor began to talk and the session rapidly became a great deal more than the demonstration of a technique. In the safe climate of Rogers' total acceptance, he began to shed his masks, hesitantly at first and then more and more easily. As each mask fell, Rogers welcomed the one behind it unconditionally, until finally we glimpsed the beauty of the doctor's naked face. I doubt that even he himself had ever seen it before. By that time many of our own faces were naked and some of us had tears in our eyes. I remember wishing that I had volunteered, envying

Rediscovering the Lost Body-Connection

this doctor the opportunity to be received by someone in such a total way. Except for a few moments with my godfather, I had never experienced that kind of welcome.[1]

■

(Ed continues:) As my training program with Dr. Rogers' progressed, I came to realize that what he was teaching us as potential healers stood out for me as the missing link within pastoral Christianity for empowering each person to tap into the gift of *agápe* love within their own body. As we have repeatedly emphasized throughout this book, this means first learning to develop a healing relationship with my own body and its emotions. Such a quality of presence creates an initial sanctuary for homeless feelings inside myself.

While practicing such a growing habit within my own life, this emerging teacher can then invite others to learn how to begin giving sanctuary to whatever has gone into hiding, been denied, unloved or devalued inside themselves. I found it so freeing and hope-filled that a fellow psychotherapist could not only practice but grow personally through his research, knowing in my Christian bones that this might be the closest I would ever come to experiencing in my own body the human qualities of a presence in *agápe* love that so many with open hearts must have felt in the presence of Jesus.

Like Dr. Remen I, too, have worked for decades in a culture where the human spirit and heart too often go homeless. When St. John wrote in his First Epistle that "*agápe* love is brought to perfection *(maturity, completion)* within us," it gives my faith the boost of courage and hope it needs to continue changing and growing in the quality of *agápe* love shared with my own scary feelings as well as helping others to do the same. I find it wondrous to continually experience within myself and others that this *agápe* love is a relational process and, as St. John said so clearly, it is *developmental* and therefore meant to be *integral* to the maturing of our own humanity as this divine process slowly unfolds within us.

A Baptist minister recently wrote when applying for our 3 Month training program, "What a revolutionary notion that *the way to heal is not to enforce change* but *to love the hurting, broken parts*; even to bring the Caring, Loving Presence to all our resistances."

Agápe Love as An Expanding Sense of Identity

Dr. Carl Rogers spent his professional career researching *the quality of human interaction and presence* which facilitates inner wholeness and healing. When children struggle to mature, or the emotionally wounded do not know how to connect with stuck feelings, his study becomes increasingly relevant.

In Chapter 7 we introduced an exercise to help you discover the body-feel of your own Affection Teacher. We began with affection because your developing sense for *agápe* love first appears *in your body* through an experience so simple as affection. When a little boy or girl cuddles a puppy, they experience themselves as *folded into* the puppy and the puppy feels folded into their own body. Our Affection Teacher appears as an early developmental herald raising into awareness this body sense of *enfolding* or *being enfolded*. You don't just think affection in your mind. You directly feel and experience such enfolding from within your own physical organism. In Dr. Maslow's words, "The strawberries tasted better in my child's mouth than they did in my own." Our experience of affection raises a physical sense of tied-in-ness to the world and one another. Recall, as well, Alan Watt's comment that, "...the clearly defined crest of a wave *goes with* the smooth and less featured curve of the trough." An experience of the *"goes with"* lies within your body's awareness. Your physical organism provides you with your actual *feel for the road*, as much in a car as within your explorations into God.

In a similar manner, the New Testament teaches that Christ has enfolded Himself into us as we find ourselves enfolded into Christ. Once again, however, *we can only know such experience through, with and in our bodies.* We may mentally *understand* a teaching *about* such revelation, but the actual experience lies within our own body-knowing. There we discover the New Adam, the *Christ-in-us* and *we-in-Him*.

The rise of spiritual hunger, therefore, foretells the developmental birth of a new sense of identity, not separate from, but *enfolded-into* some Larger Body. The "...wider self through which saving experience comes...",[2] which William James identified during his investigation of religious experience, expresses itself within a New Testament Christian faith perspective through *agápe* as the *embodied language* of this developing new sense of human identity.

How, then, within our direct everyday awareness, does *agápe* express itself in our bodies? Toward what experience must we now turn our attention? Can the findings of contemporary psychology assist in our search for the embodied roots of being enfolded into something greater than ourselves?

Carl Rogers' research outlines specific characteristics in a quality of presence that people universally experience as sacred, being in a holy place, or walking on hallowed ground. We find his effort especially significant for the Christian community because it provides better understanding and a convenient vocabulary with which to comment on the gifted invitation of a developmental experience that can appear within the human body. The apostle Paul constantly prayed for this gift when asking that the Christian community might mature in the experience which New Testament revelation describe as the gift of *agápe* love.

Three Psychological Characteristics of *Agápe*

We are now better able to examine Bishop Robinson's comment about the Body of Christ as *a developmental experience* for persons of Christian faith seeking to explore that "...common organic functioning, as the new tissues take on the rhythms and metabolism of the body into which they have been grafted." [3]

Within a Christian faith context, *agápe* expresses an *interactive* human experience, whether felt within oneself or through interaction with others. It blesses both the one who gives and the one who receives. When experiencing such moments as either giver or receiver, we find ourselves drawn or *enfolded* with/in one another.

The issue of human wellness and healing, or wholeness, revolves around an experience of inner *congruence* directly experienced and felt within the human organism. For us, congruence means, *being able to feel your feelings physiologically and allowing them to symbolize themselves accurately.* Developing a body-sense of congruence *within yourself* and learning to take care of your inner environment balances your inside ecology so you can then bring this same caring quality of presence toward your outer environment. The process of your inner congruence then becomes your teacher for how you present yourself and interact in the world around you. But this process first begins *inside your own body.* Your developing sense for inner congruence, or wholeness, can then guide your quest for growing in *the body-experience* of being an integral part of something greater than yourself.

We introduce the topic of congruence here because a growing inner sense for this experience directly relates to maturing in the capacity for *agápe* presence. For our purposes, we can identify three defining characteristics of maturing *agápe* love from inside your body's knowing by using some of the helpful terminology developed in Carl Rogers' client-centered psychology and descriptions of congruence. While the three may be discussed separately, each still remains an integral part of a much larger, interacting process. The three are: (1) *An Experience of being Fully Received*, (2) *Empathic Presence* and, (3) *Unconditional Acceptance* or, as Rogers would phrase it, being the recipient of an experience of *Unconditional Positive Regard*.

(1) THE EXPERIENCE OF BEING FULLY RECEIVED: Have you ever attempted to share a deep personal longing or issue with someone, and while making that effort felt they were unable to be fully present to you? It might not have been their fault. Perhaps the other person had no basis in his or her experience to empathize with your unique situation. Even though they could hear your words and understand the gist of your meaning, something in their body-response did not radiate back in a way that you felt truly touched and *heard on the inside*. You did not experience a body-sense of being *fully received*.

When training small group companions to become team members with us during our program, we teach them to ask themselves a simple question while working with participants in their groups. This question has helped our facilitators to enter more fully *inside* their participants as each shares his or her story. The question: "How is this other person *in* what he or she is saying?" By this we invite the trainee to direct their attention not just toward the dictionary meaning of spoken words, but also to include a careful listening inward to the body-feel of how each speaker experiences the sharing of his or her words in an inside body way. "Does she carry herself in a lonely, excited, wondering, or sad inner way?" "Does he feel angry, challenged, depressed, or perhaps feeling a quiet moment of self-realization? What is the body *tonality* of each person who speaks their innermost self?"

We then teach our trainees to respond verbally, if possible, using the speaker's own words as to how that person inwardly carries the *felt-meaning* of their words within their own body. "That felt really scary for you." "You seemed all alone in that situation." "It felt like a heavy burden lifted from your shoulders." This ability to reflect back *felt-in-the-body-meaning* with accuracy lies at the heart of helping a person to feel more fully received. The speaker then knows not only that the content of his or her words have been heard, but also the more intimate, personal body sense which goes along with them.

Being fully received allows a quiet bond of *trust* to grow between persons who can share and receive not only accurate information, but also the deeper felt-senses in one another's lives. While it is a blessing for anyone to be heard in this way, it is also a privilege to walk with another in the intimate depths of his or her sacred inner world. *Agápe* interaction is what opens up this entire universe of human experience for exploration and personal growth. It forms a solid ground for building healthy, peace-filled community experience because it grounds the relationship in trust.

(2) EMPATHIC PRESENCE: expresses a special quality of your body's attention directed toward your own or another's inner world of meaning, feeling, and felt-sensing. It communicates companioning, an accompanying *presence* in that world, not so much as an analyzing, but an inviting, supportive, attentive listening. The person who shares their inner feelings experiences a sense that you can be truly present, companioning them *in your body* as they speak, because you are comfortable enough with who you are that you can find yourself free and not afraid to enter into their world. You know you will not lose your own identity and can therefore companion them in their hurting, scared or angry inner world. The capacity for such inward listening is the polar opposite of someone fussing with things on their desk, glancing about, or looking out the window while you pour out your deeply felt story.

We teach the importance of empathic presence and caring listening to our new companions because the quality of their own bodily-felt relationship to participants in their small groups actually *models* how those same participants must then learn to relate to the sad, scary, lonely, and often frightened, or angry feelings inside themselves.

Frequently, your hurting inner world may at first be quite *hidden* from you, especially when you have not yet developed any habit of taking care of your own important feelings. For this reason, noticing and nurturing how your body carries such feelings helps to build the essential foundation for a healthy, living Christian spirituality. Whole people beget whole people. Fragmented, disconnected persons tend to spread their own inner dissociation no matter to what church or spiritual organization they belong or who their pastor may be. It takes the process of community-building going forward *inside* each one of us before any lasting communion can occur within the social order around us.

Initially, anyone's difficult feelings may need to experience an empathic presence from someone who can respond in a receptive, caring, way. An experience of such presence will then serve as a blueprint for how the person receiving such caring attention may then begin relating to his or her own inner feelings in much the same manner, inviting their own Affection Teacher to guide them. Gradually, under the influence of this change in relationship to themselves, some degree of forward movement or felt inner processing can begin to unfold.

We all experience empathic presence within the body and communicate it through the body. This quality of presence does not arise as a purely mental or conceptual exercise. It emerges from within your body and can be felt by the one toward whom it is directed. Yet, it remains strange how we can more readily respond in an empathic way to the needs of a total stranger than we do to our own familiar, so-called *enemies* who populate the seldom companioned underworld of our own neglected feelings.

Carl Jung once described a tragic paradox he had observed in the lives of many Christians. It appears as an unsuspecting choice made very early in childhood, triggered largely by observing how our parents, teachers and other peers relate to and push away their own feelings, especially those emotions labeled as *bad* or *unacceptable*. Such uncritically introjected modeling raises protective walls within each person, cutting them off from a caring presence for their own feelings and felt-senses.

Christ taught us, "You have heard that it was said, 'You shall love your neighbor and hate your enemy.' But I say to you, love your enemies and pray for those who persecute you." (Mt 5:43 RSV). Yet, what about the enemies we have already created *inside* ourselves from among the inner feelings we so often reject, push away, neglect, or otherwise disown? What about the separations, inner division, and disconnections that we, more than likely maintain unintentionally and even protect inside ourselves? Jung commented:

> That I feed the hungry, that I forgive an insult, that I love my enemy in the name of Christ—all these are undoubtedly great virtues. What I do unto the least of my brethren, that I do unto Christ. But what if I should discover that the least amongst them all, the poorest of all the beggars, the most impudent of all the offenders, the very enemy himself—that these are within me, and that I myself stand in need of the alms of my own kindness—that I myself am the enemy who must be loved—what then? As a rule, the Christian's attitude is then reversed; there is no longer any question of love or long-suffering; we say to the brother within us "Raca," and condemn and rage against ourselves. We hide it from the world; we refuse to admit ever having met this least among the lowly in ourselves. Had it been God himself who drew near to us in this despicable form, we should have denied him a thousand times before a single cock had crowed.[4]

Into the jumbled world of such confusion within much of our Christian world, your Affection Teacher opens a doorway into the possibility of discovering the gift of God's Presence and grace at the heart of what we fear and avoid most inside ourselves—namely the very feelings and physical body we have so often made into our enemies.

Recall how St. John reminded us that, *"God is agápe."* He describes *a quality of presence in relationship* that brings new life. But from what source does such blessed experience arise? *Empathic presence* and a sense of *being fully received* embody two psychological ingredients which hold the potential to unveil an even Larger Life-Giving Presence that can surface from within the habit of noticing and nurturing your important feelings in an *agápe* loving way.

The essential point which Christians overlook, because we have never been taught how to have *agápe* for our own hurting body, puts the cart before the horse by first trying to love our external enemies. Yet, the doorway into such transforming experience lies right within *the relationship to our own body's feelings.* The tragedy which Jung described lies in the simple fact that Christian spirituality misses this open doorway even though, as we shall see in a chapter ahead, St. Paul already recognized and described it nearly 2000 years ago.

But for now, let's move forward and consider a third aspect of *agápe* by looking into a final phrase Dr. Rogers used to characterize yet another quality of personal presence which he found brought greater healing and inner wholeness into people's lives.

(3) UNCONDITIONAL ACCEPTANCE: What the recipient feels in their body is your authentic availability to care for him or her as a person without you needing or demanding that they first become someone other than who they are before you will enter into their world of felt meaning in order to companion them.

Such a person feels received by you just as they are *in this moment*. A person capable of *agápe* love can allow other people to be different from them while at the same time still accepting such persons and companioning them with all their differences. A distinct body sense comes across within unconditional acceptance and empathic presence. The listener has found security within his or her own self-identity. This means they are congruent enough within themselves to a point where they can truly listen, and not fear being swallowed up by another's confusion or pain.

The listener does not necessarily have to accept or approve the lifestyle, choices or beliefs of the one who is speaking. Rather, it is this unique person who is accepted and heard. The experience then allows a recipient of such *agápe* love to begin the slow process of turning his or her attention inward, companioning and listening to themselves in the same caring way they now find themselves being heard, accepted, and received by you.

We have found that this experience can describe, to some degree, our body's quality of physical *agápe* presence which moves wholeness (holiness) forward toward greater completion and fullness within the human organism. Once you begin developing a body-sense for such experience there can be no question but that you are walking upon holy ground. The sense of being fully received, empathic presence, and unconditional acceptance provide a convenient vocabulary describing a bodily-felt quality of physical presence which expresses how, through faith, *agápe (God)* can be directly experienced within the human organism.

Ed shares an illustration below of the dramatic effect such fully-received, empathic presence and unconditional acceptance can have upon others.

An Example of Companioning Presence

On one occasion, sponsored by the Medical School's Psychiatry Department at a University of California campus I, along with about 300 other professionals, was attending a week-long program in a very large amphitheater-like room where we all looked down upon the discussions and demonstrations involving many different approaches to healing.

On this particular occasion, a panel of world-renowned doctors in psychiatry and psychotherapy were gathered at a long table below us. Dr. Carl Rogers was included in the group. Each panelist had already made their individual presentations, and at this closing session they were all now gathered to answer questions from the audience. Each panelist was given time to respond to all questioners. Late in the afternoon of the last day a final questioner from the audience turned out to be, or to have been a graduate student in the host department at the University. Instead of asking a question, she had instead prepared a personal complaint to air publicly about her mistreatment and, as her talk unfolded, what for her had been a visibly painful experience.

She was a very large young woman with a somewhat squeaky voice, airing an inappropriate intervention, given the context of the program. So, as she continued with her tale of woe, people began to snicker and eventually laugh out loud at her ill-timed performance. As the audience's laughter and its noise grew louder, her nervousness and pitch grew higher until, finally, she just fell apart and sat down.

While all this was unfolding, I found myself caught up and carried along by the audience and panel's ridiculing reaction to her, even turning to the person beside me to offer some critical comment of my own, when suddenly my eyes were riveted by the sight of Dr. Rogers at the end of the table of experts below. He alone among all the panelists was fully present to her in her pain and humiliation, even though she had brought it upon herself. From where I was seated high above I could feel this quality of presence emanating from his whole being. I was so touched that tears began to role down my cheeks and I felt ashamed to have allowed myself to be swept along by the crowd.

One by one the panelists responded, scolding, chiding, even further humiliating her. Yet, all the while they were doing this Dr. Rogers never lost his contact with her. He never joined in any of the sarcastic wit aimed at her which brought more pain, but remained steadfast looking at her with a companioning presence and an unconditional acceptance that began to touch others in the audience as well when they noticed him.

From my position at the far end of a semicircular row of seats on the other side of the room, I could still physically feel this empathic bond as did the man next to me who also began to wipe his eyes. The sheer power of Carl's solitary, embodied connection in the face of this large crowd's swelling movement in the opposite direction began to have its impact. Gradually, others in the audience one by one fell silent. By the time it was Dr. Rogers' turn to respond you could have heard a pin drop in this vast theater of so-called wise men and women, all professional healers who had just wiped up the floor with this hurting woman. When it was time for him to speak all eyes were silently upon him and her.

Throughout her entire ordeal she had very clearly felt his long companioning presence, as many in the audience gradually began to feel as well. After allowing the silence to seep through us all and never once looking away from her, he simply said, "This whole experience has hurt you in such a deep way." And from across the room I could hear a very grateful, "Yes, Dr. Rogers, it has. Thank you for being with me," and that was all either of them said. A prolonged and very meaning-filled silence ensued before the chairman finally dared to break this hallowed sense of presence with a rather awkward and nervous, "This program is now concluded." ■

An Exercise You can often Return to as You Grow into the Habit of Bringing a Loving Presence to How Your Body is Carrying a Difficult Feeling

1. Ask yourself, "What in my body right now most needs my loving presence?" *(Pause to go inside and do the exercise)*

2. Notice where you carry that in your body and how does it feel to be carrying it. *(pause)*

3. Now, try to be with that place using the Affection Teacher your body already knows (cf. Ch. 7). *(pause)*

4. Notice how your body feels when you are with it in a caring, loving way as it carries this *pain, fear, sadness, anger... whatever... (pause)*

5. How does your body feel when it is treated this way? *(If in a group—then share)*

6. How is this nurturing experience different from the way you used to treat difficult feelings in your body? *(pause—then if in a group, once again share)*

Personal Notes

Chapter 12

Exploring Agápe Love from Inside Your Body's Knowing

The Body-Life of *Agápe* Love

TO BE EMPATHETICALLY HEARD by another and unconditionally accepted is to experience in some way that your very personhood is received and enfolded with/into the body of another, just as their caring presence for you is enfolded into your body. For a Christian, such experience in faith can represent the vibrant, embodied manifestation of Christ's prayer to His Father: "...that they may be one, as we are one; I in them and you in me, may they be perfectly one." (Jn 17:22–23). The interaction itself is the living with/in God, when shared in and passed on in faith as the very life of God-with-us, *agápe*.

The unity for which Christ prayed and which *agápe* love brings is never forced from the outside but gifted and experienced from within the body. For the person of Christian faith, empathic presence, unconditional acceptance, and the feeling of being fully received on the inside are *an embodied vocabulary* of a graced experience in both giver and receiver. The pastoral challenge, however, lies not merely in explaining or preaching *agápe* theologically, but in providing the practical support and guidance that can lead people into *an actual experience* of this graced interaction within their own bodies. This is the kind of Christian community for which St. Paul prayed that we might all create together.

Obviously, such experiencing happens developmentally and in stages. So, what we have described as our Affection Teacher is a key ingredient in this growth. While hugging their mother, a little boy or girl already begins to feel the melting of rigid boundaries within their small bodies. A spiritual journey begins with something so simple and ordinary. Tissues taking on the "...new rhythms and metabolism of the body into which they have been grafted..."

Affection gifts our journey into building and maturing the Body of the Whole Christ. It rises up as an ever-present teacher drawing us beyond rigid boundaries, perceptions, and perspectives. It represents a first step on a lifelong journey into *the Body of Agápe (God "in Christ")*, inviting us forward into a unique spiritual unfolding within our own physical organism. The gradual emergence of an entirely new identity in *agápe, (God)*, can then be felt from inside.

While working with parents, Ed wrote the following material as one possible way to begin guiding younger children into recognizing God's Presence as this kind of *agápe* love in their daily lives.

Helping Our Children Recognize God's Presence as They Grow in the Gift of *Agápe* Love

"Mommy, we learned the pledge of allegiance at school today and it said, *God*, in it. Is there really somebody called, God?" Or, as one grammar school boy put it to his mother: "I can't understand why adults make such a fuss about God if he doesn't even have a website we can visit to learn more about him. In fact, he doesn't even have an email address."

Sooner or later, every parent is confronted with their child's questions about, "Who is God?," "Where is God?," and "Why do we talk to God if we don't even know where he lives?"

Children have a way of asking common sense questions and wanting answers they can understand in simple language drawn from their own world of meaning that touches everyday experience. Over the years I must have been asked hundreds of times by parents how to respond to such questions. The struggle we all face is not only learning to recognize a new paradigm being born in our midst, but to find simple ways to share this with our children as well.

At the heart of Christ's revelatory new paradigm about God lies a profound shift in perspective. If God is *agápe* love, then God *is* a special *interaction*, a special relationship or quality of presence. This is the meaning of living with Trinitarian life—living in a relationship of love *is* our experience of the Holy Spirit. God appears or can be experienced, so to speak, in the loving way we take care of our own body when it hurts or we are scared, as well as through our nurturing relationships with one another. The paradigm shift lies in opening the eyes and ears of a younger generation to this transformed way of discovering God. It is looking for the Presence of God in what our bodies can teach us and not solely through what our minds can think about God.

So, here is my suggestion: Rather than offering abstract explanations when a child is young, you might begin, instead, by responding to the, "Who is God?" questions with a response like the following which can connect children with their own *inside experience*.

(a) *A Beginning*

You might start by asking: "What does it feel like inside when you're scared or hurting and I pick you up and hold you close to me?" Usually, the child responds with words like, "I feel better, safer, loved, and not so scared anymore." Whatever it is they try to say with words, encourage them to notice how this feels inside their body when someone is kind, patient, or caring with them—maybe a grandparent, neighbor, or special teacher.

Then, adapting the following to the child's age and the situation, I would try to go a step further by responding to the, "Who and where is God?" question with some story-like response such as the following:

When Jesus was alive, he had a very dear friend named John who understood what Jesus was trying to teach us about who God is today and how we can recognize God's presence in our ordinary, everyday lives. This friend wrote out an answer to your question whenever people like you ask, "Who is God and where does God live?" This is what John said:

"Although God has never been seen by anyone, God dwells in us if we love one another… (1 Jn 4:12). So, let us love one another, because love is from God. Everyone who loves is a child of God and knows God—for God *is* love *(agápe)*." (1 Jn 4:7–9). Perhaps repeat this again in your own words with other examples of *loving relationships* which the child experiences.

(b) *An Enrichment*

Then, depending once again upon the child's capacity to grasp what you are saying, you could go a step further at another time and explain:

"Remember I told you that Jesus's friend, St. John, says that God *is* love? Therefore, wherever there is love, there is God. So, when you have scary or hurting feelings inside you, if you can be kind, gentle, and loving toward how hard that is on your body to carry those feelings, this invites God to be there and then you will notice that your feelings can change. If you imagine yourself down inside your own body where you feel your fear, pain, or anger and then try to be with your hurting body like you would hold your puppy with love, that brings God's Presence into your body. Sometimes, your hurting body will feel better and then quietly tell you its story. Often, what it tells you comes as a real surprise.

"Wherever love—*(God)*—is part of the situation, change can happen as a surprising gift, and we can feel that change inside ourselves. We call that, *grace*. That's when we feel God very close inside our body. When you experience me loving you, and then feel less scared, or you feel warm and safe inside, whether I'm holding you or you are learning how to take care of your body's feelings on your own, then you experience God's presence inside you. When you are loving your pets or grandpa, or are being kind and caring with your sister you bring God's love to them and you can feel that inside yourself. You also feel God's presence when they love you, too. Just like John said, *'Wherever love is, God is.'*"

I can still recall the marvelous way in which one little girl translated this message into her own world when she told her mother, "Mommy, do you know what I do so I don't push my scary or hurting feelings away? I ask them to stay and play with me."

(c) *Another Step*

Because the experience of God's Presence in and as *agápe* love is developmental, then more can follow later as a child grows into adolescence and on into young adulthood. At a later time, you can further explain that this is why we don't push our hurts, tears, and fears away but, instead, try to be loving toward the pain they bring into our bodies, so God can be invited in to help our feelings tell their stories and each of us can then grow more consciously into who we really are becoming as membranes within a Larger Living Body.

That's why we want to help each other do this in our family when we have important feelings—especially ones that are scary, make us angry, sad, frustrated, really excited or curious. We know that all our feelings have a story inside them, and that God will help us hear those stories if only we learn how to hold them gently, in a loving way, and are willing to be patient and wait. Even when you find yourself hurt or scared, you know how it helps to be held with love while you wait for something to feel better inside. We can help one another to be this same way with the feelings inside ourselves so we can always be close to God and grow, even when we don't have loving people around us. As we mature through life, this helps us to carry love with us on the inside no matter what happens to us on the outside.

Older children may notice that the same English word, *love*, is used to describe a relationship to an ice cream sundae, a movie, a song, or sexual relations. So, obviously, the same word can have different meanings.

God's appearance in love *(agápe)* is perhaps best described as a certain *quality of presence* that we recognize when someone makes an effort to leave their own self-preoccupation and enter into our world of meaning and our needs of the moment. For example, they try to enter into the world of how we actually feel right now, or how we might be experiencing something that has just happened, or is happening to us. By sensing our inside world of felt-meaning (our felt-senses), that person companions and helps us in our need. We sometimes use the word *empathy* or *empathic* to describe this quality of presence. All of us can grow in our ability to develop this more empathic presence.

Parents can learn how to explain and model this in daily life for their children. Empathic presence fits in any kind of situation. For example:

When an infant is crying a mother instinctively knows she needs to have empathic presence in order to *get inside* her baby's world of need simply because the baby cannot verbally explain what hurts. An infant depends upon the mother's ability to have an empathic *body-feel* or felt sense inside her own adult body, so she can then respond to her baby's need. He's hungry, wet, hurting, afraid—whatever—and mother tries to get it right and respond. A mother needs to develop that kind of sensitive, empathic *agápe lo*ve. She must learn to notice and nurture all this inside herself, *membrane-to-membrane* in order to *bond* with her children and nourish them emotionally.

The same situation occurs all the time when people need some kind of *inside companioning* to help them because they are old, sick, don't speak our language, or have had an accident and are alone. This is how *agápe* love appears in our midst and then God lives among us. Wherever such love is present so, too, God is present. Even more remarkable, John also reminds us that *without agápe, we cannot know God.* "He who does not love does not know God; for God IS love *(agápe)*." (1 Jn 4:8).

So, to be very practical, when a child asks you about where God is or how to find God or how to know God, you might say:

"Oh, that's easy. When you see some new kid at school who maybe has no friends and is all alone eating his lunch, go over and say, 'Hello,' and offer to show him around school. Notice what it feels like inside you to be responding to his inside feelings, perhaps his loneliness or, for a moment, sensing how it might feel not to know English very well, or to feel embarrassed trying to speak. Try to sense how it must feel to be laughed at, or called dumb or stupid because some kids can't speak the way everybody else does. When you care for and companion a fellow student in his pain or fear, you bring God into his life and you can notice how that feels inside yourself.

"Notice how it feels inside your body to be making an effort to let another person know that you really care, that you are not going to ridicule him or her or that you will help someone to learn something with you. Notice how that feels inside and you will then gradually begin to know God's presence within you. God can be as close to you as you can risk companioning your own tears and fears and those of others in a loving, inside way.

"Try to have this quality of caring relationship and presence for any student or older person who is having a hard time getting across the street, or carrying groceries to her car—anything that helps you get outside your own little world of needs and allows someone else's needs and feelings to enter inside you. Usually, you can sense what kind of response is appropriate in any given situation. As often as you grow in the habit of being that way with yourself it will come easier in your relationships with others. It is in this way that you will come to know and feel the presence of God in your life.

"Everything depends on how well you develop the habit of companioning your own important feelings in a loving way, giving them the time to tell you their stories and, when appropriate, how well you can then bring this same quality of presence to others." Experience has shown that two very important learnings can result from such companioning presence between parents and their children.

- Trusted, open communication between parents and children for life—especially in their teen years. There is less need to argue or pry into private areas when sharing this kind of companioning, especially when a child or teen matures to the point where such companioning presence often grows to become *mutual* between parents and young adult children. Family members can learn to help one another listen inwardly to how each feels, especially when this involves differences of opinion and conflict. It helps them to discover God and grace in their interactions so that family becomes the primary relationship where their faith in God is born and continues to be nurtured.

- *A Faith-in-the-Bones Foundation for Life:* By the time young people go off to work or college and run into teachers and friends with persuasive arguments against the existence of God, your children will already carry within their own bodies an experience of the opposite. They have a body-feel for grace and God's presence that will carry them through many tests of their faith. Throughout life, the parental relationship should be a child's first foundational experience of God.

■

Affection rises up in our awareness through ordinary, daily interactions. But the more subtle, *bodily-felt* back-and-forth, the *in-between* of our affectionate interacting seems more muted, soft, or indistinct. We easily miss its appearance in all our mental analyzing. The language of God becomes lost in the whirlwind blizzard of our incessant everyday thinking and planning.

The missing link lies buried beneath all this surface head-chatter. The hidden message in the *agápe* love we hunger for is not more ideas, explanations, definitions, or constructs of the mind. We long to experience God in a very real, felt way as part of our lives, an Interacting Presence known within our own bodies.

Our Violent World Cries Out for an Experience of God-with-us in Our Hurting Bodies

After spending more than 35 years helping people use the gift of their Affection Teacher by turning this capacity for caring toward their bodies' so-called negative feelings, we have found this to be *the* necessary step for therapeutic healing, growing inner wholeness and any lasting peace. In our view, it has also become *an obligation* for the larger Christian faith community. *The key to diminishing violence in our world is to begin by decreasing it inside ourselves.* This mandate stands out as especially urgent for parents of younger children. We encourage them first to make the connection for themselves, by together going through this workbook—perhaps with another couple or two. Then, begin to develop and pass on this same habit to their children as early in their lives as possible—even around the age of 2½ to 3 years old.

Insofar as we can tell, children do not automatically hold their body's pain with its tears and fears as they might cuddle their teddy bear or puppy unless parents or nursery school teachers help them learn how to do this. We need to build an inner bridge, first modeled and then encouraged by the adult community, before children will find motivation to build that same bridge inside themselves. Each child needs to find his or her own body-feel for how to be caring with their own physical organism when it is hurting, frightened, angry, or sad. It means developing an entirely new habit of calling upon their inner Affection Teacher Resource to help them take care of how their body carries its feelings throughout all the stages of life.

As children enter into more adult life relationships, the body-feel of this early childhood experience will further expand and mature. But the initial habit they learn to use when taking care of their body's burden of tears and fears will ground their faith in the experience of God discovered within the Body of the Whole Christ, which includes their own bodies. They will have learned that they are never alone, and will know *in their bones* how to find God in the experience of adversity.

The larger Christian faith community can then celebrate the birth of Christ in every child by passing on the gift of this habit as a patient and loving contribution to building up the Body of Christ in each new membrane of the Whole Body. For Christians, this happens in our day-by-day passing on of the gift of God's *agápe* to each new generation, a first and most important exercise of our common priesthood through baptism into the not yet fully perfect and whole Body of Christ. It represents a special aspect of our daily living of Eucharist, and our daily celebration of thanksgiving for the indwelling of the Holy Spirit within us. We learn to empower every child to utilize their own body-sense for loving their doll or kitten in order to develop that same love for their own hurting body's tears and fears inside themselves.

The older we grow the more inflexible and structured our habits can become, making tears and fears into new enemies inside ourselves. The rigidity of these familiar patterns make it difficult to change such obdurate habits. Yet, in spite of the many obstacles, which continue to divide and separate our Christian communities, we must find ways to commit ourselves to helping one another build the inner and outer bridges necessary to rediscover *together* the gift of God's *agápe* within our bodies.

We are never too old nor too divided to realize this. With faith, we can help one another in Christ as we struggle to *rewire* old habits of neglect into new routines and faith-filled traditions of caring for all our feelings. People everywhere from all walks of life are hungry to be noticed and nurtured in the Body of Christ. But we need the support of one another to build these new bridges of inner habits inside ourselves. That is a huge piece of what the Larger Christian Community is called to become—together in Christ.

Once this fresh perspective begins to grow, the grace of this entire new paradigm can be released within our bodies and into the communities around us. Inner disconnection and incongruence can begin to switch away from an ever-present potential for violence and destruction, becoming a dynamic movement toward unity and peace, greater freedom and creativity, wholeness, and an awareness of living a more grace-filled human life. Just imagine how such a transformation, accomplished through the gift of *agápe* love within Christian communities, could literally change the face of the earth. Such a 180 degree turnaround within heretofore splintered Christianity might well bring about the most dramatic step toward world peace in human history.

Exploring *Agápe* Love

Another Pauline Prayer from Inside Your Body's Knowing Based Upon *Ephesians 1:18–19*

O God, I pray that the eyes of my heart may be illumined by *agápe* love, so I may know in my body what is the hope to which You call me. May the eyes of my opened heart experience Your Presence in my own body as a living cell in the Body of the Whole Christ.

I pray that I may develop the habit of noticing and nurturing my important feelings so this gifted doorway enables me to pray, simply by being inside myself in a loving, empathic and unconditionally accepting way without words or thinking. Amen.

A Brief Reminder—An Exercise After Reading This Chapter

Once again, just a reminder to pause at the end of this chapter, or any time something touches your body while reading because it surfaces feelings—an idea, a memory, a story, a relationship. If some deeper felt-sense meaning calls for you to return later because you have an appointment or need to do something else, be sure to use your personal note page to leave enough of a reminder that when the time is right you can quickly return to that inner felt-sense once again.

By now, you have probably found the format that best enables you to develop a habit of noticing and nurturing your important feelings (felt-senses). So, we want to encourage you to use the opportunity of this and the remaining chapters to grow and deepen this habit in your body. Much as you already know when you need to stop and think something through for yourself, you will also eventually know just as easily and regularly when you need to notice and nurture a felt-sense. The two approaches become like breathing in and out...both vital to staying alive and becoming more human in Christ. ∎

Personal Notes

*A **Fourth** Body-Learning*

■

Living Christ's New Commandment of Loving as God Loves

Maturing into the Gift and Freedom of Loving as God Loves Transforms Our Self-Awareness of Who Christ Really is Today and Who We are in Christ

Chapter 13

Loving God or Loving as God Loves?

AN AMAZING PIECE of New Testament revelation, though familiar, still conceals an as yet little recognized piece of common sense data, an *in-the-body-knowing* which lays down a very clear and simple guideline for where the rubber hits the road within ordinary, everyday Christian experience.

But in order to appreciate the powerful significance of this text we need to work our way into it slowly by walking through an experience of Ed's which both summarizes much of what we have shared in our book thus far, while simultaneously pointing our attention toward a particular quality of personal interacting and faith that can bring God's grace into clearer focus within everyday human awareness.

A Special Little Boy

On the morning of September 11, 2001 along with the rest of the world Ed watched television images of what three hijacked jetliners had done to thousands of people in the World Trade Center Towers and the Pentagon. Words from a book he had been writing ten years earlier flashed through his mind. About a week later, he then wrote the following to our Institute members.

■

> I want to share an experience with those among you who are today's parents, child caregivers, teachers and counselors because several days later as the terrorists were being identified, I suddenly realized that when I had written, *Beyond the Myth of Dominance—An Alternative to a Violent Society,* as a wake-up call, several of those killers were still children themselves. In fact, one pilot responsible for the death of thousands was, at that time, only 12 years old! My book feels even more compelling and connected today than it did when I first wrote it.
>
> One afternoon toward the end of a six day program that Pete and I were conducting, a young woman stopped me in the hall and asked if

Loving God or Loving as God Loves?

I had a few minutes to talk. She identified herself as an elementary school principal and told me that one of her jobs was dealing with problem children. Then she quietly looked at me with tears in her eyes and said, "I just want to say, thank you, for all the children you have reached this week." I guess I looked a bit confused, so she continued:

"I am in charge of a school in an upper middle-class area, largely populated by professionals—hardly what anyone would call a *deprived* class of people. These kids appear to have everything. Yet, during this program I have realized more than ever before just how deprived they really can be, which is something I have been suspecting for a long time, but just couldn't put my finger on what my instincts were telling me. Gradually, as this workshop unfolded, I have come to understand what a very special little boy said to me only a couple of weeks ago. This child is so bright, sensitive and promising, and had always been a top student when things started to change a few months ago.

"Increasingly, homework was neglected. He was becoming a troublemaker with other children, even in his family as well, and his parents were mystified and asking me for help. In the classroom his behavior and cooperation were deteriorating every day. Just a couple of days before I came here, I called him into my office again, not really knowing what to do. As he sat there before me with eyes cast down and his shoulders slumped, in desperation I said, 'Can you tell me how I can help you?'

"Without looking up, he shrugged with an, 'I don't know,' but seemed to go deep inside himself for a long time. I didn't break the silence. Then, ever so thoughtfully out of some place deep down he said, 'Inside me it feels like a mistake that I was born, because everybody wants me to be somebody else.'"

I stood there stunned as my own eyes watered up, too, listening to her story. Finally she broke the silence. "I suppose another reason I stopped you was to tell you that I now know how to be with him, so maybe he can find support for holding on to himself. Maybe, through me, he will feel someone does prize him for who he really is. Perhaps, someday, he might grow to feel inside that he isn't a mistake."

Rediscovering the Lost Body-Connection

Even deeper than the fear of starving, of being abandoned or of never being able to grow up because of some war or environmental disaster, lies the fear of never being able to grow into the person who you are really called to be. Children the world over, but especially in more affluent, technological societies, often feel deeply afraid and confused by this fear. Yet, more often than not, they are out of touch with this feeling at the conscious level, even though they still carry it in their bodies.

As they grow up with this fear and confusion, it can affect entire cultures, like our own, because all their relationships—family, school, community, work—each is affected. It tones everything with an underlying tension and violence, continually erupting onto the surface within health problems and socially destructive acts. The little boy in the principal's school is no isolated example. Too many little boys and little girls all too often grow up carrying this ticking time bomb inside them.

How well I remember the hundreds of hours I spent as a counselor in a college prep high school, listening to the confused pain of this profound deprivation in so many of the boys who came from *fine backgrounds* and were being given one of the best educational opportunities available. Yet, over and over again, I was hearing confusion and pain, as if every cell in their being was telling them they were born on this earth to discover and be true to their own spirits while the whole world around them seemed hell-bent on blocking that journey.

When any of us are taught to deny, reject, or in some way numb out what we feel because it doesn't *fit in*, which is not the same as acting-out in a destructive manner, it feels as though the very core of our being, the entire organism's sense for why one exists at all, is being violated. Great masses of the world's helpless children feel trapped, helpless, profoundly violated and denied their very identity by the way our adult world often deprives them of their spirit.

Most people really want to love their children. It's just that they only know what they were taught as children, and then pass this on over and over again—the same old myth of dominance. But there is an alternative. By companioning a child into the wonderful world of noticing and nurturing the unique story-connections within their innermost feelings, their spirits can come alive once again and we are all made more fully human. This book is about helping you to make this happen.

Things are not What They at First Appear to Be
What Does it Really Mean—to be Human?

What was it within that principal, within the caring quality of her presence that could invite and draw forth from that small boy the deeper felt meaning and truth of his life? She had been extremely vulnerable because she really didn't know what to do. He was vulnerable because within the embrace of her felt, loving concern he could sense, perhaps for the first time, the stark truth of himself and become authentic enough to blurt it out bluntly, boldly before growing quiet to rest in the felt-sense of what he had just rubbed up against inside himself. Within that moment of *mutual vulnerability* grace quietly entered in. This moment opened a door. Something about her caring quality of presence modeled for him how he needed to be present to his own inner pain and confusion so it could move forward—symbol interacting with a felt-sense, a new felt-sense arising in his body. Symbol and metaphor playing their age-old pivotal roles at the body-interface where new meaning and direction can rise up from inside the human heart. An ancient way of knowing reappearing in modern language and clothing from within a remarkably contemporary gestalt.

More and more today, many have developed a body-sense for being part of something greater than themselves, a maturing environmental awareness. Global warming alerts us to the fact that we humans are having a negative impact upon planet earth in ways that can destroy both our habitat and ourselves. But we need to heighten awareness of our inner environment as well. As Adam Kahane has already reminded us,

> There is not 'a' problem out there that we can react to and fix.
> There is a 'problem situation' of which each of us is a part, the way an organ is part of the body.[1]

Stumbling into a new paradigm is a little like waking up and realizing that someone has moved all the furniture in your room. Everything looks and feels different. Your body and mind need to adjust. The lines on the tennis court have changed. You find yourself challenged with a different perspective. Secure and familiar ways of thinking and perceiving the world and yourself have been shaken. In short, you have entered upon or been thrust into a newly experienced pattern—one where you face foreign and uncharted rules for surviving.

And might it not be the same with our very understanding and experience of God? Today's generation of Christians face the extraordinary challenge of finding their way into a new perceptual framework of Who Christ is today and who they are becoming in Christ.

Gestalt images are not always immediately self-evident. You must often live with/in them for a time before being surprised one day when you finally catch a glimpse of the dynamic interactions which tie figure and ground together in alternating ways within your body's perceptions. It is, perhaps, a blessing that we cannot quickly *think* our way through to experiencing the Larger Whole. We must always wait upon some gifted felt-shift within the body's perspective that finally opens a window on an entirely new world inside and around us.

The mind will probably never be our premier guide for determining what is *spiritual*. It's function is to understand, predict, and control for purposes of human survival. But physicists, philosophers, and theologians have all come to recognize the deeper *interactions* and developmental tendencies which tie the real world together. There are always frustrating anomalies that won't quite fit themselves neatly into our clearly defined little boxes. Things merge, interact, develop and then break out from our mental categories in surprising, often irritating and unpredictable ways.

The physicist, David Bohm, reminded us that: "...a sharp distinction between space and time cannot be maintained."[2] Karl Rahner clearly recognized that matter evolves toward spirit in a truly developmental fashion:

> What happens when we combine the ideas of the unity and the duality of spirit and matter, keeping in mind that both realities are *moments* in a dynamic history? We can then say that *matter of itself essentially develops toward spirit.* We here presuppose the existence, in general, of evolution. A true evolutionary dynamism does not consist of pure transformation from one form to the other on the same level of reality. It is rather *an increase of reality*, an actual reception of greater fulness of being.[3] *(emphasis ours)*

Loving God or Loving as God Loves?

We never seem to escape from *pleroma,* (πλήρωμα), that *fullness* which completes — a rare word of obscure meaning mentioned earlier which appears within the New Testament bearing the *developmental* sense of an unfolding manifestation of the *fullness of God,* (πλήρωμα τοῦ θεοῦ). Rahner describes this increase of reality in theological terms, but the actual experience can express itself in a little boy talking to his teacher and, from within the support of her caring love, finding his way home to himself. *Matter developing toward spirit.* We have barely yet begun to explore the significance for life and theological investigation which lies within that evocative phrase, *the fulness of God*, for the future of Christian experience. We are in the infancy of our own understanding…

One finds undertones here of that remarkable evolutionary hymn described in Paul's letters to the Romans:

> Up to the present, we know, the whole created universe groans in all of its parts as if in the pangs of childbirth. Not only so, but even we, to whom the Spirit is given as first fruits of the harvest to come, are groaning inwardly while we wait for God to set our whole body free. *(Rom. 8:22–24 NEB)*

A Compelling Realization of Who You are 'in Christ'

Back in the 1960's, during a period when we both pursued doctoral studies in the psychology of religion, we chanced upon the writings of a Canadian scripture scholar, John Barry Wheaton. His exegesis of texts from the Gospels of St. Mark and St. John were impressive not only because of the surprising conclusions he drew from them, but also because these same conclusions were beginning to shed light upon some of our own psychological investigation into the nature of health and pathology as this appeared in religion and religious practices.

We had already published our first book, *Becoming A Person in the Whole Christ*,[4] in 1967 which made an initial integration of the work of Dr. Carl Rogers into a Christian perspective.

In 1969 we co-authored a second book, *The In-Between: Evolution in Christian Faith*,[5] which went a step further. In the Foreword to this book, we asked a question of our readers:

Is not our attempt to fashion the secular city but a projection of what we struggle to create *within* ourselves? And if a particular expression of God has died, is it not because we have outgrown something *within* ourselves which needed the support of a certain historically conditioned image of the deity; an image which now no longer speaks to the new way in which we are rapidly finding ourselves?

Perhaps in order to discover the true language of Christian experience we must penetrate deeper into the very dynamisms of human growth which underlie the constantly changing expressions of ourselves. Maybe it is something just this basic, something shared by every human being simply because we are human, that is needed as the starting point in Christian renewal? What could be more fundamental to the Incarnation and what more universally shared by all as the starting point for expressing an "enfleshed" faith, than simply our humanity itself? (6)

A firm conviction at that point in both our lives and our research had led the two of us to conclude that a significant transformation was in the process of occurring within human self-awareness. It had developed to the point where it clashed with our old, familiar understanding and experience of God to such an extent that Christians and others were being challenged to explore a more ancient way of knowing *in-the-body* in order to move forward on their spiritual journey.

It was in this second book that we first introduced the work of John Barry Wheaton. But at the time we found ourselves unprepared to make any actual integration with a psychological process that our readers might use and explore for themselves in order to promote their own health and human wholeness on their spiritual journey. Then, in 1985 we went a step further in a third book, *BioSpirituality: Focusing as a Way to Grow,*(7) by integrating the contribution of Eugene Gendlin's work on the Focusing process into our ongoing investigation. In the preface to this work we wrote:

> ...we have found buried within the Judaeo-Christian tradition some neglected and little used information that may well unlock the secret of consciousness evolution. In this book we plan to describe certain teachings from this ancient heritage which contain clues about the nature of consciousness and its evolution. These clues are equally applicable to non-Christians as well as to Christians *when they can be approached*

out of a bodily-felt perspective. That perceptual shift makes all the difference. It opens a refreshing new direction for anyone interested in spirituality.[8]

By developing a deeper appreciation of the body's perspective in the experience and practice of religion we attempted to open the door on a new and largely unexplored frontier in spirituality. Now, in this our current book we reintroduce Wheaton's scriptural exegesis once again because it offers even greater richness and significance to the experience of "...your body as it is felt from inside."

That little phrase can open a transformational starting-point which provides a fresh approach to your experience of yourself. It offers a creative opportunity, both for personal and community renewal as well as a heightened capacity for finding God in all things.

Introducing the body's knowing and felt-sensing potential into the spiritual journey unveiled an amazing new gestalt. And most surprising was to find that this view from within the body's knowing brought into vivid relief within experience some of the most ancient, yet often neglected aspects of the Christian tradition—such as living with Trinitarian life which, paradoxically, offers a new approach to the interactive experience of being made in the image and likeness of God. Herein one could discover a world filled with rich metaphoric potential for opening our *eyes to see and ears to hear* an ongoing, day by ordinary daily revelation of finding God in all things.

A little boy struggling to discover, maintain and grow his own unique identity stands out as an integral membrane within the weaving of a much larger, personal, spiritual fabric. It is never something apart because *there is no longer anything apart. "When we try to pick out anything by itself, we find it hitched to everything else in the Universe."* John Muir's words are woven throughout an even larger tapestry. An ever-renewing life in Christ animates the Christian worldview. Humankind has now grown to the point where it recognizes that we are somehow all together one, even though we still maintain our different tribal affiliations, separated churches and religions, as well as insisting upon glass ceilings and walls to segregate ethnic groups or genders or whatever other divisions we still hold onto. But the bottom line remains within the gestalt which is Christ that there are no longer any divisions between Jews or Gentile, freed men or slaves, males or females. Yet, after more than 2000 years, the full implications of this simple, clear mandate still call out to be drawn forth to their fullest extent within everyday living and governing so that this transformation can eventually impact our behavior, as well as the cultures and communities which we create.

With this as background, then, let's now consider the work of Barry Wheaton and examine a few biblical texts along with some of his exegetical comments.

Christ's New Commandment

We will begin with two familiar passages from the gospels of St. Mark and St. John which, when viewed from within, "...your body as it is felt from inside," can introduce fresh meaning into the message of Jesus.

> Then one of the lawyers, who had been listening to these discussions and had noted how well he answered came forward and asked him, 'Which commandment is first of all?' Jesus answered, "The first is, 'Hear, O Israel: the Lord your God is the only Lord; love the Lord your God with all your heart, with all your soul, with all your mind, and with all your strength.' The second is this: 'Love your neighbor as yourself. There is no other commandment greater than these.'" The lawyer said to him, 'Well said, Master. You are right in saying that God is one and beside him there is no other. And to love him with all your heart, all your understanding, and all your strength, and to love your neighbor as yourself—that is *far more than any burnt offerings or sacrifices.' (A remarkable statement since sacrificial offering was a central act in the Hebrew religion!)* When Jesus saw how sensibly he answered, he said to him, *'You are not far from the kingdom of God.'* (Mk. 12:28–34, NEB) (comment and italics ours)[9]

These two commandments from the Hebrew Scriptures have traditionally been taken as the basis for a Christian's relationship to God and neighbor. But the hidden significance of this passage from Mark is that here, for the first time, these two commandments of the Old Law (Deut 6:5) and (Lev 19:18) had been put together, side-by-side. When Jesus linked these two, he added a new dimension to the Old

Law and the intelligent lawyer caught the implications and could exclaim: *"...this is far more than any burnt offering or sacrifice!"* The lawyer had made a significant step forward in regard to his understanding of the Old Law. But Jesus responds to his perceptive insight in a rather surprising way by saying, *"You are not far from the kingdom of God."*

This curious comment of Jesus,

> ...adds up to the somewhat unexpected result that the two commandments are presented by him and accepted by the scribe as *the essence not of Christian life* (the life of a follower of Christ), *but of the Jewish Law, the Old Covenant.* This is why Jesus says to the scribe who has accepted his teaching; "You are *not far from* the Kingdom of God." Jesus means, You have seen what is most important in Jewish Law, but you are *not yet* my follower! [10]

Then, at the Last Supper, Jesus pronounced a totally New Commandment which was a radical departure from the Old Law.

> I give you a new commandment:
> love one another;
> *just as I have loved you,*
> *you also must love one another.*
> By this love you have for one another,
> everyone will know that you are my disciples.
> *(Jn. 13:34–35, JB) (emphasis ours)*

Commenting on the significance of this text, Wheaton wrote:

> This, Jesus says, is a "new" commandment—new, because we are not told to "love God with all our heart" but to "love one another;" new, because we are not told to love our neighbor "as yourself" but "just as I have loved you." This is the *only* (one commandment) sign by which we can be recognized as following him—*"by this love* you have for one another." And if we still persist in thinking that loving God is a greater love than this, then we are mistaken, for Jesus tells us: "A person can have *no greater love* than to lay down his life for his friends. This is my commandment: love one another as I have loved you...What I command you is to love one another." *(Jn. 15:13, 12, 17).* [11]

The conclusion and further implications to be drawn from this bit of dialogue are even more intriguing, as well as paradigm-shifting:

> We are now at a point where the first commandment of the Old Law has apparently disappeared. In reality, it is no longer something that we specifically strive for. The reason is that the love *(agápe)* which Jesus commands is *not that we love God, but that we love as God loves*...Now we come to view all of life, not as our love for God and neighbor, but as God's love in us.[12]

The last two sentences open an entirely new perspective for Christian living. In the New Testament God is not revealed as some object within our awareness but rather as a new experience of living, relating and interacting. Developing new eyes to see and ears to hear now demand that old perspectives need to be transformed. *"God is a verb, not a noun!"* One discovers the experience of God *within an embodied interaction, agápe*, living with and in *the life of God* as this can be felt from within our own bodies.

Our more Western perceptions and expectations are attuned to search for God as though we were seeking some other individual like ourselves. But the New Commandment of Jesus offers a striking alternative. Christ speaks, instead, about living with a new kind of *life* — a gifted life, we might add, that is known in your body, "...as it is felt from inside."

This new revelation and commandment are simple, straightforward, and clear. God **IS** love *(agápe)*. The God whom we experience *in agápe* appears more like the breathing in and out of our own lungs. Without our minds yet fully comprehending the scope and significance of such a realization, our bodies have already been *immersed* within the interactive experience of God's grace-life already resonating throughout our body's knowing.

As *agápe* we discover God embodied within the ordinary, everyday *in-betweens* of our daily interactions inside ourselves, with one another, and the world around us. A Christian's life and prayer are meant to develop a new *habit* of awareness—the "eyes to see" and "ears to hear" an *Abiding Presence* rising up into conscious awareness from within our body's knowing.

Loving God or Loving as God Loves?

Jesus redrew all the lines on the court with his New Commandment. He set up advanced, state-of-the-art rules of engagement for His New Testament paradigm—a worldview pointing the disciples attention toward a quality of personal *agápe-presence* based neither upon gender nor ethnic background, tribal affiliation or social status. His message highlighted an experience of being caught up within the very life of God in our everyday interactions. He led us into the rising column of air.

The challenge, therefore, remains as it always has if we choose to recognize it. What inner resources of caring presence have we yet failed to uncover on our journey into God? What important feelings lie still neglected and unheard inside ourselves? What old habits continue to lock us in frozen and rigid perspectives which block this realization from emerging into awareness as a daily habit? We will have much more to say about this last question in the next chapter.

The change in perspective, habit and experience centers upon the presence of God appearing not as some *object* in our awareness but as a Graced Presence unfolding from within our interacting relationships—much as Christ was recognized in the breaking of the bread by his disciples as they ate together with him on their journey to Emmaus.

> And their eyes were opened and they recognized him; and he vanished out of their sight. They said to each other, "Did not our hearts burn within us while he talked to us on the road, while he opened to us the scriptures?" *(Lk 24:31–32 RSV)*

From this more inward physical perspective, we experience God as the very life of our bodies interacting in *agápe*.

Christ's New Commandment offers a complete transformation in perspective and experience. Not *looking* at God but discovering your being *within* God, "…as you take on the rhythms and metabolism of the Body into which you have been grafted." A transformed physical sense for the felt meaning of *Incarnation* lies waiting to unfold from within your own body's knowing.

There are parallels here with the dramatic shift in perspective precipitated by Copernicus and Galileo. *The old center no longer holds.* We find ourselves seeking new bearings within an ever expanding universe. It is perhaps only at this unsettling juncture that we dimly perceive answers which no longer lie exclusively outside ourselves. The telescope, finally, must now be turned *inward* as well.

In the opening lines of his Letter to the Hebrews, Paul sharpens our understanding of the Incarnation by describing *a growing interiorization* of the revelation of God-with-us in Christ as this had developed from the age of the prophets into the times when Jesus lived.

> "When in former times God spoke to our forefathers, he spoke in fragmentary and varied fashion through the prophets. But in this the final age he has spoken to us in the Son whom he has made heir to the whole universe, and through whom he created all orders of existence..." *(Heb 1:1–2 NEB)*

"In this final age he has spoken to us in the Son...," in whom "...we live and move and have our very existence." (Acts 17:28) Paul points our attention toward the *embodied* experience of our *membraneship* within the Body of Christ as the new, interacting resource unveiling the presence of God-with-us at the heart of our everyday living.

In the light of this revelation, the tactical challenge facing Christian communities becomes quite clear. It is to uncover practical, simple ways for moving beyond all the old routines and habits that continue to lock-in our more familiar yet often frozen and rigid perspectives, the mind-forged manacles which can block an unfolding of this new revelation and commandment. What are the important feelings that yet lie neglected and unheard inside ourselves? What closed doors hold us back from this transformed perspective? What new habit must we acquire in order to live and find God in a new way? What historically-conditioned divisions among ourselves and with others cry out to be transcended and finally grown beyond in the light of Christ's New Commandment?

"I live, now no longer I but Christ lives in me," (Gal 2:20) was Paul's blunt, yet visceral way of stating his awe at recognizing the gift of *agápe in Christ* that made it possible both for him and for ourselves "to love as God loves."

The renowned theologian, Karl Rahner, shone a laser-like light upon the revelation of Christ's New Commandment, bringing it into even sharper contemporary focus when reflecting upon the significance of John's gospel and epistle for the entire Christian community:

> "In John we find the first reflective justification of love of neighbor as the root of the whole of Christian existence. Otherwise, love of neighbor could seem merely a pious exaggeration and be so watered down that it would become only one element of the Christian demand. According to John, we are loved by God and by Christ *so that* we love one another; this love is Christ's new command *(Jn. 13:34)*. John draws the conclusion that the God who is love *(1 Jn. 4:16)* has loved us, not so that we love him in return, but so that we love one another *(1 Jn. 4:7, 11)*. For we do not see God; we cannot reach him in a gnostic or mystic interiority *(1 Jn. 4:12)*. Thus the 'God in us' in our mutual love is the God whom alone we can love *(1 Jn. 4:12)*. Indeed the compelling argument for John, if usually none too illuminating for us, is that '…he who does not love the brother whom he has seen, cannot love God whom he has not seen' *(1 Jn. 4:20)*." [13]

In addition, we would add that the human body itself remains the unacknowledged key for unlocking this ancient but still fresh revelation. We state in this book that the first step must always be taken inside ourselves. The relationship to ourself and our own body's knowing is intrinsic to all our relationships. It is foundational for the new *agápe* commandment of *loving as God loves*.

■

The long journey into a more profound "loving as God loves" begins when you can finally bring a caring presence to all those enemies you have created over the years inside yourself. The new relationship you develop with such feelings and your own body suffering beneath this burden becomes the key to uncovering new ways of relating to all those around you.

Learning how to grow into such a fresh relationship lies before you as your first step forward. We suggest in this book that the immediate, practical and first step forward involves developing a new habit of noticing, nurturing, and caring for the enemies you have created inside yourself.

"Can I foster a caring relationship with my own body as it struggles with the burden of scared, hurting, angry or confused feelings?

"Am I able to companion my own body carrying such feelings, just as I might be with an abandoned baby, or as I was with a loved pet, my teddy bear, or a favorite doll when I was a child? Can I learn to let my Affection Teacher guide me? Can I find a way to be with my own body and its feelings as teachers rather than as enemies?"

Everything inside that you shun and push away, everything you numb or from which you distract yourself has some opening that will allow you to make a caring connection—even with your most difficult feelings.

They want to be heard, too, because they have something important to tell you, or you wouldn't be feeling them. None of this will ever change, however, until you find some way to create a more open, caring, *agápe* body-connection with whatever you're pushing away—at the very least offering an inside body-to-body handshake, so to speak.

Without some caring, bodily-felt link, some physically felt availability, those hurting, hiding places inside will remain forever outcasts howling in the night. Their stories will remain untold. Their enduring pain of not being heard will continually rise to the surface of your awareness, much as oil leaking from a rusting hulk at the bottom of the sea drifts slowly upward toward the light, eventually soiling the surface and everything that touches it.

All of creation, all of nature struggles toward a unity and life-giving connections that our minds will never fully grasp. The untold, still disconnected stories within all of our unheard feelings are no exception.

This slow, day-by-day struggle to grow into greater wholeness within our own bodies, "...as they are felt from inside," can open a fresh way to love ourselves, one another, and the planet which sustains us—*as God loves*. Your body itself continues to offer you the key to a remarkable cellular awareness of who you are in Christ and who Christ is today.

"The stone which the builders rejected has become the main cornerstone." *(Lk. 20:17, Ps. 118:22)*

One Woman's Journey into Loving as God Loves

If you are a woman reading this chapter, something of the profound implications for your own freedom, not just to grow more fully as a woman but to discover your own deepest self-identity in God may be stirring inside you. Let me (Ed) share with you what this chapter stirs in me with a story of how a retreatant, whom I companioned many years ago, helped me to connect inside myself through her own journey with a hidden felt-sense of the earthshaking significance of Christ's new commandment of loving AS God loves.

This woman was a middle-aged Catholic nun on a year's sabbatical to allow her time for rest and then to check out and apply for the program she felt would offer her the best preparation for a new type of ministry she now wanted to pursue. Previously, I was told by other sisters that she had spent her entire adult life in just about every high administrative office she could hold within her religious community as well as in their schools and hospitals. Moreover, outside her congregation she was widely admired as a most capable CEO, as well as a much loved leader.

So, when we sat down together she told me that she had decided on what she wanted to be trained in, a field very different from administration, and she had filled out the application almost ten months earlier, but still could not bring herself to sign and mail it—and that was what her sabbatical had really turned into—being stuck in that same place after retreats, prayers, visits to therapists, spiritual counselors, etc. Now, she only had three weeks left before she was due to report back at the mother-house in order to tell them where she had applied and had been accepted.

Needless to say, this very competent woman had years of experience and the well-developed habit of resolving problems by gathering all the facts pro and con and then assuming the responsibility for making a decision. So, it took me quite a while just to support her in noticing how and where her body was carrying all this anxiety, confusion and embarrassment at the fast-approaching deadline. Once we got that far, she could easily remember growing up on the family farm with many baby animals she loved to hold, play with and feed. Then it was relatively easy for her to use her body's memory of holding and caring for these little pets as her body-way *now* of being with the physical and emotional pain she was carrying in her body as I companioned her that afternoon.

As she quietly held her pain this way I could see the physical changes and easing of tension on the outside, so I invited her to notice on the inside how her body was feeling now, having its pain cared for like she once cared for her childhood pets on the farm. Her answer was an easy smile with eyes closed. So, I encouraged her to take her time being present in this loving way and to let me know whether anything came that felt connected. She grew very still and deeply present to herself.

Then it happened. As tears began to run down her cheeks, followed by deep gut-wrenching sobs, I said nothing but was fully with her as the tears continued to flow. After a time, she told me that the feelings inside had told her what they had wanted to say for many years and that it was now time to stop. So, I helped her go through a simple *before and after checking exercise* as a way to notice whether there had been any changes that she could physically sense inside. Using her own words for the inner, physical changes she was describing, I offered the option that she might want to take time quietly and gratefully to companion these healing changes in her body as her own uniquely personal body-sense of God's intimate presence within her.

After more quiet moments she then opened her eyes and I inquired whether she preferred to remain quiet about what had happened, or if she wished to share anything of her experience. This is what she told me.

She had four older brothers and all of them had grown up together on this very large, isolated, midwest farm with the many after school, vacation and harvest-time chores of such a lifestyle. There were no neighbor girls her own age to play with, so as young children she had played with her brothers, especially the oldest who built a swing for her, carried her around on his shoulders, built her a dollhouse and her own tree house, and who was always there to help her with homework and put her to bed with loving hugs and reading stories when her mother was still working in the kitchen. She adored him and knew from her earliest memories how much he loved her.

Then one year, her father told the whole family that he needed everybody during the coming summer months to help him clear some acreage of forest in order to increase more productive farmland. This large project was a rare event in the children's lives because it meant bringing in neighbors and a caterpillar tractor from outside to pull out tree stumps and a portable sawmill to cut lumber for another barn. Their secluded lives would become very full of new people.

So, on the first day of summer vacation they all got up early to begin the entire project, made lunches to eat out in the woods to save time and as all her brothers were piling into the truck she had her own lunch and even a new pair of work gloves to help pile brush, when her dearest older brother yelled at her as she was climbing aboard, "You go back to the kitchen with Mama. This is men's work, *you're just a girl*"—and when she remembered those words the dam broke and she could feel an enormous release and flood of grieving tears.

Then continuing, she reminisced: "I guess I've spent my entire life trying to prove to myself and to my brother that there really isn't anything wrong with me because I'm a girl. It feels now like I never owned how much that hurt me and how the challenge of going back to school now, becoming a student again after 35 years away from the books, has surfaced this hidden suspicion that maybe my brother was right and now that will finally show up—that there really is something the matter with me because I'm a girl. All of this probably came together in my not being able to sign the application which I very much wanted to do." We talked a bit more and then both walked to the dining room for supper.

The next day, she stopped me to say, "It's OK now. I've signed and mailed the application and will call and visit the campus when I leave here." Several months later a kind note of thanks came along with news about how much she was already learning and enjoying her new challenge.

When she uttered those words, "You're just a girl," in that moment I, too, changed. I believe this experience stands as one of the principal inner motivations which has kept me working all these years to develop practical steps, exercises, and ultimately this book, in order to help all Christians experience God not as a male, patriarchal, dominant king whom tribal cultures have created for their survival in the past, but which now no longer fits within our rapidly globalizing world. Such tribal, male imagery, along with gender-oriented male God language creates an horrendous model-barrier as well as a confusing obstacle. This remains true not just for women, but for all of us in our struggle to develop and pass on a healthy Christian spirituality that nourishes our humanity as

Rediscovering the Lost Body-Connection

we learn to help each other love as God loves—the new post-tribal, post monarchical, post-imperial Good News of God *as a Loving Presence within Whom we all participate* opens a new way of living in all our relationships.

Those words, "You're just a girl," have come back to me over and over again, helping to remind me that what is perhaps the greatest inherited barrier today for actually living Christ's New Commandment of loving as God loves—is this symbol of God as a dominative male figure. How can women, as well as men who have been abused by dominative males, not feel repelled, frightened, ill at ease or unconsciously confused when they hunger for God's love and the experience of being able to love God in return. Yet, they find themselves surrounded with imagery, language, prayers, rituals and art which constantly remind them that God exists as this overwhelming super-male figure instead of a quality of Loving Presence whom they can begin to notice and nurture in their relationships to their own body's pain, fears, emptiness or confusion? The meaning of Christ today is that now God is truly with us in our bodies, available to be discovered in whatever is real in our lives if we can only help one another learn how to find that Loving Presence in all things.

One late afternoon a few years ago, while sitting alone on a side bench in the Sistine Chapel after the tourist crowds had gone, and resting my head against the wall I could relax and easily look up to absorb Michelangelo's huge, male, body-builder image of God the Father with his flowing gray beard on the chapel ceiling above me. Once again, those words, "You're just a girl," hit me. But this time, it was my eyes that now filled with tears. I felt embarrassed and filled with grief to the core of my being because the grandeur of such remarkable Renaissance imagery has blinded us to the true simplicity and paradigm-shattering significance of Christ's New Commandment.

Most of all, however, during my time in the Sistine Chapel, I felt especially saddened for how young girls must feel in their hunger for an experience of God when all the pictures associated with God are masculine—a male God to be served as king, even in heaven. What must that do to their own developing sense of self-worth as female?

A Brief Reminder Exercise After Reading This Chapter

Remember to allow yourself a moment for growing quiet inside, noticing how your body responded as you read through this chapter. Was there some phrase, a quotation or description that called forth anything from inside you? Perhaps you could feel a wondering, a question, some yearning or feltness that might indicate an opening, an invitation drawing you to listen deeper into your personal history or what your future might hold for you. Each time your body responds a potential door appears. Listening in to these felt openings can lead you into the sacred spaces of your own inner story—the pilgrimage of your unique spirit's homeward journey into love.

> "…we forget that there is a hidden door, a secret room in all our lives. The force behind myths, fairytales, parables, and soulful travel stories reveals the myriad ways the sacred breaks through the resistance and shines forth into our world. Pilgrimage holds out the promise of personal contact with that sacred force." [14] ∎

Personal Notes

*A **Fifth** Body-Learning*

■

Process-Skipping

Growing Beyond Process-Skipping Habits

Which Lock in Addictive Patterns,

Block the Body-Sense for Grace and

an Experience of Living

Within the Larger Body, 'in Christ'

Chapter 14
What is Process-Skipping and How do We Grow Beyond it into Loving as God Loves?

Pete's Process-Skipping Story

MANY YEARS AGO it became clear that my mother needed to be moved into an assisted living facility. The personal inner struggle triggered by this experience led me on a journey through unowned aspects of my own experience that, at the time, I scarcely even knew existed.

After spending several days moving mother and getting her settled I finally left the care facility, but with an uneasy sense inside; a feeling that was nothing compared to *the guilt* that soon surfaced. Finally, I couldn't take it any more and drove the 350 mile roundtrip back to visit her. The guilt ceased *for a time*. But soon a phone call or some anniversary would come and the familiar pattern repeated itself. Guilt inevitably returned. Fairly soon a predictable sequence became evident, not to me, but to those who knew me. Something would trigger feelings of guilt about mother being alone in the care facility and my response, in order to alleviate this feeling, would be to drive the long trip to visit her.

I never set time aside to enter into my body, holding my guilt in a caring way, listening into what it might want to tell me. I simply reacted. *Guilt—go visit mother.* In fact, I soon became *addicted* to visiting mother as a way to *deal with* my guilt. Some people use work, eating, sex, alcohol, or drugs, even religious practices to deaden such feelings. Others have such an overpowering *need to please* that they fall into all kinds of addictive behaviors as a way to ease their inner pain, insecurity, and confusion. (By *addiction,* here in this context, we mean the use of any action, person, group or thing as a substitute for growing into a more truthful relationship within myself, with the world around me and within God.)

What is Process-Skipping?

All these approaches become tactical maneuvers through which we distract ourselves from difficult feelings or numb the pain they cause so we don't feel them as much, allowing us more easily to ignore them or substitute more acceptable feelings in place of those that embarrass or confuse us.

Throughout the pages you have already read, you learned that the direction toward a felt-sense always lies in moving *into and through* your feelings, never *away* from them. Yet, for me, every time I felt guilt, I escaped in the opposite direction, trying to handle my difficult feeling by visiting mother—doing a good thing, but for unhealthy inside reasons. I would skip right past the point of entry into my own process and unfolding inner story—*(see process-skipping illustration, facing page)*. I never penetrated beyond the top of the iceberg. Quite literally, I became *addicted* to visiting mother as a way of numbing and therefore *controlling* the feeling of guilt. I substituted this distracting activity in place of *entering into and through my feelings* into my body's felt-sense of it all, thereby failing to dispose and open myself to receive the untold story hiding beneath the feelings.

Coming right up to the threshold of my guilt, without even being aware of it I then took an action which made some form of addiction inevitable. I failed to enter through my feelings into my body's felt inner meaning. I completely missed the visceral significance of it all. Instead, I substituted visiting mother in place of being in touch with how my body actually carried the uncomfortable feelings which no one had ever taught me how to be with, either when I was a child or throughout all my years of Jesuit education and formation on the way to becoming a priest.

Rather than becoming more congruent with what was real in my body, thereby allowing it to unfold and tell its story so my body-sense of that issue could then unfold, move forward and be carried in a different way, I chose a different path. Ultimately, however, this path took me away from the very experience of finding myself *in Christ* as well.

Millions of people make this same tragic choice every day of their lives in situations far more complex than the simple example Pete shares here. But the psychological process remains the same. We seek to control the so-called bad feeling, to make it go away or

Rediscovering the Lost Body-Connection

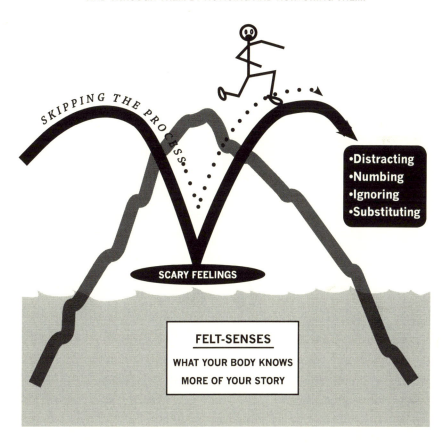

substitute something better in its place. While doing this, however, we fall prey to the very psychological mechanism of escape we have stumbled into or perhaps deliberately chosen. It soon becomes our jailer, locking an addictive pattern of distraction or avoidance in place. Inevitably, we become its slave in order not to feel our real feelings.

We can now put a psychological label on this pattern. It is *a Process-Skipping Structure.* The label, of course, cannot help us to change. But a better understanding of this addictive escape mechanism can

What is Process-Skipping?

alert us about where to look within experience for our own process-skipping habits. These rise up, both as major obstacles as well as valuable opportunities for healthy relational, emotional and spiritual growth, if one can take advantage of how to grow *through* them into the greater freedom of noticing and nurturing all our important feelings so their felt meaning can surface and become more explicit inside us.

Pete concludes his personal reflection above as follows:

> When I finally took time to create a caring presence around my guilt and other negative feelings, and did not just continue to react in an addictive way, my incomplete stories began to unfold. What eventually surfaced was deep anger and resentment over unfinished issues from childhood—painful family separations and being sent away to boarding school when I was only seven years old because of war and illness over which my parents had no control. But I still felt those absences and the pain of them.
>
> These resentments were deep, carried around for years inside my body. My mind had long since arrived at its own adult *explanation* and understanding. *But my body's as yet unheard story was still only seven years old.* If only someone had known how to help me as a child to be with all my unprocessed feelings around lengthy illnesses and wartime separations, I'm sure I would have carried these experiences through life in an entirely different way. When we divorce our body's knowing from our human story, history and our spiritual journey, we introduce *a radical disconnection* into life that will follow us to the grave unless we find some way to develop the habit of allowing our important feelings to tell their stories and be heard.
>
> With Ed's support, I deliberately took time to allow the many unheard feelings and felt-senses to unfold. This made a tremendous difference in the quality of my personal presence during visits to mother. When compulsively visiting the retirement center, I was invariably there to get the monkey of guilt off my back. I fulfilled a duty but was rarely present with that deeper capacity for authentic communion and easy sharing that characterizes true companionship. I know mother felt this in some way. But as I listened in a caring way to the unheard narratives within my feelings, I found over time that guilt and anger began to tell their stories and change in how they felt inside. With this inner forward

movement came a whole new way of appreciating and *being present* to my mother. I could sense a genuine adult friendship maturing during our visits together. We shared much in common and were both blessed with a similar sense of humor. A surprising and wonderful gift appeared when I could finally discover my mother as a friend.

Why Have We Placed Process-Skipping Toward the End of Our Programs?

Here's what we have found happening within most people if we explained process-skipping long before they had developed any body-sense for how the human organism knows and learns through the habit of noticing and nurturing important feelings. Essentially, we were asking them to put the cart before the horse because information alone rarely, if ever, provides the actual *bodily-felt steps* into acquiring a new, physical habit which first needs to be developing inside them before it can then take the place of an older process-skipping habit.

An outdated or unhealthy habit in the body can never be removed by a good idea or accurate analysis. One first needs to develop an equally *embodied* habit that can eventually replace the one that isn't healthy or no longer works. Slowly going through the Body-Learnings in this workbook until you gain some experience of what this type of more physical learning actually *feels* like in your own body provides the necessary foundation for motivating you to keep on track, noticing and nurturing how your body feels and, perhaps, still carries more old process-skipping habits. This all comes together not just in your mind, but *inside your own body* as the process deepens your Christian faith and trust in recovering the lost body-connection within your spirituality. The experience of learning a new habit enables you to persevere in replacing the old, unhealthy habits which block both the body-feel for grace and an experience of living within the Larger Body "in Christ"—because the very sense for God's Loving Presence may be discovered right within an experience of growing beyond process-skipping. That appears to have been St. Paul's experience, as we shall see in the next chapter.

Understanding your process-skipping, as well as how your own physical organism carries it, becomes integral to your maturing sense of self. We have observed that people who try to live the learnings in

What is Process-Skipping?

this workbook often find themselves astounded at how much of their previous behavior, even their religious practices, has involved process-skipping. Yet, by patiently companioning yourself and one another on our unique journeys into loving as God loves, a deeper, healthier faith community becomes possible at a level of experience where it feels much better physically and emotionally to live Christ's new commandment rather than to continue being enablers of process-skipping.

Our formerly rejected or stuffed feelings can then become our teachers. Christian spirituality can then be lived as it is meant to be—a daily continuing embodiment or incarnation *within our own bodies* of the living Spirit of Christ's Larger Body in us. Our tears, fears, hurts, loneliness, human limitations and failures become our teachers and open doorways into the Body of Christ—no longer our enemies.

No matter what our age, there is spiritual and health-care wisdom in knowing how to prevent children (as well as the child still alive inside all of us) from continuing to fall into habits of process-skipping. As Christian communities, we are called to learn how to companion ourselves and one another beyond this pathology. As you have read so often throughout these pages, knowing in the mind is never the same as a process of changing in your body. This fundamental learning lies at the heart of the still-new paradigm shift that Christians need to rediscover in order to recover the lost body-sense of Christ within their own bodies.

Process-Skipping has sunk deep roots into our culture because our one-sided approach to scientific advancement has taught us that cognitive understanding of our problems, together with an ability to analyze and name them, provides a kind of power and control over what has become outdated or needs to change. But over time, we both gradually came to realize how we all have been slow to recognize that our preferential nod in the direction of head-knowing and thinking not only slants our perspective but rarely brings about any desired change in the way *our bodies* actually carry difficult feelings and the visceral, physical experience of them.

The threefold, scientific methodology of understanding, prediction and control certainly does resolve many types of problems. But our culture has naively fallen into the trap of assuming that this one approach represents the only modern way to resolve *all* problems.

And, of course, it does not—most certainly when the life-long challenge of becoming more fully human involves the close cooperation of our body's felt-sense knowing as one of our *two* primary knowledge resources for personal and social community building.

The gradually-developing inner world of connecting through our body's felt-sensing within some Larger Body's loving, gifting Presence can never be contained within an intellectual concept nor effectively learned through an inductive or deductive reasoning process in the mind alone. Cultures highly impacted by the scientific methodology easily become seduced and sidetracked into believing that we gain control over all our problems and our lives by thinking about and analyzing them as much as we can. The development of such knowledge, of course, represents an important tool on this journey, But without the *balance* of our felt-sense knowing, wisdom fades. Learning to integrate the body's knowing into both daily life and spiritual experience remains a key ingredient in the maturing of any healthy spirituality. Insofar as process-skipping distracts and draws our attention away from this central task, it poses a serious impediment to spiritual development, global peace and the diminishment of violence.

What helps me (Ed) the most in my own rediscovery of God's Loving Presence in my own body is the simple morning exercise I shared with you at the end of Chapter 9. It relates directly to this chapter, helping you to understand what we mean by process-skipping as well as tying it into the process and steps you already know, so you can begin noticing and nurturing how your body feels about your own process-skipping and how to grow beyond it.

As I said at the end of chapter 9: When awakening in the morning before rising and beginning to plan and think about the day's work, I ask myself: "What in my body right now most needs my caring, loving presence?" Then, of course, I pause long enough and silently to go into my body, waiting to notice whether I can pick up any felt clue that needs my loving presence.

As time goes by, I am also finding this simple question very helpful at other times of the day or evening when I start to worry about something, get upset with some situation or someone's behavior, don't feel too well or don't know how to write what I know inside. I am finding that as this habit grows, it nips in the bud any tendency to slip into some new process-skipping structure.

Even after some of my most obvious process-skipping habits have been given time to tell their stories and fade into history, I have found that this exercise alerts me to any new or old fragments of skipping away from feelings which still call out for my attention.

In our world today, process-skipping has become programmed into us as a cultural value through advertising and entertainment. It lies woven throughout much of our media messaging where we are told on a daily basis what spells success. It colors our obsession with the lives of celebrities and what it really means to be human. Television screens barrage us with high impact images and computer generated creations that seep into our world-view, daily telling us what life is all about. Into this high intensity environment of someone else's questionable version of reality and values, I find my own body's organic Christian faith truly a balancing breath of fresh air, a dose of healthy common sense and a life-sustainer and savior. Knowing that we can support and journey together with one another in the development of such experience can bring into the lives of each of us a profound and satisfying meaning. The gift of learning to love as God loves is the engine which makes this possible.

Dr. Gendlin's recognition of *process-skipping*, along with his coining of the phrase, offers not only an accurate and clever label for identifying another psychological virus eating away at the challenge of continuing to grow more fully whole as a person. It lies at the core of what so ravages and corrodes our effective witness of living Christ's New Commandment to love as God loves within Christ's Body through our own bodies.

Repairing the Relationship to Our Difficult Feelings

Rewiring our habitual relationship of pushing difficult feelings aside instead of embracing and listening to what those same feelings try to tell us, both in body as well as mind, obviously will not happen overnight. It takes time and practice to grow beyond this slavery to fear, replacing old habits by first beginning with a new relationship to ourselves. Happily, we have found that this can be done. However, most people need support in their development of this new body-habit, discerning what eventually can replace all those old fears and the sense of helplessness which literally enslave us in a dead-ended, hopeless and unhealthy relationship to our own feelings. Unfortunately, a destructive form of process-skipping interaction can so dominate our behavior and diminish our relational world that we only connect with those feelings which we have been brain-washed into believing are acceptable.

Remember, that in themselves feelings are neither good nor bad. The moral issue comes into play when you choose to act out such feelings in a way that becomes destructive to yourself, others or the common good of our life-sustaining environment. Your so-called negative feelings have as much important information to tell you, as do your positive and likable feelings. But *how you relate* to your more difficult feelings brings attention directly to bear upon where you begin the process of transformation beyond unhealthy habits. Noticing and nurturing your important feelings becomes the knife that can slice through this knot, offering a change that promises huge personal and social benefits which bless both you and the society in which you live. Growing into a practical body-sense for the implications of such experience represents a large part of what this book tries to convey.

Any religion we have ever come across, including our own Christianity, has seriously neglected to understand fully and develop simple, practical steps for how to work with *the body itself* as our most fundamental building block for achieving human wholeness (holiness) within our educational and spiritual formation programs. Our marriage preparation classes, parenting programs, formal schooling and training for ministry, along with religious education etc., need to free people from the pathologizing habit of process-skipping in their bodies. Until we achieve this in a practical, hands-on way we will continue talking the talk instead of putting our bodies where our good intentions are.

The psychologist, Carl Rogers, once reminded us from his long experience as a therapist, of his consistent finding that beneath every socially expressed and unacceptable destructive feeling in a client there invariably lies a deep hurt. When we treat our feelings as alien invaders to be fought off, conquered, or controlled, we smash the phone or kill the messenger because we fear or cannot comprehend the message.

What is Process-Skipping?

As Christians we must, eventually, make a crucial choice. Will we continue to use prayer and asceticism as a way to *control* and *contain* our feelings, or will we listen deeper into the hurts and frustrations, the sense of unfairness, resentment, loneliness, anger or feelings of near despair that often lie within such feelings. Unheard felt-senses always await our attention, longing to speak and struggling to tell their stories. They call out for respect and a caring presence, yearning for the touch of grace and healing. Our futile attempts at control from the outside never really work.

Experienced counselors know that the low self-esteem people carry inside is a primary cause of destructive behaviors. It blocks the maturing of inner potential, creativity and personal wholeness. Children seldom grow beyond such inner blockage and repressions unless they find help for getting in touch with the felt meanings that lie deep within their feelings—especially the more difficult ones. Learned habits of avoidance, which quickly become *process-skipping* substitutes that unfortunately replace inner wholeness and congruence, forever cut us off from all our deeper, untold inner stories still waiting to unfold. Our failure to listen with a caring presence into those hidden stories cuts us off from a maturing, embodied experience of God's Presence in all things—even our tears and fears.

Deliberately Noticing Your Process-Skipping Patterns

Consciously or not, each of us develops unique stratagems for avoiding, running away from, numbing or otherwise attempting to control our troublesome inner lives. We find ways to make them invisible instead of opening ourselves to listen for the narratives that lie buried within. After a few years of this, an embedded pattern of process-skipping around or away from your feelings runs on automatic pilot. You rarely even notice when this habit turns itself on, forcing you to overlook opportunities for further growth as you escape from inner pain or substitute other more acceptable feelings in place of those that trouble you.

Let's illustrate this problem with a chance experience Pete once had which alerted him that the principal roadblock to noticing and nurturing his important feelings was a deep, already entrenched habit in his body. This experience became an important personal metaphor for him as he struggled to comprehend and work with his own inner *blind spots.*

The Flinch

One evening while enjoying a quiet stroll on a deserted country road, I noticed a small, stuffed ball lying next to my path. Picking it up, I continued walking, idly tossing the ball in the air and then catching it as it fell. It struck me how rarely as an adult I had taken time for such a simple boyhood pastime.

Frequently, my toss was off, and I needed to run a bit to catch the ball. It was then that I became acutely aware of something—a persistent pattern. As I tossed the ball and it fell back toward me I would follow with my eyes until it was a few inches from my hand, when suddenly my gaze would *flinch* and veer away in the last split second before the ball actually came into my grasp. "Keep your eyes on the ball!" The words came back from grammar school softball experiences—but this time I really heard them.

For the next several moments I disciplined myself to watch the ball fall all the way into my hand. I could immediately feel a different body-sense in the experience. When my eyes veered away, there was a sense of wincing, pulling to one side—an avoidance. But when I followed the ball all the way into my hand, I could feel a kind of newness in the experience, something fresh which felt quite firm and novel, as though I had never noticed this before. At that point, I fell into one of those precious moments of reverie where things began falling together and my experience took on a meaning far more significant than what appeared in this idle pastime.

Most of us know that we have feelings. *What we don't know is how to follow an important feeling all the way down into the story in our body whenever that feeling needs to change.*

Psychologically, a process-skipping habit draws us *away from* the fully attentive, caring presence which enables us to stay connected with our difficult feelings long enough in order to sense the deeper, hidden felt meanings waiting to unfold from within them. Process-skipping introduces *a psychological wincing*, drawing-back, defending ourselves or retreating from some imagined or anticipated threat.

What is Process-Skipping?

But there are far more potentially devastating consequences here. Process-skipping habits not only pull you away from the path of healthy human growth and fuller human functioning within your own body. They obstruct any maturing in your unfolding awareness of opening up and listening into your body's more veiled felt sense for *being part of something greater than yourself*, being an integral membrane within a Larger Living Body.

Entering consciously into your own body's growing sense for *felt inner personal wholeness or congruence* lays the experiential groundwork for beginning to explore a more extensive world of connection *within an even Greater Whole*—for Christians, the Body of Christ. An expanding awareness of both inward and outward environmentalism, an organic incarnation both personal and cosmic in scope guides the healthy development of human evolving. The two seem meant to go hand-in-glove together, mutually supporting one another.

Unfortunately, just like my eyes following the ball, most of us *flinch* and turn away when brushing against negative feelings we abhor or from which we instinctively recoil. Our gaze veers to one side, drawing attention away from the possibility of any new unfolding of feelings and felt-senses changing and moving forward together. Because of this process-skipping flinch, symbols cannot effectively touch and invite hidden stories to blossom from within your body's knowing.

Most of the time, your process-skipping habits operate without you ever even becoming aware of them—just one big blur rushing past on autopilot. But when deliberately slowing down and learning to *notice* enough, you can soon begin feeling for and observing such habits as they kick into action. You eventually find yourself in a far better position to begin listening further into your unexplored, deeper felt-senses which you could not access before because your more disruptive emotions drew you away from listening to hidden felt meaning inside your body. Dr. Gendlin puts it this way:

> It seems quite striking and universal that we feel guilt, shame, and badness, *instead* of feeling that concerning which we feel shame, guilt, and badness. It is almost as if these emotions themselves preclude our feeling what it all is to us—not so much because they are so unpleasant, as because they skip the point at which we might complete, symbolize,

respond or attend to that which centrally we feel. ...These emotions seem to complete but actually "skip" the incomplete implicit meanings. ...the preoccupation with these emotions is not to be confused with the felt meaning which, though connected to these emotions, needs the focusing.

One client describes it in terms of a hurricane: "If you only go so far into something, it's like going into a hurricane and getting terribly blown around. You have to go into it and then keep going further and further *in* till you get to the eye of the hurricane. There it's quiet and you can see where you are." This beautifully expresses the fact that the direction of focusing is definitely into the emotions, not away from them, yet also that focusing involves something qualitatively very different than merely "being blown around" by the emotions. The illustration also captures something of the centrality, depth and quiet which one finds—the quality which others have called "being in touch with myself." [1]

As you make a deliberate effort to become more aware of your process-skipping mechanisms you also open the possibility of rubbing shoulders with how your own body carries the experience of your habit of avoiding your difficult feelings. This can reveal yet another path for you to follow in making a physical connection inside yourself. How does your body feel *about* your process-skipping habits? For example, you may find a body-sense of sadness around all your process-skipping. Perhaps you find yourself puzzled, curious, angry or somewhat apprehensive. Becoming more aware of your own unique process-skipping ways offers a surprisingly simple approach to slipping right into *how you actually feel about* the very habit most responsible for your chronic disconnection from yourself. Pete never even suspected his complete out-of-touchness with a boyhood sense of anger and resentment at long separations from his family. His hurricane of guilt obscured the unprocessed felt meaning within his deeper childhood feelings of loneliness and separation which still needed to be heard and companioned in a caring way so they could finally tell their story and begin to change. ■

For a process-skipping exercise, please turn the page

What is Process-Skipping?

Growing Beyond Process-Skipping: An Exercise

Steps to Help You Notice and Nurture How Your Body Carries The Burden of Process-Skipping

*(A key body-learning for noticing & nurturing your important feelings is to become aware of your habitual ways of **NOT** listening to them. Use this exercise until you have listened to all that your body wants to say about your process-skipping habits, and then check-in daily on other felt-senses.)*

Preparation

Take a moment to close your eyes, growing quiet inside by letting your attention settle into the center of your body.

Noticing and Nurturing

1. Ask yourself: "When I feel depressed, sad, scared, angry, anxious, afraid of failing, teary, etc., what process-skipping habits do I automatically fall into in order to make myself feel better?"

(Give yourself whatever time you need to let an answer come that feels on target.)

2. Ask your body, "What feeling usually comes inside just before I automatically process-skip in order to get away from it?" *(Pause)*

3. Now ask yourself, "How does my body feel about my process-skipping and not listening to what these feelings are trying to tell me?"

*(Give yourself plenty of time to listen for how **your body** carries the answer to this question. Don't just "think" an answer. Let yourself feel it.)*

4. "Where in my body do I most feel and carry the effects of this neglect?"

(Take time to notice how your body tells you the answer.)

(1)

Rediscovering the Lost Body-Connection

5. When feelings surface in response to these questions, then take care of them so they can tell you their story and help you to grow beyond process-skipping. Allow time now to let your Affection Teacher help you hold this burden in a caring, gentle way so your inside place can feel that you are trying to say: "I really care and won't leave you alone. I'll try not to neglect you any more and be available."

If practical, you might want to place your hand wherever you physically feel any of this in your body. Let your hand express your caring rather than only intending or thinking it in your mind.

(Spend as much time as you can together with this place, just as you would with someone whom you care for and love.)

Ending

6. When it's time to stop, try to build a special bond with anything that feels unfinished. Ask your body, "How do you need me to be with you so we can continue our journey together? Is there anything further you want to tell me before I stop?" Then listen for whatever may come from inside your body.

(Wait for anything to surface that might feel connected.)

7. Just before stopping, allow a few moments to be inside yourself with gratitude and reverence for the silence, for the time to be together with your own story, thankful for any movement that may have occurred, grateful simply for the gift of it all ... whatever feels right for you. Then, when you're ready, you can stop.

*** *** ***

The authors, the Institute for BioSpiritual Research and its members do not teach the habit of noticing and nurturing important feelings as a substitute for professional psychotherapeutic or psychiatric care for those who need it, nor as a substitute for training and licensing in the above health fields.

(2)

Personal Notes

Chapter 15

Paul's Astonishing Discovery 'in Christ' '...When I am Weak, Then I am Strong...' (2 Cor 12:7–10)

Opening a Door on 'Inner Dwelling'

"...I was given a sharp pain in my body...Three times I begged the Lord to rid me of it, but his answer was: 'My grace is all you need; power comes to its full strength in weakness.' I shall therefore prefer to find my joy and pride in the very things that are my weakness; and then the power of Christ will come and rest upon me. Hence I am well content, for Christ's sake, with weakness, contempt, persecution, hardship, and frustration; for when I am weak, then I am strong." *(2 Cor 12:7–10 NEB)*

WE FIND IT INTERESTING in several translations of the above passage from Paul's Second Letter to the Corinthians that the Greek verb, *episkeinósei* (ἐπισκηνώσῃ), is translated as, "the power of Christ...*will rest upon me*. ..." (2 Cor. 12:9 NEB) Yet, the more accurate meaning of this verb is to *take up quarters, take up one's abode, to dwell in*. The translation, *"to rest upon,"* fails to convey the full sense of being viscerally soaked, bathed and caught up in an *embodied* intimacy and closeness with/in Christ's Body that the use of this Greek word implies.

What we're really discussing in this workbook is how you can discover *a new way to dwell inside yourself*—within the truth of how you really carry your feelings. Learning to notice and nurture your important feelings means bringing a caring presence (Christ's *agápe*) to all the unheard stories that lie hidden within your own body. Bishop Robinson's earlier quoted reference to *membranes* rather than *members* of the Body of Christ emphasizes his graphic attempt to describe a far more intimate, embodied, or in-corporated and less separated way of being within and finding yourself, *"in Christ."*

Earlier translators, perhaps steeped in their immediate historical experience of monarchy, perhaps sought a more *distancing* kind of translation for the text from 2 Corinthians. Maybe they wanted to avoid what might have been viewed as an inappropriate closeness or intimacy between human and divine, much as a king might deign to reach down and rest his hand upon a lowly subject. "the power of Christ "*...will rest upon me. ...*" (2 Cor. 12:9 NEB).

But Paul's language and choice of words are far more grounded, visceral, and even democratic. His sense for the reality of Christ and our radical *membraneship* within His Body does not allow for any careful, discrete distancing that a more royalist-leaning translator from another time and social experience might seek to impose!

The fascinating shift that Christian churches in our time find themselves challenged to make within their experience and appreciation of the Body of Christ will flow from a newly emerging interiority which individual Christians gradually begin to become aware of and grow into within themselves. It is perhaps akin to the inner felt transformation from being the *subject* of a ruling monarch and then finding oneself anew as a free *citizen* within a pluralist, democratic society. The texture of *self-awareness*, the quality of self-esteem, the inner sense of spirituality and even church itself become significantly transformed. As bishop Robinson has already noted, we are not like so many peas in a pod but more like branches within the same tree. An emerging new experience of *individual self-awareness within the Body of the Whole Christ* may well open an unexplored ecumenical path for the future of effective dialogue not only among the various separated Christian churches—but within an even more extensive dialogue among serious spiritual seekers within the human family at large.

Recall, once again, bishop Robinson's earlier comment about the Apostle Paul twisting the Greek language in order to include the entire Gentile world within the Body of Christ:

> ...The Gentiles are fellow-heirs (**συν**κληρονόμα), and fellow-members of the body (**σύν**σωμα; Mersch: 'concorporate'), and fellow-partakers (**συν**μέτοξα) of the promise in Christ Jesus' (Eph. 3.6).[9] *(**bold** emphasis ours).*

This sense for participation within some Larger Living Body expresses itself as a universal human phenomenon, not the private preserve of a privileged few. The human body itself offers a common path for the journey which lies ahead. Learning how to love as God loves knows no boundaries.

At this point in your reading of the book, the pieces of a much larger puzzle can begin knitting themselves together. If the human organism itself offers a unifying point of focus, then process-skipping habits which lead us away from our true selves also lead us away from a growing, congruent awareness in our own bodies within which we can begin to discern ourselves as membranes within some Larger Living Body. We don't *think* our way into God, rather, as Paul bluntly put it:

> ...they should seek God, in the hope that they might feel after him and find him. Yet he is not far from each one of us, for 'in him we live and move and have our being'... *(Acts 17:27–28 RSV)*

Or, as The Inclusive Bible—The First Egalitarian Translation translates this text:

> ...human beings would seek, reach out for, and perhaps find the One who is not really far from any of us—the One in whom we live and move and have our being. As one of your poets have put it, 'We too are God's children.' *(Acts 17:27–28 TIB)*

The Greek text, "*might feel after him*" (ψηλαφήσειαν) translates as, *to touch, handle; feel around for, grope for*—a wonderfully visceral sense of fumbling or groping in the dark, a consciousness with our eyes tight shut inviting an awareness in our fingertips to guide us forward on our pilgrimage "into Christ." With *agápe* in our hearts and dwelling within a graced, embodied, felt-sensing awareness of being a living cell within something greater than ourselves we follow an inviting Call from within, moving us all forward *together* on our common human journey into God.

Puzzling Interactions

There was great puzzlement during the 19th century when scientists noted that passing a magnet near a compass made the needle jiggle and dance. To the naked eye, there was no visible, physical connection between the two yet, obviously, they somehow interacted with one another. Placing a magnet beneath a rigidly held sheet of paper upon which iron filings had been randomly scattered soon revealed the hidden shape of an invisible magnetic field as the metal filings rearranged themselves in orderly patterns around the poles of the magnet. Puzzling and little understood experiences like this were often called *unexplainable interactions*.

In his Second Letter to the Corinthians, quoted above, Paul wondered about a puzzling interaction in his own life. The experience was not drawn from an observation of some external event. Rather, he was stunned by an experience right within his own body "...as he could feel it from inside..." What is most interesting about the origin of Paul's unusual interactive experience is that it arose as a direct result of his futile attempt to use prayer in order to *process-skip* around his own painful and difficult feelings.

Paul's Process-Skipping Experience

> ...I was given a sharp pain in my body...Three times I begged the Lord to rid me of it, but his answer was: *'My grace is all you need; power comes to its full strength in weakness.'* I shall therefore prefer to find my joy and pride in the very things that are my weakness; and then the power of Christ will come and rest upon me. Hence I am well content, for Christ's sake, with weakness, contempt, persecution, hardship, and frustration; *for when I am weak, then I am strong.*
> (2 Cor. 12:7–10 NEB) (emphasis ours)

Three times Paul prayed to have his pain taken away. Just as Pete attempted to control guilt by visiting his mother so, too, Paul attempted to control his pain by asking the Lord (someone more powerful than himself) to take it away from him. But Christ refused to cooperate with this process-skipping evasion and offered a curious alternative: *"My grace is all you need; power comes to its full strength in weakness."* (2 Cor. 12:8–9 NEB)

In this incident, Paul shares a personal experience, but without any attempt to explain it. He offers no comment as to the actual inner process whereby he moved from begging God to take away his pain before suddenly finding "...my joy and pride in the very things that are my weakness." He does, however, hint at the importance of *contrast* in his discovery of Christ's presence within the experience of his weakness. Somehow his own weakness became the *gestalt background* against which the power of Christ became even more sharply evident and clearly manifest within him. Paul appears very aware that the transforming power he experienced was not of his own making—*"My grace is all you need; power comes to its full strength in weakness."*

The central learning for Paul, however, was that he found Christ not by running away from nor gaining power over his weakness but, paradoxically, by owning and journeying even deeper into it. Through this inward pilgrimage he discovered a radically new kind of empowerment right within the very feelings from which he had initially sought to escape, even asking Christ to help him. Without yet being able to identify and describe the inner psychological steps he had taken to stumble into this alternative graced direction inside himself he had, nonetheless, been drawn into a whole new world upon hearing the words, "My grace is all you need; power comes to its full strength in weakness." (2 Cor 12:8–9 NEB) From that moment on, his attitude toward all the tears and fears of life, and even the burden of his own limitations dramatically changed!

Paul moved beyond his more dominative approach of always trying to fix and control his so-called *negative* feelings, opening himself to a force he literally could neither imagine nor visually experience, yet which clearly was already at work within his own body. Even more startling, Paul discovered this new power rising up from right within the very weakness itself from which he was trying to escape. After this experience Paul's world was quite literally turned upside down.

> Most gladly, therefore, I would rather boast about my weaknesses, that the power of Christ may dwell in me. So I am content with weakness, with mistreatment, with distress, with persecutions and difficulties for the sake of Christ; when I am powerless, it is then that I am strong. *(2 Cor. 12:9–10 JB)*

In this unusual experience Paul found himself brushing up against a force and interaction at work within, from which he then drew new inner strength while at the same time recognizing that he was not in

'...When I am Weak, Then I am Strong...'

charge here. Paul was neither alone, nor did he move forward on the basis of any abilities of his own which he could muster from inside himself. He had stumbled into an upsurge of pure gift or grace, an updraft changing everything in an instant, making all things new.

Put another way, *it was like discovering himself living within a whole new kind of Body!* Here was an experience which would draw from him the memorable cry of faith: "...it is no longer I who live, but Christ who lives in me..." (Gal 2:20 NEB) It reminds one of the baby hawk's world immeasurably enlarging and filling with awesome potential in the experience of being drawn upward within the rising column of air.

Paul's remarkable exclamation grew not from teachings and information learned in his mind. Rather the cry emerged from within an *embodied* experience in which he knew he was powerless, yet at the same time discovering an unexpected strength gifted from within the very weakness and pain he had so resolutely determined to avoid inside himself. The experience changed his entire relationship to his own hurting body. Paul's prayers so often ask that we, too, may be gifted with that same changed relationship to our own hurting bodies.

There are remarkable overtones here of Bishop Robinson's earlier comment on "membranes" in the Body of Christ. This time, though, the experience becomes suffused with individual self-awareness as each membrane "...takes on the rhythm and metabolism of the body into which they have been grafted."

One finds a curious resonance, too, with the flock of birds or schools of fish being able to act in unison as a single body through some power at work in them reaching far beyond their more separated ability to fly or swim independently on their own. While remaining in their own distinct bodies they simultaneously act together in unison as integral parts of some unified Larger Whole.

It is also much like the gestalt we viewed in an earlier chapter. Interaction surges back and forth between one side and the other. The experience of strength-IN-weakness opens a further crack in our familiar, everyday perceptions, setting ajar for an instant the tightly shut door separating one world from the other. Flocks of birds can become symbol and metaphor for something even more profound occurring inside ourselves.

'...When I Am Weak, Then I Am Strong...' *(2 Cor 12: 7–10)*

The unambiguous *contrast* in this experience is what sharpens the appearance of a previously unnoticed, largely unrecognized power at work in Paul's body. *Weak* and *strong* are like the black and white in a gestalt. Lines here are clean and clear-cut when one is a background for the other. The back and forth stands out unblurred, unambiguous. It was like Pete's *"que sera sera"* experience. His feelings clearly changing as he recognized with certitude that there was absolutely nothing he could possibly have done *on his own* in order to make this change in his feelings occur.

So often when people bump up against their human limitations we have heard phrases and cries like: "How can I ever get control over this whole situation?" "It will take so much time to learn how to do this!" "How am I ever going to be able to heal and get beyond all this pain?"

The habit of immediately turning to control, willpower, and an exercise of sheer brute force to move forward with a problem is so ingrained in us that without even thinking we fall into this pattern of perceiving and acting. Yet, there remain such vast areas of human living and experience that in no way bend to such an approach. Can you directly *will* self-esteem into being? Have you ever forced love and mutual vulnerability to occur? Can you control the inevitability of your own or a loved one's dying? On a more positive note, have you ever been so touched by a piece of music or the sound of a beautiful aria that you sense spontaneous chills running up and down your spine and feel goose bumps rising on your arms. As we asked earlier, "Have you ever deliberately tried to will a goose bump?"

We can't even make goose bumps happen yet we attempt to control, dominate, power talk, and power walk our way through so much of our day-to-day living. Noticing and nurturing your important feelings and developing a new kind of relationship to all the unheard inner stories and painful, hurting places inside your own body lies quite literally beyond this carefully crafted world of dominance and control overshadowing so much of our waking awareness. That's not to say there can be no place for control in life. As we often remark, "God help you if you have no control in your life. But God help you even more if ALL that you have is control!"

'...When I am Weak, Then I am Strong...'

The capacity for good management as well as organizational ability is necessary for community development. Yet, these same skills are powerless to enable any of us *to evolve*. Evolution points toward, and requires a capacity to be drawn beyond old, outdated patterns of survival that no longer work for us. Our current situation as a species now demands that we survive by evolving within ourselves in order to discover the fresh answers called for by our times. It is from within the depth of our own felt-senses that we will eventually begin discovering an ever-renewing source of unexpected direction and gratifying surprise.

Finding a fresh way to move beyond stale, outmoded patterns of perception and acting is always the real challenge in human evolution and spiritual growth. The first step in responding to that challenge is to notice and nurture your own important feelings—your body's language for connecting to the world of Spirit and inspiration. But in our culture today this means developing a new habit, an entirely new way of relating to our own bodies and their felt-sensing. Then we will discover the gift of a surprising experience of power and direction maturing from inside our body's knowing which does not originate from our addiction to controlling everything with our minds.

That is what Paul discovered with a little nudge from his Mentor. *"My grace is all you need; power comes to its full strength in weakness."* (2 Cor. 12:8–9 NEB) We are each called to develop a new habit of *disposing ourselves* for gift, grace, inspiration, hunch, intuition, creativity, and surprise. As already noted, we can neither force nor control evolution. Grace is always pure gift. We can never produce it on demand.

But we can learn, and need to discover a new way of being in and relating to ourselves, especially to our own weaknesses and brokenness. We face the challenge to uncover *a new kind of interiority* that can open unexplored doorways, direction, and answers which we can never achieve by just thinking about them. The Apostle Paul has invited us to discover this power of *a New Body* being born from within our own body.

When St. Paul encouraged the early Christians that they needed to find and develop an entirely new identity *"in Christ,"* he challenged them to add another dimension to their everyday experience of themselves. This reflects the same wise approach that Albert Einstein offered and we have already referred to in Chapter 10. Whenever you face difficult questions and thorny, irresolvable issues he reminded us that, "...you can never resolve them at the level where you first experience them. Rather, you must first add another dimension to your experience of the problem, and only then will you begin to discover a solution."

We need to give Paul a chance to get through to us. He sincerely attempted to add just such a new dimension of awareness to our human experience by offering to humankind the missing key to who Christ is today and who each of us is in Christ. "When I am weak, then I am strong." (2 Cor 12:10 RSV) We have read these words for centuries. Now is the time to experience what Paul's message actually feels like and can mean in your own body. But rather than just discovering new ideas, this generation finds itself called to develop a whole new sense of what it means to be "I" as we stumble upon the dynamic experience of a body-feel for grace that can guide us into a global community of brothers and sisters yearning for a unity which today seems even more elusive than ever before in an age of confrontation, perennial divisiveness and violence.

Our world seems to flounder so helplessly as it faces the specter of necessary political, environmental, social and religious change. Yet, Paul's paradoxical experience within his own body, finding himself strong inside as he owned the stark truth of his feelings *"in Christ,"* could well model for us how we, too, in our time can turn our own world upside-down. Nations find themselves beset on all sides by the control of greedy politicians, corrupt, power hungry leaders, and violent religious terrorists, with weapons of mass destruction and the threat of global climate changes looming ever larger in the background. There has never been a more urgent time than now for Christians finally *to gather together* in order to introduce into this chaos the most radical step in evolution ever proposed in the history of humankind. We are called to give witness to a maturing sense of the Incarnation of Jesus Christ within our own bodies, by recognizing and owning our addictions to process-skipping just as Paul did. Then, our growing unity through companioning one another as One Body, *in Christ,* could plant the seeds of a newly-born global awareness of the entire earth's common good.

We, like Paul, find ourselves challenged to find some new doorway into an intimate experience of God's Presence within us by entering through our important feelings into the *More* of all the untold stories in our lives, just as Paul has described in his letters to the early Christians. He wrote of being imprisoned, scourged, beaten with rods, stoned, shipwrecked, adrift at sea, hungry, cold, overworked, frustrated in his ministry. But most of all, Paul found that the key to discovering Christ *was to notice and care for all these important feelings in his own body by entering into a new relationship with them.* They became his teachers and friends in Christ's Body—his own body. Paul prayed that the same experience might happen to us. His personal story of discovering the body-connections within Christian spirituality by changing his relationship to his own hurting body, holds a potential to unveil for us today how the Body-Learnings in this workbook can dispose us to receive the graces of growing beyond process-skipping into a new experience of ourselves within the Body of the Whole Christ.

Paul clearly owned his personal process-skipping way of praying when he realized that Christ was telling him, "Don't ask me to become an enabler of your own process-skipping. My grace is all you need." The power of healing change comes to its full strength when owning the truth of yourself in the how and where of your own body bearing your frustrations, hurts, imprisonments, hunger and weaknesses.

This critical inner step of noticing precisely how and where your body really feels or reacts, and then nurturing this with a physically caring and loving presence, instead of process-skipping, opens a door that then invites the power of God's Presence into the entire relationship with its inner process of unification and potential for fuller human living. This, of course, is the long-term goal of this workbook.

When such realization sinks in, then our relationship to, with, and in the Body of Christ radically changes. A new level of Believing in Yourself *in Christ* can then gradually be born. Such experience holds a powerful potential to become the bedrock of your own self-esteem and personal identity.

Maturing self-esteem must first be grounded within a congruent in-touchness and acceptance of *Who-I-Really-Am* within my own body, "...as this is felt from inside." A new identity in Christ awaits such emerging experience. *This missing piece has been left out of Christian spirituality!*

Paul's experience of the meaning of Christ and the significance of Christ's response to his attempt to use prayer in a process-skipping way provides a vital key to the future of Christianity. The lesson here is that we are not to use God to rid ourselves of how we feel about our weaknesses. Instead, we are encouraged to find Christ and his strength, peace, and wholeness by holding these same felt-weaknesses within ourselves in loving faith, waiting for the graced appearance of their personal meaning and hidden stories which then become part of our new identity in Christ. *"My grace is all you need; power comes to its full strength in weakness."* (2 Cor. 12:9 NEB)

All too often, when seeking the missing link for believing in ourselves "in Christ," we have found that simplistic moral labels have been used in ways that turn attention toward our mind's thinking rather than into the depth of our body's knowing. At the same time, however, Christian fables have continually surfaced throughout history, suggesting that we should remain steadfast in our searching beyond all these moral imperatives. Here is one such ancient fable, reset within the context of today's new inner exploration, with which to close this chapter:

■

Once upon a time, when God had finished making the world, he wanted to leave a piece of divinity behind for human beings as a promise to us of what we might find if we really put some effort into it. So, God looked for a place to hide this spark of divine essence because, as he told his staff, "What humans can find too easily will never be valued by them."

"Then you must hide this part of yourself on the highest mountain peak on earth," said one of the staffers. God frowned, "No, the human person is an adventuresome creature and will soon learn to climb the highest mountain peaks."

"Hide it, then, O Great One, in the depths of the earth."

"I think not," replied God, "for humans will one day discover that they can dig into the deepest parts of the earth."

"In the middle of the ocean then?"

Again, God said, "No. I have given humans a brain, you see, and one day they will learn to build ships that cross the seas with ease and explore into the depths of the mightiest oceans."

"Where, then?" cried the staff.

God smiled. "I'll hide it in the most inaccessible place of all, because humans will never think to look there. I will plant it deep within their own bodies, especially within their deepest feelings which they fear the most and instinctively push away from themselves."

Five Questions that will Help You Evaluate the Psychological Health of Spiritual and Growth Practices

1. Does the practice support you in *owning* your feelings, or does it merely make you aware of emotions without helping them to be in process?

A couple during marriage counseling were advised to sit together and identify all the feelings that existed between them in their relationship. At the end of the exercise they found themselves staring at one another over a huge pile of mostly negative emotions and asking: "Now what do we do?" Just because you're aware that you're angry, doesn't mean your anger will change. Change does not happen simply because you become aware of your feelings, but by entering into them in a caring way under the guidance of your Affection Teacher. This then allows deeper and often unrecognized felt meanings (*felt-senses*) to move forward and unfold within your body's knowing. Such felt inner movement, the telling of their story, then allows your emotions to change *from the inside*.

2. Does the practice keep you in touch with your own feelings in a way that allows them to unfold, or does it try to substitute other, more acceptable feelings in place of those that are troublesome?

Many angry people don't like being that way and try to change by cultivating more positive feelings to replace their anger. For example, they aim to acquire the *ideal opposite*—being *compassionate*. But while action based on ideals appears satisfactory in anticipation, it is generally unsatisfactory in performance. The anger is never processed, merely cloaked with a thin veneer of respectability. Lancelot Law Whyte put it this way: *"Ideals which seek to deny their shadows eventually exhaust their own power, at which point the dissociated balance becomes unstable and the dark component seizes control!"* [2] *(emphasis ours)* You must learn to notice and nurture the deeper felt-sense or *felt meanings* that lie within your negative feelings. Substituting a better feeling in place of one that is difficult will not bring transformation. Rather, you first need to establish a whole new relationship with feelings that are troublesome, thereby allowing deeper felt layers of your inner story to unfold. Lasting change cannot be imposed from the outside. It will emerge from within when feelings can be heard and tell their stories.

3. Is the practice one that actually facilitates change in the feeling of some issue in your body, or does it merely provide you with information that affects your ideas and thinking about that issue?

Careful, exact analysis of a problem, and precise information about the direction toward change may satisfy the mind, but it is powerless to transform the structure of habit in your body. A neurotic may know he's neurotic, but in itself such knowledge is powerless for helping that person to change. Gendlin puts it this way: *"Knowing is not the process of changing!"* Information in the mind is never the same as a process in your body. The direction toward further change means entering into whatever feelings call out for your attention. A structured *habit* of process-skipping in your body can only be addressed by returning once again to the *habit* of noticing and nurturing your important feelings. Ideas are ineffectual distractions from the hard work of developing this new habit.

4. Does your spiritual or growth practice achieve its effect in you through self-engineering and control, or through self-surrender in openness to a gifting *(graced)* process in your body—one that unveils direction and hidden meaning in your feelings and felt-senses?

An entire universe lies waiting just beyond your limited world of control. Tragically, many never find their way into this realm of gift and surprise. Being with your feelings and felt-senses *without trying to fix them* represents the bottom-line issue in this process. A profound faith can mature here when you stop trying to arm wrestle your feelings into submission. Building this new relationship to yourself lays the foundation for entering the world of gift and grace as this can be known and experienced in your body, not merely reflected upon in your mind. The habit of noticing and nurturing your important feelings disposes you for the gift of seeing and experiencing in a new way. This becomes the basis for an entirely new identity not based exclusively on control.

5. When using a practice to grow beyond stuck feelings, is the level of positive change that occurs in the way an issue feels in your body something that endures after the exercise, or must you keep *repeating* the practice in order to maintain the level of change that occurs?

Some spiritual and growth practices may seem to work temporarily, simply because they distract you from pain. But you must always remember that both religion and growth work are themselves never exempt from process-skipping. They, too, can easily turn into additional ways of skipping around habit-protected places inside ourselves. However, the old Biblical saying also remains true: *"By their fruits you shall know them."* If your practice leaves you with old, unprocessed feelings still firmly locked in place, if there is no sense of forward *movement* in stuck places, then you need to reexamine what you are doing, and how effective an approach it really offers in your life. We easily become addicted to whatever helps us process-skip around our pain. ■

Personal Notes

Chapter 16
The Habit of Noticing and Nurturing Your Important Feelings in Christ Enables You to Mature Beyond Addictive Spiritualities

It has taken us the better part of our lifetime to discover various pieces of research that needed to be integrated together into a practical alternative that could help Christians grow their spirituality beyond some of the pathologies acquired over the centuries. This resulting workbook, with its Body-Learnings and exercises now aims at deep, organic transformation within both individuals and, with time and patience, Christian communities themselves.

Now that you have begun to understand and, hopefully, to experience with the help of these chapters something of the lost biology of Christian spirituality, especially how much has been lost through *process-skipping*, it will help you to grasp the deeper implications of a changing relationship to your own body as integral to your maturing faith experience in the Body of the Whole Christ when you reflect upon all this from within the broader context of addiction.

In this chapter, we will only make brief reference to some relevant characteristics of addiction found in other research because so much has already been written on this topic. Our point here is to help you acquire an overall sense for how any spirituality grows out of and is created by people who are part of their societies and the cultures which they reflect and embody.

Whenever a society embodies addictive behaviors without clear recognition and understanding of this pathology, and without the development of carefully researched alternative behaviors implemented within its formative social structures such as family, education and religion, then spirituality easily becomes an integral part of what continues to support addictive behaviors rather than offering a healthy alternative. Addicted people create addictive spiritualities and societies, largely through ignorance and fear of the truth of their own addictive tendencies and behaviors.

The purpose of this workbook is to share with the entire Christian community, from both scriptural and psychological perspectives, that Christian spirituality is meant to be and can be a healthy, healing antidote to an addictive culture. To achieve this goal, however, both accurate knowledge of the addictive process as well as a changed relationship to our own bodies and feelings become necessary. Within previous chapters you have been introduced to various exercises that will help you begin changing the relationship to your more difficult feelings. Let's now turn our attention toward better understanding the roots of addiction in spirituality and the role this knowledge can play in helping us to reevaluate not only the relationship to our own bodies and feelings, but also the relationships and interactions we promote within our societies, our churches, our spiritualities as well as in our interactions with the earth and all of creation.

In this chapter, we want to situate the habit of noticing and nurturing important feelings within the context of our western Christian culture and spirituality which includes the piety, education, values and sometimes the structures of governance in that culture. First, we will consider the widespread proportions and subtlety of the crisis which addictive attitudes and behaviors bring to Christianity. Second, we plan to identify some characteristics of addictive religion. Finally, third, we will briefly summarize how the body-learnings in this book offer a productive and challenging alternative to such destructive patterns of addiction.

The Origins of Addiction in Spirituality

When one smells smoke fire burns nearby. Where process-skipping arises, addiction never lies far behind. Hand-in-glove these two burrow together deep within the human psyche, weaving their destructive effects throughout our lives. We have learned much about substance abuse during the last century but still have a long way to travel in our more complete understanding of the *psychological* origins of addiction and addictive practices in religion. Process-skipping, in our view, remains a key player in the psychological generation and maintaining of addictive habits, becoming double-deadly when insinuating itself deep within the domain of spirituality and religion.

From your reading thus far you have already started to understand and, hopefully, begun to experience something of the lost biology of Christian spirituality. In many instances it has become too easy to use God, church and religion as a convenient way to escape from the responsibility of owning and listening to the many untold stories within our own body's knowing, stories which offer the potential to become an integral part of *finding God in all things*.

Our position and research conclusion is that Christianity as a culture—i.e., a system of thought, of relationships, behaviors, piety, governance and education—has over the centuries become an environment within which addictive behavior has become an acceptable way of life. Our experience leads us to conclude that the more one is born, raised, educated and as an adult caught up in any religion that is not grounded in practices of emotional health, the more difficult it becomes to view that religion objectively. Therefore, it is almost impossible to recognize any sickness from within, let alone to begin a recovery process. Like the emperor without clothes, many of us are so caught up within the subcultures of our various religions that we cannot see them as they really are.

Like most educational, corporate, business and political systems, Christian churches are susceptible to the addiction of control. In our culture, Christianity has become just as addictive a system as have other social institutions, perpetuating addictive behavior in those who emulate, model and try to succeed within it. Churches, too, can call forth and invite addictive disorders, clearly exhibiting characteristics of the alcoholic addict as we better understand this disease today.

To say this is not to condemn, but to recognize that if we love the Body of the Whole Christ, the most caring thing we can do is not to go along with a denial of the disease. We must confront and offer an alternative—"Tough Love." As Anne Wilson Schaef has pointed out,

> "An addictive system is essentially a *closed* system in that it presents few real choices different from the past to individuals in terms of new roles they may take and new directions they are supported in pursuing." [1]

Schaef goes on to note that the addictive system as a whole manifests the same characteristics and behaviors we have come to recognize as addictive within the individual. A church is much like a hologram, with every part in the whole and the whole in every part. Tough love means that as individuals change and grow, they inevitably challenge their churches to do likewise.

So, once again, let us recall our definition of addiction. By addiction we mean the use of anything, anyone or any group as a substitute for a growing truthful relationship with myself, others, the world around me and with/in God. We will elaborate on the definition as we go along.

For now, we can begin by examining the origins of this addictive process in our culture. The pattern we see emerging into adult addictive behavior has its beginnings, for the most part, in what we refer to as mixed signals during childhood. What we refer to is a young person's experience of sometimes getting positive feedback from parents or early significant authority figures, and at other times receiving signals that are interpreted as saying, "You're no good, not worthwhile, something is wrong with you." An absentee father, a workaholic father, for example, clearly signals his priorities to a child because he prefers work to being present to his children. Inconsistent moods, emotional swings from one end of the spectrum to the other, are often taken by children as, "Something is wrong with me that mother or dad treat me this way."

The social expectations of any given period also play a role in this inconsistency. For example, up until very recent differences in the perception of some women, most young girls were told by the media, romance novels, magazines, peers, movies, etc., that a romantic marriage with a child or two would make them happy. Then, with an absentee husband away from home most of the time and too tired for much romance or presence when he was there, as well as children who didn't bring the magic fulfillment, generations of mothers have implicitly or very explicitly projected much of their unhappiness onto their children. The child experiences this unhappiness as rejection, mixed with guilt, perhaps, and then conflicting with some positive nurturing. Such mixed signals or inconsistent nurturing all lead to a very confused sense of self, with no positive self-esteem solidly grounded and maturing out of these early years. Daughters in particular were getting the message in their peer culture that marriage and a man would bring happiness, while from their mothers they often received the opposite message—don't trust a man, it will never work, it can never last. In the midst of such conflicted signals, there emerges an empty space where deep, positive self-esteem should have been growing, along with a maturing ability in discernment which the habit of noticing and nurturing important feelings supports.

All of this, of course, is a question of degree in each person's life, and everyone can expect to receive some mixed signals while growing up. But the problem in our culture is that the extent and depth of such signals within the primary parental relationship have reached catastrophic proportions in this and the previous century. Unhappy and disappointing relationships with romantic expectations of the opposite have been the norm for generations.

A second culturally-devastating factor contributing to addictive personalities is that there has been no culture-wide, inherited, *psychological process* for developing emotional health passed on through the family, school or church for growing through this confusion. Emptiness and low self-esteem have become the order of the day. The phenomenon of mixed signals during childhood is deep and widespread in our culture, along with no inherent support system to process and grow beyond this experience.

The stage has been set on a massive scale for an addictive society at all levels and in every participating social and religious group. The pain, emptiness, loneliness and low self-esteem arising from this unsatisfied basic need create the predominant behavior and motivation that then become manifest in our culture—namely, somehow to find something or someone to deaden the pain. We see today, emerging with a vengeance that only this kind of inner agony can call forth, the various expressions of addictive behavior in religion, politics, terrorism, obsessive-compulsive over-consumption of foods, clothes, electronics, music and entertainment.

The underlying addiction, of course, lies in controlling the pain of lost meaning and lost self-esteem by using something or some relationship to fill up the void or process-skip around our emptiness and the hurt or confusion that one feels inside. It represents a desperate effort to deaden this suffering, making it change or somehow numbing the feel of it. One might put labels on four broad areas where such process-skipping addictive behavior expresses itself in our culture. These are substance abuse, codependency, fundamentalism and narcissism. We will return to these in a minute, but first let's add a final note about the underlying addiction to control.

The need to be in control, apart from any experience of inconsistent nurturing, is part of the human condition which leaves us very vulnerable to be drawn into the control mentality and behavior whenever we stumble into the slightest provocation. The problem in our culture, as we have already briefly mentioned, is that our primary nurturing atmospheres of home and family, church and school neither teach nor support an *effective* processing of and growing beyond this tendency to control for the wrong inside reasons.

If we had been taught as children how to *process* the normal negative feelings that are part of growing up—then life might have been different. But if anything, our training has pointed us toward trying to deny, distract ourselves from or control our difficult feelings. So, it should not be surprising that the same addictive need for control will find its way into educational, religious and social structures and systems which these same children, as adults, will eventually staff and create for the next generation.

In our society, education is aimed primarily at learning information and skills in order to achieve control. That's what the *scientific method* is all about—understanding, prediction and control. In religion, both piety and spirituality have come to function in much the same way as a means to control behavior. So, the child's support system in each of these areas stands ready and waiting to foster and further extend any addictive patterns coming out of the home.

However, children need to learn from their earliest years in the family, further reinforced by their church and school, how to *process* the story of their lives in order that new meaning and direction can unfold and will not precipitate the same old addictive patterns. *Processing* is totally different from *controlling*—just as *process-skipping* is totally different from *growing more whole, more human*. Order emerges from processing not because such order has been imposed, but insofar as hidden meaning is allowed to surface through noticing and nurturing important feelings, thereby stabilizing an otherwise incomplete or unfinished situation. That's why most of us need to learn the difference between processing an issue and repressing or process-skipping around it as a means to gain control over it.

If we do not understand and practice this difference, our family life, our religion, the educational systems we create and social values we pass on to the next generation easily degenerate into becoming addictive systems of control. Falling into the addictive pattern is simply, *fitting in*. It becomes the approved inculturation process for a child. It gets accepted as *normal* growing up in order to be part of the system. However, by the early teen years, we sense a pressure to *make it*, to fit in and succeed beginning to take their toll emotionally and physically on many young adults. The pain of not being able to control everything grows more acute. Situations get out of control. Young people are often just barely *hanging on,* as they say. The pain doesn't get any better. Anxiety, stress and many suicides begin to surface. We are all too aware of these symptoms in teenagers and young adults— just as we become painfully aware of the many dead-ended and often dangerous paths they explore in their often fumbling attempts to grow into their potential and discover who they really are as unique persons. Societies of addictive control either break or make martyrs of the most creative and promising in their midst.

Areas of Addictive Behaviors

Now, let us say a brief word about each of the four broad areas that one might use to describe addictive behaviors. The first area, substance abuse, includes the use of alcohol and other drugs. So much as been written popularly and researched in this area that we will not elaborate on this form of addiction. A second area we referred to is narcissism. Here we are speaking of addictions to possessions, entertainment, to clothes, to sex, to money and to work—a basic addiction that misuses people and things. Again, the tendency to destructive behaviors in these areas is obvious.

The third area, codependency, or the enabling role, expresses itself as an addiction to helping others. This more subtle pattern of addictive behavior involves addiction to a person, a church, an organization or a relationship that in itself has become diseased with addiction. It is characterized, for example, by the martyr wife who excuses, covers up for and puts up with the abuse of her alcoholic or workaholic husband. In other words, what is basically a good thing, i.e., helping others, is used by the codependent to block growth in a truthful relationship to oneself, to another person, to a church, job, family, community, etc.

Sharon Wegscheider-Cruse, an alcoholism counselor, has defined co-dependence as an addiction to another person or persons and their problems, or to a relationship and its problems. The same may be said of society as a whole. Not only can co-dependence be supported and encouraged by our culture; it is often seen as the positive way to function within it. An addictive system views codependency as normal, proof that one has embraced the system and everything it implies. Schaef continues:

> Invariably, co-dependents are good people, devoted to taking care of others within the family system and often beyond, as professional caregivers...They frequently have feelings of low self worth, and find meaning in making themselves indispensable to others. They are willing to do whatever it takes to be liked. As a result, their caretaking often progresses to the point of workaholism.[2]

> Co-dependents are sufferers—Good Christian Martyrs...servers, volunteers, people who set aside their own physical, emotional and spiritual needs for the sake of others. They end up overburdened and exhausted, and we see them as heroes...They are selfless to the point of hurting themselves. They work and care for others to such an extreme that they develop all kinds of physical and emotional problems.[3]

> Co-dependents not only have relationships with addicts; they exhibit many of the same characteristics as addicts. They may not use alcohol or drugs, but they do use other substances compulsively and addictively. Co-dependents are frequently anorexic, bulimic, or have other eating disorders. They often smoke heavily or drink gallons of coffee. Co-dependence is simply another side of the same old coin.[4]

Within the setting of religion, co-dependence can be very subtle and difficult to recognize. In fact, it is perceived quite differently by our religious culture. Alcoholism and other addictions are viewed as negative and bad, but co-dependence is actually promoted. The co-dependent receives little encouragement to get better because the disease supports the culture and is in turn supported by it. As Schaef observes:

> The addictive system could not survive without its co-dependents. They are the people who keep it going; they are its advocates and protectors ...the addictive system invites us to be co-dependents, to refuse to see people and things as they are. In doing so, we are fundamentally disrespectful of them. It is only when people are seen as they are that they can accept and honor and take responsibility for themselves. It is only when they own who they are that they have the option to become something else.[5]

Then, as we wrote in our brief definition of addiction, a truthful relationship with myself, others, the world around me and with God can emerge. In this kind of truth, reality ceases to be based upon the need to please or the need to control. One no longer acts out of inner emptiness which fosters addiction, but from an inner truth that ultimately sets us free.

The fourth area of addictive behavior we mentioned earlier is fundamentalism in religion. Many people are attracted to a religion that asks for the jettisoning of personal responsibility, a religion that has all the answers, that demands blind obedience, not personal questioning. People desperately seeking security, who want control rather than the uncertainty of growing, are attracted to the kind of religion where everything is worked out precisely and clearly for them. The addictive personality is drawn to fundamentalism in religion because such a person cannot stand ambiguity. He or she is threatened by any developmental process that asks for the uncertainty of growing and by any religion that doesn't provide answers neatly served up in an emotionally satisfying package. We will return to the issue of fundamentalism more at length in a moment.

Some Characteristics of an Addictive Use of Spirituality and Religion

Obviously, all the things we have mentioned above—alcohol, drugs, money, sex, work, helping others and religion need not be abused in any addictive way. But when someone misuses any of them in order to feel good about himself or herself, or to assuage the pain of low self-esteem, then the use can easily become obsessive-compulsive abuse that is self and socially destructive.

Tragically, addictive behavior permeates Christianity at all levels—individually and as a system. In fact, it so colors our spirituality, our education, our piety, our governance, our quality of relationships, our social structures, that we don't even recognize the disease because we are already living in it as part of the disease. As Schaef puts it, "The addictive system, like the hologram, reflects the individual, who in turn reflects the system." [6] Both have all the symptoms of the alcoholic, including the reliance on denial, a need to control everyone and everything, and the tendency to lie frequently and habitually.

These characteristics are obvious in the drug or alcoholic addict. But many are evident in the person addicted to co-dependency within a system—in other words, to a helping relationship that supports the addictive system. Co-dependents become addicted to enabling because they do not have a strong positive identity apart from their relationship. They quite literally need the addiction of the person or system to which they are attached. Serving this person or system becomes the primary way they find meaning in life in their misguided attempt to heal their own inner hurt and emptiness.

What, then, are some common characteristics of the addict which emerge in the addictive use of spiritualities and religion? The first is a facade of stability and respectability erected at any cost. It includes the denial that things are not really working and an unwillingness to recognize that something is radically wrong at the very core, in the very heart of the system, individually and collectively. It involves a kind of blindness to the illness, to the disease itself—and above all, it involves an equal blindness to the process-skipping mechanisms which hold their addiction in place and make this pathology so psychologically resistant to change.

Within the Christian churches, for example, people are asking, in fact begging for a process to help them develop a healthy Christian spirituality, and instead what the churches all too often offer is nothing more than endless information and religious theater. The body's role in personal growth and spirituality continues to remain totally unrecognized, let alone incorporated into pastoral care.

Addictive Spiritualities

The primary mission of Christianity includes far more than just communicating religious information. It involves the facilitation of a lifelong process of wholeness within the human body which in religious terms we call *holiness*. Holiness is not an idea, pious theologizing or ritual, but a process of embodied transformation inside people within their relationship to themselves and the world around them. However, observe where so much of the creative juices, generosity, money, dedication, love, time and effort are directed in Christianity. We spend an enormous amount of time on the Word of God but how much time do we spend supporting the organic wholeness of the hearers of the Word of God? As a religion that celebrates the embodiment of God in the human body at Christmas, how much attention, research and commitment do we put into more effectively communicating *the body's role in spiritual growth*? This ought to convince anyone how often our priorities get turned upside-down within an addictive culture. There is quite literally a blindness exhibited in so many priorities that get set within Christianity.

Another characteristic of both addict and the addictive system which surfaces in spirituality is self-centeredness. This becomes evident in so many Christians where the acceptability of everything *outside* their system is measured only in terms of its value for the system. Whatever does not somehow support the system is viewed either as enemy or of little value. A siege mentality and perspective can easily develop which encourage this kind of self-centeredness or us-against-them mentality. We see it in attitudes toward change, toward new ideas, whether in science, psychology, humanism, politics or whatever. A healthy conservatism that maintains traditional values and does not allow itself to be blown aimlessly by every passing fancy or fad offers a basic balancing value in itself. But when an underlying suspicion about *anything different* is always present, when there is hesitancy about whatever is not from the past and clearly supporting the past as well as the system itself, then growing men and women begin to wonder and to feel that something is profoundly off-track.

Refuting this narrow view almost 20 years ago, Karl Rahner wrote a superb essay on *The Theology of Risk* in which he reminded his readers that, *"It belongs to the essence of Christianity not only to preserve its heritage but to press on to the new things of the future."* [7] Such an affirmation of *hazardous venturesomeness* is, of course, anathema both to the addict seeking total control as well as to those in religious fundamentalism seeking absolute security.

Without freedom and encouragement to be open to one's own inner world in order to process anger, despair, loneliness, fear—the only remaining alternative is rigidity and control. Despite protestations to the contrary, if fundamentalism reeks of superficial spirituality, neo-orthodoxy's blinding quest for control *excludes both spirit and grace*. That is the bottom line. Those mired within an addictive environment never really experience themselves and all of God's *groaning creation* within the Body of Christ in a way that supports them in maturing and deepening their faith.

Recovering that experience of living in the Spirit of Christ's Body must begin with a changing relationship to our own body because our Christian faith is meant to empower and free us inside ourselves to grow and change within the *Larger-Body-of-the-Whole-Christ*. We find *ourselves in God* within the very process of becoming more human. The stability, order and security we all crave are then experienced within the graced process of unifying change inside ourselves. Addictive spiritualities block us from such biospiritual experience.

Another characteristic of an addict which breaks out in the addictive use of religion and spirituality is an illusion of freedom. An addictive system cannot risk empowering people because that would mean destroying the system. So, it promotes elaborate diversionary maneuvers to give the impression of actually supporting such empowerment. This is not recognized as a charade because it is promoted and viewed as self-interest, survival or the protecting of some value from being destroyed. Orthodoxy becomes identified with resistance to any change. The last thing an addictive system seeks is change, and that characteristic marks the addict as well. To protect the addiction at all costs and by every means available becomes the number one priority of an addictive personality and culture. In religion today, this tendency characterizes extreme conservatism and fundamentalism.

A further characteristic of the addict and the addictive system is widespread physical and emotional deterioration from the stress of the addiction. We see this today among those holding positions of responsibility in the churches as they frantically attempt to keep the system going. In time, if addictive patterns don't change, most addicts experience that the physical, emotional and other energy resources necessary for change have been badly eroded by the addiction itself. Little vigor seems left after a while with which to do the hard work of recovery and rediscovery. Ultimately, an addiction of any kind becomes destructive of both human and environmental life, along with their innate spirituality.

One very growth-blocking characteristic of addictive religious spiritualities is the widespread inability to connect something known intellectually with how at the same time this is known in our bodies—a basic schizoid tendency, to *think* feelings rather than to *feel* them. It confuses an idea with a feeling. Alcoholics Anonymous acknowledges this as a common problem when an alcoholic goes through the 12 Steps. Perceptive AA members know the difference between committing themselves to the steps only intellectually *("dry drunks")* or going through them both intellectually as well as in an embodied way *("12 Steppers")*. Any effective owning of the powerlessness over alcohol and turning one's life over to *"A Higher Power"* must be more than an intellectual operation. When intentionality is restricted to the chin on up, frequent lapses are experienced. AA and other programs working with addictions need to incorporate a highly-researched and specific body-processes, like the habit of noticing and nurturing important feelings, into their healing care of others. Without something like this, a definite weakness in the therapy for many will inevitably manifest itself.

This culture-wide confusion around thinking feelings rather than feeling feelings becomes deeply ingrained within the addictive system and preserved within the addicted person through psychological, process-skipping mechanisms. As Dr. Schaef points out,

> An addiction keeps us unaware of what is going on inside us; we do not have to deal with our anger, pain, confusion or even our joy or love, because we do not feel them or we feel them only vaguely. We stop relying on our senses and start relying on our confused perceptions to tell us what we know. In time, this lack of internal awareness deadens our internal processes, which in turn allows us to remain addicted. At some point we must choose to recover—to arrest the progress of the

addiction—or we will die. This dying process does not happen only at a personal level; it is also systemic in our culture.[8]

Another blocking characteristic of any healing in an addict/addictive system is the inability to assume responsibility for what is wrong. Every addiction dulls and distorts sensory input. The addict neither receives information clearly nor processes it accurately. Addicts do not feed it back or respond to it with precision. Since they are out of touch with themselves, their assessments and judgments are usually inaccurate. In the language of AA, they *con* people, even those closest to them and those whom they love the most.

Many sensitive Christians are already aware that something is very wrong, but because they have become so involved in the addictive system they conclude that it could not possibly be their fault and that someone else will have to make the necessary changes. When other people fail to assume that responsibility, which of course they do not, then the blame still goes on with nothing changing. "If others would only do what they should do, then everything would be OK." So, some religious people are forever leveling accusations, constantly blaming others for something that is internally wrong within them as well as the system itself. An addiction absolves us from having to assume responsibility for our own lives—as well as for the relationships within which we choose to live.

Finally, the most common addictive pattern we have encountered over the years flows out of the addiction to control. We might call this characteristic, *the outside manipulator* addiction. By this title we identify a deeply personal resistance to letting go of *always remaining on the outside* in order to retain control—the direct antithesis of mutual vulnerability. The need to control dominates any allowing of oneself to become vulnerable by empathically entering *within*, whether that within-ness includes the world of another person or even one's own inner world.

This characteristic can easily be recognized within the depth of loneliness so widespread throughout our culture. Interpersonal relationships remain, for the most part, locked in patterns of external manipulation and valuation. In our work over the years, no theme has emerged as loud and clear as this one. It is the deprivation caused by not having a parent, spouse, friend or group *to journey with* me when fear, pain or risk become too much for me to *go it alone*. This, of course, says nothing about the further need we all have for enrichment, depth and the joy of mutual self-discovery. There is life-enhancing creativity when we can share our ordinary daily lives with another or a small group in an *inside way*.

Nothing has been more painful for us than experiences of trying to help married couples learn to lead one another through the noticing and nurturing of their important feelings when one spouse risks vulnerability in the *letting go into* and the other remains addicted to staying *outside*. Inner availability to grace and connecting remains blocked. Widespread addiction takes its inevitable toll. Substance abuse, suicide and divorce are so often spawned from the depth of loneliness and this conflict, which addiction brings into countless lives. It is the most unrecognized destructive force ripping apart all the community building relationships from marriages to viable democratic expressions of governance in societies today.

Within Christianity and its spirituality, too, the addictive pattern clearly manifests itself in the widespread anxiety, lack of leadership and resistance to providing *inside, embodied* ways to grow in prayer and worship. Generally speaking, Christians often seem addicted to manipulating God through prayer. The incessant *talking to* or *asking for* kind of praying, although theologically indisputable, nonetheless *psychologically* can feed an addiction to control. It easily becomes open to abuse, to the *godfather approach* which seeks to find someone with more power than I possess and get them on my side. Then, once again I can regain control. In this mode of praying, nothing whatever is learned about *owning the truth of myself* as I carry my weakness and fear in a bodily-felt way. There is no maturing into an embodied surrendering that can directly counteract or begin to move beyond the addictive pattern into the refreshing learning and experience with which St. Paul was blessed, "…when I am weak, then I am strong." (2 Cor 12:7–12)

Psychologically, so much of religious piety actually nourishes and holds in place addictive patterns and behaviors. No wonder then, when people struggle to break with their addictions, they eventually jettison involvement with so much of organized religion. Struggling to clarify their *felt need* for healthy surrender to the truth of themselves *in God*, they often find themselves greatly confused about what their church involvement has done to them on the inside.

There still remain a number of important characteristics of the addictive uses of religion and spirituality which can provide you with a sense for the connections between addiction, process-skipping and the alternative offered when you develop the habit of noticing and nurturing your important feelings. We will continue next with some final reflections, showing how the healthy process we present in this workbook offers an alternative to using Christian spirituality in an addictive fashion.

The Road to Recovery

> What is now defined as the disease of co-dependence is the result of years of careful grooming—basic training for the addictive system. They cannot exist without each other. When people refuse to be co-dependents, addictions do not get the support they need to continue. When addicts are recovering, they cannot tolerate living with or being around co-dependents. When both make a system shift as part of their recovery, the addictive system begins to collapse.[9]

Insofar as we can tell, the most effective approaches to recovery from any addiction always start with owning the disease, not just intellectually but as this is carried in the body. In other words, how the body knows and experiences the effects of addiction, not just how we think about it in our minds. This workbook directly addresses that issue by integrating a healing body-process within our embodied potential to discover who we are becoming in Christ—a single, holistic process.

How one can relate in a healthy fashion to any addictive system must flow out of some graced process in the body such as the habit of noticing and nurturing your important feelings. The impetus and direction come as gift, as grace, but these arise as a profound experience felt within the human organism itself, an unfolding resource, an abiding presence, a *rightness* known in the gut.

In many ways, the body-learnings in this book have been around since the beginning of human history. But the fact that they can now be spelled out more clearly today than ever before in human evolution is not accidental. We have been reminded of Christ's Incarnation over and over again in fresh new ways throughout history. The timing, the clarity, the simplicity of Gendlin's process and the coinciding of some hundred years now in the scientific study of the scriptures and of psychology—all these seem truly providential. To use a medical image, the Body of Christ in which we all participate together lies in the intensive care unit and extraordinary measures must be taken for our recovery. Ironically, what complicates our situation today is that the hospital, the doctors, the nurses and staff, all find themselves equally as patients along with the rest of us.

Anyone who regularly perseveres in *the habit* which this book shares will find that it provides a concrete structure, the practical disposing and psychological climate which allow God's grace to make you whole enough so you can love as God loves within the gifted process of growing more congruent and whole inside yourself. The grace that transforms your relationships also changes your underlying motivation, making it possible to serve and love within a growing sense of freedom. The inner landscape changes. Living the truth always frees. The key contribution this missing link offers in the recovery of your body within Christian spiritual experience lies in the owning of what is real and the bringing of a loving presence into how your body carries all this *as an act of the whole person*. Whenever each of us practices and lives the developing body-habit into which this workbook guides you within your own body, *in Christ*, then deep, organic transformation can be gifted in response to this perseverance and commitment.

Out of such experience can mature a radical sense of empowerment in our truthful, mutual vulnerability with one another as companions *in Christ*. Knowledge like this arises within awareness as the polar opposite of an addiction to control. We become freed and gifted, not hooked-on nor dependent upon using something or someone in order to feel good about ourselves. From within such experience an entirely new identity can be born, an identity for which Jesus prayed:

> May they all be one.
> Father, may they be one in us,
> as you are in me and I am in you,
> so that the world may believe it was you who sent me.

> I have given them the glory you gave to me,
> that they may be one as we are one.
> With me in them and you in me,
> may they be so completely one
> that the world will realise that it was you who sent me
> and that I have loved them as much as you loved me.
> *(Jn 17:1–23 JB)*

Through the living gift of *agápe* love our personal horizon expands to include an experience of the Larger Body. An environmental transformation within the experience of one's inner self can then begin to occur. "…it is no longer I who live, but Christ who lives in me…" (Gal 2:20 NEB) "God is love *(agápe)*; a person who dwells in love is dwelling in God, and God in that person." (1 Jn 4:16) In time, the individual and his or her life support system becomes, "a new creation," in the language of St. Paul. Empowerment grows from within the vulnerability of truthfulness, "…for when I am weak, then I am strong." (2 Cor 12:10 NEB) By maturing beyond the addictive need for control, and instead, through a daily loving presence to how our body carries the truth of ourselves, Christian companions in Christ can change the world in ways our minds could never conceptualize. As St. John put it, "Though God has never been seen by any person God dwells in us if we have *agápe* love *(for ourselves)* and each other. Thus God's love is brought to perfection within us." (1 Jn 4:12) *(emphasis ours)*.

Beyond the Stumbling Block of Fear and Pain Lies Hope-Filled Paradox

As you may now realize, this book has offered you more through steps taken within your body's knowing, rather than through any analyzing or reflecting within your mind's thinking. Amazing as it may seem to many of us who have grown up in an information-oriented and heady culture, learning how to find God in all things is very much *a felt-sensing body-journey*.

From the very moment when we were born, crying out in pain from our need for air and food, physical and emotional pain in our bodies has been something we want fixed right now—or, if not fixed, at least numbed. So, in our helplessness, we cry out and search for fixers. Obviously, St. Paul was no exception, praying to have his pain taken away.

And yet, the response he received was not what he expected nor prayed for—"My grace is sufficient for you, for power is made perfect in weakness." (2 Cor 12:9 RSV) In the light of this reply, Christians today are challenged to learn from Paul's experience that their need to use God and prayer in order to process-skip needs critical evaluation because of the ease with which it gets us off track.

Like Paul, we, too, must discover a further alternative by first owning our need to process-skip, recognizing that ultimately it damages our health and blocks our body's ability to feel God's Loving Presence. Instead, as you have been learning throughout this workbook, you can allow yourself to be drawn into the world of grace inside the process of noticing and nurturing how your body is physically carrying fear and pain, especially how it responds to your caring, loving presence. Both faith and the gift of your ability to care and love even a little, can come together, freeing up the hidden story in what previously you would have pushed away. No denials. No process-skipping around Good Fridays. Instead, a bodily-alive faith within the Body of the Whole Christ—as this can be felt from inside.

This workbook is meant as a companion to be used over and over again so that this new habit can grow in your body. It has been written in order to support your filling in the gap left between Paul's description of his process-skipping prayer, followed by his "boasting" about his own infirmities because then the power of Christ's Body was made manifest within his own body.

Unfortunately, insofar as we know, Paul never described either psychologically or physiologically what went on inside his own body that could bring him to such a sudden change in perspective. Yet, there had to be some *embodied* felt shift from within, enabling him to view his experience in a totally different light—some contrasting experience that led to his surprising, paradoxical conclusion. Paul found God *in all things* because a transformative change occurred within his body's knowing. We now know psychologically what could have precipitated such change and what that change might have been. We are no longer left hungering for some concrete, practical body-learnings and exercises telling us how to follow in his footsteps. We, too, can now grow into the living paradox that Paul became within his own humanity.

The two of us have found that the missing link in the lost biology of Christian spirituality lies in a broken relationship within our own bodies, most especially within the physical pain and often paralyzing fear that confounds us. We have never been taught how, in a caring way, to treat the burden of pain in our body. The deeper paradox, however, lies veiled within the simple fact that answers we so often seek, hide themselves inside the very pain and fear we most avoid inside ourselves. This is the paradoxical puzzle which drew the Apostle Paul into his own process-skipping attempts at imploring God to take away the "thorn in his side." But the baffling response recorded by Paul in his Second Letter to the Corinthians, 12:9 casts only a dim light upon a neglected facet of our human body's knowing—a knowing which has lain waiting to be rediscovered behind the shadows of our inner pain and fears.

In a somewhat oversimplified illustration, process-skipping and the weak/strong experience offer an unexplored body-bridge into a more *environmentally expanding* sense of self. If you want to use a loose, analogous sense, it's a little like learning to drive a car. At first, you don't have any clear sense for where the front, back and sides of your car really are. Your body and the car's body have not yet morphed into a single sensory unit. You don't spontaneously *feel* when your wheels are on or over the line. You cannot immediately *sense* whether you are close enough to the curb for parking. When Pete began training to be a school bus driver as a young Jesuit he needed to become accustomed *physically* to sensing from within his own body what seemed like a cavernous, huge Yellow Body trailing along behind him.

Process-skipping and weak/strong experiencing carry this expanding environmental experience well beyond the mere *spatial* edges of modern day vehicles. The experience adds *another dimension* to our widening inner sense of, "…the body as it is felt from inside." In a similar manner, sensory awareness broadens within the experience of *gratitude* which can arise when being blessed by a surprising gift of grace. Gratitude includes a sense that, "I didn't do that. I cannot make this happen on my own. In this moment I am truly blessed because I'm not in control here." In other words, I become aware of *something more* working away inside me, an outright gift over and above any of my own limited ability to understand, predict and control many of my everyday realities.

The sheer contrast between my own experienced weakness and the appearance of this more gracious power at work within my life shakes up the familiar frontier edges of my imagined inner environment. I gradually learn to discover myself more as *membrane* within some wider, extended reality rather than as a distinct, autonomous member standing on my own—"...it is no longer I who live, but Christ who lives in me." (Gal 2:20 RSV) There are moments when I find my body-knowing caught up in and surprised by something far more broadening than my more accustomed and independent existence. Many have described this as a felt-sense of *Presence* or a profound experience of no longer being alone.

We cannot emphasize strongly enough that this new sense of "I" matures in conjunction with a potentially new habit that can form itself within your body—an entirely new way of *being within* your own physical organism as it is felt from inside. This is fortuitous because the addictive habit of process-skipping can never be replaced simply by acquiring new information in your head. That blunt fact unveils the radical limitation of just talking-the-talk. Process-skipping as habit can only be grown beyond by replacing it with another *equally embodied habit*. You can never *talk* yourself out of process-skipping. The next forward moving, evolutionary step in human transformation is *organic*. More than developing new ideas, it includes the maturation of new physical habits of consciousness within the human organism itself.

We all-too-quickly learn process-skipping as a short-cut way to survive. You make a choice to escape, to numb, to distract yourself—conning yourself into believing that you have removed something you don't like from your awareness. Such a habit you either deliberately choose or spontaneously fall into as an instinctual response to pain or fear. Yet, this decision soon becomes set on automatic pilot. You no longer even advert to what you're doing. In the end, you create your own prison by reaching for *a numbing out-of-touchness* as the illusion you grasp on to in your attempt to escape from pain. Rather than filling the gaping hole of your misery, the dead-end of process-skipping, which you fail to notice, then furthers your lack of wholeness, blocking the process of change you long for.

Process-skipping represents a delusion, but as you become more aware of your own process-skipping mechanisms, while at the same time learning a new body-habit of noticing and nurturing your important feelings, you begin entering into the hidden stories which your body always carries inside. You learn a new habit, bringing affection and a caring, *agápe* love into the hidden places where fear or pain have prevented you from entering. In that experience you cross over an unexplored threshold inside your own body. The language of Alcoholics Anonymous says it well. You finally begin *walking-the-walk* instead of just *talking-the-talk*.

Your former process-skipping experience has become the vivid *background* against which a new *foreground* may now more easily be sensed and observed, a springboard on your journey of continued connecting. From this latter, somewhat surprising vantage point, process-skipping then offers an illuminating light or stark *contrast* against which you can more readily sense *something more* at work within you. "When I am weak, then I am strong for then is the power of Christ (the Larger Body) made manifest within me." (2 Cor 12:9)

The radical paradox which Christianity offers through the writings of St. Paul lies in the arrival of a surprising alternative when the gift of *agápe* love dramatically transforms the relationship to your own body. This changing relationship within individuals carries immense social implications because laying down the weapons of war against one's own body and feelings opens a door for revolutionary metamorphosis within the social order as well. Paul tells us that we no longer need to go down this path. He has opened a workable alternative, a practical course to follow, yet one which most find themselves slow to approach because of its seemingly preposterous, paradoxical nature—"When I am weak, then I am strong."

Who would imagine that the wholeness and inner peace we long for can be found right at the heart of what we fear and avoid most inside ourselves? Yet, when we begin treating the feelings which we hold at arms length as teachers and friends trying to tell us something important about ourselves, that very transforming change in relationship alters our inner landscape. New possibilities emerge. More often than not the concern or fear I reject and push away has something to tell me which also contains the seeds of an answer along with some inner movement or resolution for which I yearn. Does it not make sense, then, at least to give this a try?

We have become so accustomed to controlling from the outside that we never really notice how often things spontaneously unfold from the inside. And when they do, we just feel relieved and move on without ever stopping to wonder about what just happened. Most of us don't even bother to turn and look back. Yet, the attitude of *noticing* and *nurturing* tills the soil in an entirely different way from violently ripping it apart with brute force. We must learn to open our feelings using a more gentle approach that allows them to breathe, inviting something *more* to grow and spring forth from within.

The challenge lies in gaining access to that *more*, learning how to notice, nurture and listen even when—especially when—it is the imagined enemy within whom we have held at bay inside ourselves. The only way to move forward when patterns from the past no longer work for us lies not through using force from the outside but by tapping into resources for change which lie within. That is what healthy Christian spirituality is meant to be about. We start by learning *a more effective pedagogy* for listening on the inside. The path for growing beyond a process-skipping, addictive culture emerges from within the daily work of noticing and nurturing your important feelings.

This so-called *information age* of ours finds itself caught up in a wrenching tsunami of process-skipping and addiction. Individual personal turmoil brought on by this massive internal crisis inevitably spills out into the social order. The old, the poor and middle class watch in anger, feeling trapped and afraid without hope as major institutional systems within finance, government, religion, the job market, education and healthcare keep breaking down. Senior citizens watch helplessly as their life savings evaporate.

Yes, the old patterns from the past are breaking down—but this is caused by a new development that *only a few have begun to recognize*. The pain of attempting to control the complexities of our modern cultures are finally forcing more of us to realize that laws and the brute external force—government or military—are simply not enough to rein in the destructive powers that can devastate our societies over and over again as well as destroy any long term attempt at a truly democratic way of life. There is no data to support the position that the old externally imposed patterns of control from our tribal, monarchical past can supply the necessary social order and community development for *evolving* human beings.

We need some new and radically different alternative—a real paradox that will appear to many as literally insane. That is what St. Paul and the early Christians faced 2000 years ago when the working model of success was the Roman Empire. But what might happen in our time if we turned the energy of our capacity for loving presence, which is available right here and now, toward our own difficult feelings and toward the hurting people around us as well as all that gifts us with life—the water, air and soil that grows our food? What might happen if we took the time and turned our attention toward accessing this untapped inner resource as a response to solving our external problems by listening to our own body's story as a living cell of the Larger Body in which "…we live and move and have our very existence?" What wise and loving answers might come our way?

Of course it's a challenge. Of course it raises the specter of a terrifying mutual vulnerability. But is this not the realistic stuff of a genuine caring for the common good, a support for inner and outer peace, unity, oneness and wholeness, being part of something greater than ourselves—in a word, faith in *agápe* love, God's Presence?

Charles Dickens opened his *Tale of Two Cities* with the memorable line, "It was the best of times. It was the worst of times." Not a bad comment on our contemporary situation. For the Christian community to bring the paradox of Christ to life within us would show the world another alternative that has never been tried by using what we now know about *the biological roots of Christian spirituality* and *the process of human wholeness.* Day by ordinary day, month by month and year by year, every one of us personally and as a community of *agápe* are called to pass along to each new generation an unfolding of the Christ paradox—*as this can be felt and known from inside our own bodies.*

A Closing Exercise

You might want to pause for a moment, asking yourself: "Is there anything in my body right now after reading this chapter which needs my open, listening and caring presence?" Allow yourself a moment to grow quiet, noticing and nurturing anything that has stood out for you in these pages. Allow time for listening into how your body now carries all this inside. ■

Personal Notes

A *Sixth* Body-Learning

■

Creating Families and Groups of Companions in Christ as Cellular Models for Living Christ's New Commandment to Love as God Loves

Chapter 17

Recovering the Lost Biology of Christian Spirituality

Looking Back Over Your Body's Journey into Finding God in All Things

YOUR VENTURE SO FAR through this workbook has perhaps been more pilgrimage than journey. Pilgrimage because you travel into a sacred space inside yourself—walking the holy ground where spirit and matter, mind and body agree to meet and dialogue as equal companions journeying together on their lifelong exploration into both self and God.

Let's now take a brief look back at places we have touched on this journey into *Rediscovering the Lost Body-Connection Within Christian Spirituality*, taking time to note a few underlying themes and melodies woven throughout these pages which easily become lost beneath the pressures and distraction of everyday living. Each interactive exercise begins with you working with yourself—all the while remembering that far more lies hidden away here than at first meets the eye because every exercise is only just a beginning.

You essentially function as an integral part within a much larger systemic whole within the world in which you live. Everything is a gestalt. What brings wholeness into your individual body brings wholeness into the Body of Humankind itself. When you discover reconciliation inside yourself everyone benefits from your discovery. The introductory exercises throughout this book represent tiny baby steps, not solely in the direction of realizing your own personal wholeness, but into a growing inner unity within yourself which then becomes a window within experience through which you gain access into a much larger sense of cosmic congruence. "When we try to pick out anything by itself, we find it hitched to everything else in the Universe."

That's the point of this final chapter, as it has been of your journey with the help of this workbook. We all live together within a more extensive environmentalism, a Greater Body, a Larger Living Organism, and our *agápe* relationships are the evolutionary force moving everything forward. The practical side of that revealed truth lies in what we mean by the Sixth Body-Learning: *Creating Families and Groups of Companions in Christ as Cellular Models for Living Christ's New Commandment to Love as God Loves.*

A huge part of the missing, and generally misunderstood link in Christian spirituality is that *agápe* relationships are meant to operate at all levels—within individual persons, in families, societies, ethnic groups, between races and nations. *We are all systemic together*, all part of the same gestalt, figure and ground for one another, all caught up within *the same common good* and *common-agápe-life in Christ*, on our journey into God.

> I am the bread of life.
> Your fathers ate manna in the desert,
> but they died.
> This is the bread that comes down from heaven,
> and if you eat it you'll never die.
> I myself am the living bread
> come down from heaven.
> If any eat this bread
> they will live forever;
> the bread I will give
> for the life of the world
> is my flesh. *(Jn 6:48–51 TIB)*

For a Christian, noticing and nurturing their body's enfleshed feelings expresses a first step within an organic act of appropriating and owning their very flesh and blood, discovering the truth of who they really are which *also includes* their own unique, individual identities within a Larger Body—the Body of Christ. Through a faith-filled organic transformation, Christians are called to discover themselves as the living flesh and blood of the Body of Christ—membranes together with and in one another within this Larger Organic Body, thereby becoming a living expression of the flesh and blood of Christ alive in our world today. "...the life that I now live is not my life, but the life which Christ lives in me." (Gal 2:20 NEB)—a living Eucharist.

In a very real sense then the Body of Christ today, the bread of life which comes down from heaven (gifted to us by God), is the gift to us of ourselves—*in Christ*. Our day-by-day living this faith invites us to allow this gift to become born again and again in us by owning and neither denying, repressing nor negating what our own body's intelligence knows is real. Then, and only then can the identity and experience of having our being within a Larger Body be gifted to us within a body-knowing and not just a head-understanding of our membraneship in Christ. Then, as Jesus tells us, when we eat of this bread, we shall find our way through to the gift that we are in His Body—and then we shall never die.

Yet, what so often blocks us is the ongoing difficulty of grasping an actual *experience* of this Reality from information alone. We can never fully absorb such knowledge solely through the mind analyzing. Somehow it needs to *mature within our bodies* as well. Just thinking about it doesn't work and never has. Growth in our body's way of understanding calls out for a different way of knowing, a more embodied manner of learning, an entirely new pedagogy along with the development of a transforming set of often unfamiliar habits in our bodies. In his Foreword to *Theory U*, Peter Senge reminds us that:

> ...significant innovation is about doing things differently, not just talking about new ideas...Too many books continue the "downloading" of unexamined assumptions and beliefs, even while challenging us intellectually with new ideas. The question is always one of practice—of doing, not just thinking.[1]

Theology, sermons and ritual make sense to the extent that one nurtures first and foremost some development of an *embodied* sense, a *felt* experience of presence and connecting within the human organism itself that serves as the visceral foundation upon which any further theological interpretations or ritual acts may then be framed. Without the stability of this embodied inner process, healthy Christian spirituality rests upon shaky ground.

Too many people assume that intellectual brilliance and clarity of ideas carry the Christian message forward most effectively, while in actual fact the motivation which moves the message into our hearts lies within the body and the body's knowing. Ultimately, it's all quite visceral—the Body of the Continuing Incarnation in us. This does not reject rationality and ideas. The goal is discovering that delicate *balance* between thinking and our felt-sense knowing. It also means rediscovering the role of paradox and grace as twin catalysts moving us forward beyond patterns from the past that no longer work for us.

Yet, still today, few would even think that an experience of *affection* could become your most valued teacher, or that *process-skipping addictions* might silently worm their way into our bodies and psyches when we least expect them. There's always a great deal more going on in the background of everyday living than most people seem to notice or even care much about. But to be fair, usually no one has ever taught us how to notice and nurture our body's intelligence. This has been one of the reasons for this workbook and the lifelong research and experience it has required.

How many people in their families or churches have ever been helped to practice a spirituality that daily opens them to discover their own personal metaphors in life, symbols which so touch their body's knowing that they can feel new meaning, direction and purpose rising up from inside them? Where can one today find churches supporting small groups of *companions in Christ* because they realize that in order to grow in Christian faith, we need the personal, loving presence of one another in order to help us not make enemies out of our difficult feelings? This means learning an inner process of discovering *our own* unique, personal symbols or metaphors *in Christ* as Paul did, not just symbols drawn from times past and now imposed upon everyone living in another age and culture. Effective symbols which gift us with our own unique body-sense for grace come through each individual's life. We need to reorganize in order to take the time for giving one another the support which allows this to happen. Through such interrelationships our Christian faith is meant to become incarnated and renewed, continuing to be further discovered and deepened throughout our lives.

For the Christian faith to be relevant for any growing child or adult it must be developmental and organic, flowing out of each person's changing relationship to themselves and the world around them. As

St. John points out in his First Letter, each individual person's growing experience of God is *developmental*, "God...dwells in us if we love one another; his love is brought to perfection within us." (1 Jn 4:12 NEB) Thus, the experience of *God as the loving (agápe) relationship gifting us with this fullness of our own self-identity in the Body of the Resurrected Christ is what makes it possible for us to love as God loves*—that is, to live Christ's New Commandment.

This workbook recognizes that if we are growing, our experience of ourselves is always evolving and our bodies play a key role in the ever-unfolding awareness of what comes next for us. The exercises in this book are designed to help you notice and nurture all this background activity bubbling away inside your own body—whatever your age. So, when you complete your reading of these chapters, if they have in any way worked for you it might well be time to go through this journey again because now you are no longer in the same place where you began. One way to keep moving is to invite others either to start or continue their pilgrimage with you. As Albert Einstein was reputed to have said, "Life is like riding a bicycle—to maintain your balance you need to keep moving forward."

So, as you gain more familiarity with the experience of noticing and nurturing your important feelings, this will help you to support others among your family or friends to begin following their own inner paths. As more and more small groups gather together to support one another in the simple act of developing such a habit in their bodies, this will impact the larger community and society. The process you have experienced in this book by its very nature supports community-building. People grow closer to one another when they companion and experience being companioned by others. The next step, then, is to create small groups of companions in Christ as cellular models for living Christ's New Commandment.

This last chapter opens a door for living Christ's New Commandment of loving as God loves. Once we begin to notice, nurture and listen into the feelings and felt-senses which we so often identify as scary or some kind of enemy inside ourselves, we become exposed to the possibility of how we might learn to companion others on their own inward journeys. Each of us first needs to develop a personal sense for this process before gathering a group and companioning them, using their own personal copy of this workbook like a diary. The book can then serve as resource, reminder and teacher. You, too, need to companion yourself each time you companion another or a group because each experience changes you as well. Your companioning of yourself and others is always your most important teacher.

Bringing Change to the Serious Systemic Problem of Process-Skipping—by Creating Small Groups of 'Companions in Christ'

In the past, people thought they remained frozen or out of touch with themselves because they feared getting too close to their painful feelings. But while working with this puzzle over the years, we finally came to realize that another, even more subtle player worked to keep us out of touch with ourselves. The veiled and murky impact of *addictive process-skipping* structures, patterns, routines and habits have become so firmly embedded in our culture that we scarcely even notice them. So, the two of us began realizing that systemic change in our cultural enablers will never happen unless people like yourself begin living the habit of noticing and nurturing their important feelings *as a way of life*.

All of us are challenged to create new social systems that do not routinely contribute to addictive process-skipping patterns which have often been uncritically promoted as, *the way things are and have always been done* in our formative systems of creating new generations through parenting, education, spirituality, health care, politics and the media we allow into our lives. Healthier, more whole (holier) people will create social systems less addicted to control, power and the wealth which routinely results in conflict, violence and inevitable wars. This realization is why we have spent the last forty years searching and experimenting with the Body-Learnings and exercises that have turned into this workbook. Some who for the first time go through our three month program have called it, *"Love 101"* or *"PeaceMaking From The Inside."*

After working with hundreds of groups as well as individuals, we have put these pieces together because we found that the psychological missing link for healthy human wholeness lies in the felt-experience of being an integral, living, organic cell of some Larger Body. This provides us with not just mind-meaning, but *organically experienced*

Rediscovering the Lost Body-Connection

direction, continuity and purpose in life. It offers a grounding within your own body for the experience of being connected consciously to some benevolent, gifting presence within your life. It motivates and builds up the organic feel for your personal tied-in-ness to all of creation and your organismic responsibility for a larger common good.

This embodied hunger for felt meaning and completion cannot come through conceptual information alone. It arrives through the body's conscious, felt relationship within this Larger Whole. That experience caused us to examine more closely the Letters of St. Paul, especially where his writings to the early Christian groups he had founded shared his own struggle to break with an addictive use of prayer by manipulating God into following his own scenario for how he thought things ought to be.

Habits of addictive process-skipping have always been a major stumbling block to recognizing when change is needed, both for healthy human wholeness as well as peacemaking in a disconnected and violent world. More than a stumbling block within individuals, process-skipping readily migrates into social systems, popular culture and tradition as well. "Keep a stiff upper lip." "Let sleeping dogs lie." "When I'm feeling sad, I simply remember my favorite things and then I don't feel so bad." Charming lyrics and, on the surface, seemingly wise sayings often mask our disconnected inner selves and our perennial flight from the pain of this experience. Massive and omnipresent, this largely unrecognized blanket of soothing habit and mass incomprehension blinds generation after generation to what our own bodies recognize inside ourselves as out of sync patterns and outdated systems. Even worse, process-skipping cuts us all off from the very resources for change which lie hidden within the difficult feelings we so often avoid and run away from—namely, our deeper, unacknowledged felt-senses which hold the promise of guiding us home to ourselves and, ultimately, into the larger world of grace and further exploration into God.

The social disaster associated with ignoring the body-side of human knowing remains clear. All our inner frustrations, unowned hurts and neglected inner pain lie blocked and pent up inside, just waiting for an opportunity to explode in violent and aggressive acts which divide, tear asunder and destroy the fabric of healthy spirituality as well as our social and global communal good. We can never emphasize enough that before such destructive explosions occur within our societies, the fuse has already been lit through the internal violence, disconnections and inner neglect we each unknowingly foster inside our own bodies through process-skipping.

The most formative social institutions we create in order to pass on what we believe it means to be human still continue to infect generation after generation with process-skipping attitudes, practices and habits. But once your mind as well as your body's felt-knowing become convinced of the personal and social havoc that process-skipping wrecks in all our lives and upon our precious earth, then you grasp in your bones how by keeping us out of touch with ourselves and our innate body-sense for environmental issues, process-skipping contributes to global, environmental disasters, the sociopathic violence of human sex and drug trafficking as well as religious fanaticism and terrorism. Rapidly increasing emotional and physical illnesses, especially in children, together with crises precipitated by unhealthy parenting, inadequate education, neglected whole-person healthcare along with the pathology that infects much of institutionalized religion—all find their origins in the negative effects produced by some form of addictive process-skipping.

However, a silver lining often appears during times of turbulence and traumatic change in social systems, such as our own, when certain individuals and groups within that society begin to develop a capacity for listening deeper into their own body-knowing. Our felt-senses offer surprising, creative and inspired alternatives for action and exploration, carrying us beyond no longer workable patterns of thinking, acting and futile process-skipping approaches to issues that affect both the common good as well as Christian spirituality.

We have written this workbook with its Body-Learnings so that it might provide practical, healthy support for the creation of families and groups of companions in Christ who could then become cellular models for living Christ's New Commandment. Our world today needs to experience who Christ really is through our bodies in His Body. Your own body is the switch which turns that light on.

Your body also knows equally well your right next forward step, even though you may have difficulty within the present moment articulating that step in a coherent sentence. As Eugene Gendlin has said, "The living body always implies its right next step."[2] Otto Scharmer calls such experience, "...learning from the future as it emerges."[3] The wonder is that such awareness emerges from within our own body's knowing.

After many years of working with diverse groups of people on several continents and from all walks of life, we find that whenever someone actually enters into the process of noticing and nurturing important feelings within their body—whether they are five or ninety-five—a wondrous gifting and healing happens, often in the most unexpected and amazing ways within the most unlikely people. Experiencing such moments when working with people has always felt sacred, as though we are walking on holy ground.

What now needs to happen is that this embodied, loving presence be kept alive in you through the daily habit of noticing and nurturing your important feelings. This is precisely how you bring God into the world around you and into all your ordinary relationships. Over time, such a habit in your body creates a felt presence that conveys the message of a living, real, loving presence here and now—not just a 2000 year old idea, teaching, belief or somebody's theology or conviction. The experience of God's loving presence to the people around us comes packaged through your own caring relationships to those afflicted with so-called negative feelings which they try to deny, numb or escape from through their various addictions.

One never fully appreciates the full range of felt meaning available within the Christian faith without this kind of body-felt-sensing. Without such experience you have nothing left but abstract doctrines, dogmas, teachings, and interpretations. In other words, you can recall *the information* in your mind as beliefs, but that will always be different from a faith-filled *felt-sensing of the experience of agápe love in your body*. The felt-sense of loving presence, therefore, becomes the key player in the actual experience of the Body of Christ.

The failure to integrate such felt-sense knowing into spiritual experience explains the puzzling impotence which religions have for so long exhibited when faced with human aggression and violence. Cognitive ideals of love, caring and compassion within religion all too often become powerless when facing the seething energy of violence where the issue arises as a felt problem *in the body*, and not an abstract idea or ideal in the mind. The challenge for Christians who value and love their faith becomes one of evolving *a new pedagogy* for actually being in touch with the origins of such experience in ourselves, not generating more abstract information, teachings and explanations about it.

In an Addictive System, we are trained *not* to be ourselves. We lose touch with ourselves. We reference ourselves externally. We deny who we are. This leaves a hole in the puzzle and a hole in the universe that no one else can fill.

Because we have been living in a system that is an addictive system, we are living in a universe that has many holes. As we begin to claim our lives, our pasts, and our selves, that hole in the universe is filled.

It is in living our own process that we take our place in the universe and the whole system can then heal.[4]

■

We are God's handiwork, created in Christ Jesus to devote ourselves to the good works for which God has designed us. *(Eph 2:10 NEB)*

So...let yourselves be built as living stones into a spiritual temple; become a holy priesthood...through Jesus Christ. *(1 Pet 2:5–6 NEB)*

(because)...the glory which you gave me, (Father), I have given to them (us), that they may be one, as we are one; I in them and you in me, may they be perfectly one. *(Jn 17: 22–23 NEB)*

Like ourselves, the Apostle Paul never personally met Jesus of Nazareth, yet he physically experienced himself as incorporated into the Body of Christ. His faith was always more than mere *cognitive insight*. In Paul's letters, he wrote of his striking conversion experience that united his Hebrew faith in a promised Messiah with his felt-sensing world of experiencing God's grace at work within his own body—a remarkable integration of his personal struggle to articulate who Christ was and is today as well as who he and we are together, *"in Christ."*

Adapting the Body-Learnings in this workbook for younger children as well as exploring ways to introduce these learnings into other disciplines and cultures holds the future potential to support a world-wide universal growth in this experience which, for Christians, can renew the profound rediscovery of Eucharist itself right within the daily offering of our own bodies in the Body of Christ, for the life of the world.

Learning from the future is vital to innovation. Learning from the future involves intuition. It involves embracing high levels of ambiguity, uncertainty, and willingness to fail. It involves opening ourselves to the unthinkable and sometimes attempting to do the impossible. But the fears and risks are balanced by feeling ourselves part of something important that is emerging that will truly make a difference.

...in times of great turbulence and systemic change...leadership comes from all levels, not only from "the top," because significant innovation is about *doing* things differently, not just *talking* about new ideas. This leadership arises from people and groups who are capable of letting go of established ideas, practices, and even identities. Most of all, this leadership comes as people start to connect deeply with who they really are and their part in both creating what is and realizing a future that embodies what they care most deeply about.[5]

Effective peacemaking and justice in the world always begins on the inside—within each person's individual inner struggle to become more whole. Unless we can first address the wars we so often conduct inside ourselves with their inner divisions and patterns of blind escape which separate us from the truth of ourselves, our attempts at peacemaking in the world will be frustrated and ineffectual. Whole people beget whole people. Fragmented people beget fragmented people. The body's role in effective, loving, caring presence is central. Loving as God loves springs from an inner body-sense of being part of some Love greater than ourselves.

When you can bring a loving presence to the burden of your own weaknesses, hurts and fears, then this flows out to others in a felt way that invites them to bring love into the way they treat their own bodies. Essentially, the Good News is communicated body-to-body. Not through technologies, electronic media, travel into outer space and other more efficient everythings—which all may be fine *as far as they go*. But the message becomes most effectively communicated through the indispensable, most basic human need we all have of *a loving presence that can be felt in our bodies*. That is who Christ is today and who

Recovering the Lost Biology of Christian Spirituality

you are really meant to become within yourself and in the world around you.

> For where two or three are gathered in my name, there am I in the midst of them. *(Mt 18:20 RSV)*

A Closing Exercise

Right now, what in my body most needs my Loving Presence? Take time to notice and nurture whatever you may discover, so this can tell you whatever it wants you to know. ∎

Personal Notes

Afterword

I HAVE TRIED to write a review of this remarkable book for some time, but found it almost impossible to do. Last week, however, I had an experience that relates to this book in a way that no summary or analysis could ever express.

On Monday morning I received a phone call at 6:10 AM from my mother's nursing home. The nurse on duty informed me that my mother's condition had taken a sudden turn for the worse and she could well be in the final hours of her life.

I immediately went into organizational mode. Ringing my father, I told him I would collect him on my way to the nursing home. I then rang the rest of my brothers and sisters as my wife and I made our way down to my father's home. Realizing that I was in a state of mild shock I gently welcomed that sense in my body—a very strange response to such an emotion. But, as I acknowledged this sense of shock it eased and something inside assured me that to feel this way in such circumstances was a natural reaction. It then became easier to be mildly shocked.

By the time we arrived at the nursing home my mother had stabilized and she seemed to be out of immediate danger. The sense of shock began to ease with this exterior reassurance. I stayed with my mother until around 3 PM. But on arriving home I received another phone call from the nursing home. My mother's condition had become perilous. The matron said she did not think my mother would survive unless she was transferred to the hospital immediately. I granted her permission to ring for an ambulance and made my way back to the nursing home in time to accompany my mother to the hospital. It was clear from the reaction of the paramedics that she was very seriously ill. The journey was not a pleasant one. Mother was admitted to the resuscitation ward of the accident and emergency department where she was stabilized.

My mother has had Alzheimer's and Parkinson's disease for many years now. The doctors at the hospital asked regarding her resuscitation status—i.e. they wanted to know what kind of medical intervention should be provided if my mother's heart should stop beating or if she should not be able to breathe independently. It was a very difficult decision to make, but as a family we instructed the doctors that extraordinary interventions should not be provided for mother if these events occurred.

She was then moved to a ward on Tuesday afternoon where we kept a vigil at her bedside as she was still gravely ill.

On Wednesday I spent the day at my mother's bedside, keeping a keen eye on the monitors that showed my mother's oxygen saturation and her heart-rate. The nurse had informed me that these were good indications of how she was doing.

It was this monitoring of my mother's condition that suddenly made me realize how I was more present to the machine beeping at my mother's bedside than I was to my own mother.

Sadness emerged, when I acknowledged that a part of me felt easier with a machine, than I did with my own sick mother. The sadness quickly passed, bringing instead a great sense of peace and connection. The rest of the world disappeared and there was just me and my mammy. At one stage she became restless, I offered my index finger to her outreached hand—she grabbed my finger and held it for a long time. I noticed how this felt in my body. In this moment of physical connection all of time was made a mockery. Within the experience of mother gently holding my finger was a lifetime containing all the care and love a mother has for her son. It included all the longing for connection that so often happens as a child separates and finds his way in the world. It held all the terror in her onset of dementia, all the caring and trying to keep my mother at home for as long as we could as her condition worsened. It had the son now scared sitting at the bedside of his gravely ill mother—and it had my mother still taking care of me, her son, as she connected once more, continuing to educate me about the world and the nature of love and connection.

After some time mother let go of my finger. I returned to the book I was reading, *My First Summer in the Sierra* by John Muir, and found the following lines:

Afterword

> We are now in the mountains and they are in us, kindling enthusiasm, making every nerve quiver, filling every pore and cell of us. Our flesh and bone tabernacle seems transparent as glass to the beauty about us, as if truly an inseparable part of it, thrilling with the air and trees, streams and rocks, in the waves of the sun—a part of all nature, neither old nor young, sick nor well, but immortal...In this newness of life we seem to have been so always. (1)

Now I can let you know what this book about Christian spirituality holds for me. At its core lies the message that there are many ways of interpreting and understanding the world. We are mistaken when we apply the schema of scientist and mechanic while trying to explore the body's knowing of what spirituality is about.

The scientific method has been inculcated into most of us. Doctors McMahon and Campbell, however, tell us that we make a category-mistake when applying our usual problem-solving techniques to the realm of spirituality. Instead, we need to develop a new habit in our bodies for approaching areas of human living that are too complex and intricate to ever provide a simple, reducible, repeatable answer. I was looking for answers on the exterior in the beeping of the machine. Fortunately, Fathers McMahon and Campbell had let me know that we also find answers when being lovingly present to how our own bodies carry emotions that connect us to life.

This book describes how to develop such a habit, and it is because I have begun to grow into this new habit myself that I was able to be with my mother in the way I described above. It has involved growing into a new relationship to my own body and its feelings. While developing this habit and rediscovering my own lost biology, my-body-connection within the Larger Body of the Whole Christ, I have discovered a perspective on the world I live in that is far richer and more filled with connection than I ever believed was possible. I have been graced with a profoundly felt, organic bond to my mother that may not otherwise have been available to me. John Muir discovered this connection through his body's relationship in the beauty of the Sierra mountains. I rediscovered it within the beauty of my mother's touch.

John Keane, (Ph.D. Candidate)
Dublin, Ireland
May 2010

Notes

Scripture Quotations:

RSV Revised Standard Version
The Holy Bible, Revised Standard Version with the Apocrypha
Thomas Nelson & Sons, New York, 1952, cited as RSV.

NRSV The New Revised Standard Version with Apocrypha
Containing the Old and New Testaments and the Deuterocanonical Books, Hendrickson Bibles in conjunction with Oxford University Press, 1989, cited as NRSV.

NEB The New English Bible New Testament
Oxford University Press, Cambridge University Press, 1965, cited as NEB.

JB The Jerusalem Bible
Doubleday & Company, Inc., Garden City, New York, 1966, cited as JB.

NAB New American Bible The New Testament—The Catholic Study Bible
New York, Oxford University Press, 1990, cited as NAB.

TIB The Inclusive Bible—The First Egalitarian Translation
A Sheed & Ward Book, Rowman and Littlefield Publishers, Inc., New York, 2007, cited as TIB.

Why This Book?

1. John Muir, *My First Summer in the Sierra,* (Boston: Houghton Mifflin, 1911). The Quotation may be found in Chapter 6 on page 110 of the Sierra Club Books 1988 edition.

2. Pierre Teilhard de Chardin, *The Phenomenon of Man,* (New York: Harper & Brothers Publishers, 1959), pp. 284–285.

3. Abraham Maslow, *Religions, Values, and Peak-Experiences,* (Columbus: Ohio State University Press, 1964), p. xiv.

4. Carl R. Rogers, from a private conversation with Robert J. Willis, Ph.D.

5. Eugene T. Gendlin, *Focusing,* Second edition, New, revised instructions, (New York: Bantam Books, 1981), p. 77.

6. Adam Kahane, *Solving Tough Problems: An Open Way of Talking, Listening, and Creating New Realities,* (San Francisco: Berrett-Koehler Publishers, Inc., 2004), Quotation from the Foreword by Peter M. Senge, pp. xi–xii.

7. Jean-Paul Sartre, *Nausea,* (L. Alexander, Trans.), (New York: Philosophical Library, 1964), pp. 170–174

continued

Notes

Why This Book? *continued*

8. From a private conversation.

9. C. Otto Scharmer, *Theory U—Leading from the Future as it Emerges—The Social Technology of Presencing,* (Cambridge, Massachusetts: The Society of Organizational Learning, Inc., 2007), pp. xiv–xv.

10. Ibid.

11. Ibid., p. xvi.

12. Joseph Campbell, *Thou Art That—Transforming Religious Metaphor,* Edited with a Foreword by Eugene Kennedy, Ph.D., Joseph Campbell Foundation, (Novato, California: New World Library, 2001), p. 1.

13. Ibid., Editor's Foreword by Eugene Kennedy p. xvi.

14. Ibid., p. xvi.

15. The Institute for BioSpiritual Research, Inc. is a non-profit organization incorporated in the State of Wisconsin. The two co-founders, Rev. Edwin M. McMahon, Ph.D. and Rev. Peter A. Campbell, Ph.D. have authored many books, videos and booklets in the field they have called *BioSpirituality* from their years researching the body's role in healthy spiritual growth. The Institute is an international network of interested persons—including parents, counselors, health care providers, hospice volunteers, clergy, members of religious communities, teachers and therapists. The Institute is not affiliated with any church, political party or country. It is a member supported, shared leadership community of *peacemakers from the inside*, dedicated to the psychological study of human wholeness and its spiritual implications. For further information, visit the Institute website at: *http://www.biospiritual.org.*

16. C. Otto Scharmer, *Theory U—Leading from the Future as it Emerges,* Quotation taken from the jacket cover summary by Peter M. Senge.

17. Eugene T. Gendlin, *"A Theory of Personality Change,"* in J.T. Hart & T.M. Tomlinson (Eds.) New Directions in Client-Centered Therapy, (Boston: Houghton Mifflin Co., 1970), p. 155.

18. Adam Kahane, *Solving Tough Problems—An Open Way of Talking, Listening, and Creating New Realities*, pp. 104–105.

19. Chris Crowley & Henry S. Lodge, M.D., *Younger Next Year,* (New York: Workman Publishing Co., 2007).

20. Henry S. Lodge, M.D., from Modesto Bee Supplement, Tuesday June 17, 2007.

21. Henry S. Lodge, M.D., *You Can Stop "Normal" Aging*, Modesto Bee Supplement, March 18, 2007.

22. Henry S. Lodge, M.D., Modesto Bee Supplement, Tuesday June 17, 2007, p. A-4.

Chapter 2
An Exercise—What Would It Have Felt Like if...?

1. Joseph Campbell, *Thou Art That,* p. xvi.

Chapter 3
A Story for the Hiding Child in All of Us

1. Abraham Maslow, *Toward a Psychology of Being*, (Princeton, New Jersey: D. Van Nostrand Company, Inc., an Insight Book, 1962).

2. Gordon Allport, *The Individual and His Religion*, (New York: The Macmillan Company, 1950).

3. Anne Wilson Schaef, *When Society Becomes an Addict*, (New York: HarperCollins Publishers, 1987).

4. William Butler Yeats, *A Prayer for Old Age*, (From Parnell's funeral and Other Poems Published 1935).

5. Edwin M. McMahon, *The Little Bird Who Found Herself*, Illustrations by Prabhjot Uppal, M.D., 2008. (Steuben Press, 4901 E. Dry Creek Rd., Ste. 160, Centennial, CO 80122. Tel. (720) 205-0864).

Chapter 4
Journeying into Your Own Inner World of Felt Sensing

1. Eugene T. Gendlin, *A Theory of Personality Change,* pp. 140–141. "There is an *interacting*, not an equation, between implicit meaning and symbols...a felt meaning can contain very many meanings and can be further and further elaborated. Thus, the felt meaning is not the same in kind as the precise symbolized explicit meaning...Implicit bodily feeling is *preconceptual*. Only when *interaction* with verbal symbols (or events) actually occurs, is the process actually carried forward and the explicit meaning formed...Thus, to explicate is to *carry forward* a bodily felt process. Implicit meanings are *incomplete*. They are not hidden conceptual units."

2. Joseph Campbell, *Thou Art That*, p. 1.

3. Ibid., Editor's Foreword by Eugene Kennedy p. xvi.

4. Ibid., p. xvi.

Notes

Chapter 7
A New BioSpiritual Way of Loving, Guided by Your Affection Teacher Through, '…the Eyes of your Heart' (Ephesians 1:18)

1. Edwin M. McMahon, *"Beyond the Myth of Dominance: An Alternative to a Violent Society,"* (Kansas City, Sheed & Ward, 1993).

Chapter 9
Ancient and Modern Intimations of a Larger Body— But How Do We Connect?

1. Dana Ganihar, *Let Your Body Interpret the Text: How to Read (Gendlin) Experientially*, The Focusing Connection, Vol. XXVI, No. 3, May 2009, p. 1.
2. Thomas S. Kuhn, *The Structure of Scientific Revolutions*, (Chicago and London: The University of Chicago Press, Third Edition, 1996), pp. 121–123, passim.
3. Alan Watts, *The Book: On the Taboo Against Knowing Who You Are*, (New York: Random House, Pantheon Books 1966), p. 11.
4. Peter A. Campbell & Edwin M. McMahon, *BioSpirituality—Focusing as a Way to Grow*, First Edition, (Chicago, Illinois: Loyola Press, 1985).
5. Peter A. Campbell & Edwin M. McMahon, *BioSpirituality—Focusing as a Way to Grow*, Revised Edition, (Chicago, Illinois: Loyola Press, 1997), p. 113–114.
6. John A.T. Robinson, *The Body—A Study in Pauline Theology*, (London: SCM Press Ltd., 1963).
7. Ibid., pp. 62–63 passim.
8. Ibid., p. 63.
9. Ibid., p. 63, *(Also note:* σύνσωμα = σύσσωμα, *used only once in the New Testament, Eph. 3:6.)*
10. Ibid., p. 63.
11. Karl Rahner, Herbert Vorgrimler, *Theological Dictionary*, (New York: Herder and Herder, 1965), p. 469.
12. Peter A. Campbell & Edwin M. McMahon, *BioSpirituality—Focusing as a Way to Grow*, First Edition, p. x.
13. John A.T. Robinson, *The Body—A Study in Pauline Theology*, p. 51.

Chapter 10
Clues Unearthed During the Last Century by Scientists From Various Fields Who Discerned the Larger Body Within which We Live

1. Eugene T. Gendlin, *Focusing*, p. 77.

2. Pierre Teilhard de Chardin, *Science and Christ*, (New York: Harper & Row, Publishers, 1969), p. 13. (*Science et Christ* was first published in France by Editions du Seuil in 1965.)

3. Ibid., p. 12.

4. William James, *The Varieties of Religious Experience*, (New York: A Mentor Book, New American Library, 1958), p. 388.

5. Ibid., p. 391.

6. Bruce H. Lipton, *The Biology of Belief: Unleashing the Power of Consciousness, Matter, and Miracles,* (Santa Rosa, CA, Mountain of Love/Elite Books, 2005) p. 75.

7. Alan Watts, *The Book: On the Taboo Against Knowing Who You Are*, pp. 61 & 80.

8. Karl Rahner, *The Love of Jesus and the Love of Neighbor*, (New York: The Crossroad Publishing Company, 1983), p. 76.

9. Anthony J. Sutich and Miles A. Vich (editors), *Readings in Humanistic Psychology*, (New York: The Free Press, 1969), in Carl R. Rogers, *Toward a Science of the Person*, p. 43.

10. Ibid., p. 42.

Chapter 11
Agápe in the Light of Carl Rogers' Research

1. Rachel Remen, *Kitchen Table Wisdom*, (New York: Riverhead Books, The Berkley Publishing Group, a division of Penguin Putnam Inc., 1996), pp. 217–219.

2. William James, *The Varieties of Religious Experience*, p. 388.

3. John A.T. Robinson, *The Body—A Study in Pauline Theology*, p. 63.

4. Carl G. Jung, *Modern Man in Search of a Soul,* translated by W.S. Dell and Cary F. Baynes, (New York: Harcourt, Brace & World, Inc., a Harvest Book, 1963), first published in 1933, p. 235.

Notes

Chapter 13
Loving God or Loving as God Loves?

1. Adam Kahane, *Solving Tough Problems*, p. 104.
2. David Bohm, *Wholeness and the Implicate Order*, (London: Routledge & Kegan Paul, 1981), p. 211.
3. Karl Rahner, *"Christology and an Evolutionary World View,"* in Theology Digest, Vol. 28:3, Fall 1980, p. 216. *(emphasis ours)*
4. Edwin M. McMahon & Peter A Campbell, *Becoming a Person in the Whole Christ*, (New York: Sheed & Ward, 1967).
5. Edwin M. McMahon & Peter A. Campbell, *The In-Between—Evolution in Christian Faith*, (New York: Sheed & Ward, 1969).
6. Ibid., pp. 7–8.
7. Peter A. Campbell and Edwin M. McMahon, *BioSpirituality: Focusing as a Way to Grow,* (Chicago: Loyola University Press, 1985, Original Edition).
8. Ibid., p. xiv *(Original Preface, unrevised edition)*.
9. Rev. John B. Wheaton, C.J.M., *Doing the Truth in Love*, (Halifax, Nova Scotia: Mount St. Vincent University, 1967), p. 5.
10. Ibid., p. 6.
11. Ibid., p. 7.
12. Ibid., p. 8.
13. Karl Rahner, S.J., *"The Unity of Love of God and Love of Neighbor,"* Theology Digest, Vol. 15, No. 2, Summer 1967, pp. 87–93. Present quotation from p. 88. *(emphasis ours)*
14. Phil Cousineau, *The Art of Pilgrimage—The Seekers Guide to Making Travel Sacred*, (Berkeley, California: Conari Press, 1998), p. 35.

Chapter 14
What is Process-Skipping and How Do We Grow Beyond it into Loving as God Loves?

1. Eugene T. Gendlin, *A Theory of Personality Change,* p. 149–150, in footnote 13.

Chapter 15
Paul's Astonishing Discovery 'in Christ'— 'When I am Weak Then I am Strong…' (2 Cor. 12:7–10)

1. John A.T. Robinson, *The Body—A Study in Pauline Theology*, p. 63.
2. Lancelot Law Whyte, *The Next Development in Man*, (New York: A Mentor Book Published by The New American Library, 1948, Third Printing, 1962) p. 203.

Chapter 16
The Habit of Noticing and Nurturing Your Important Feelings 'in Christ' Enables You to Mature Beyond Addictive Spiritualities

1. Anne Wilson Schaef, *When Society Becomes an Addict*, (New York: HarperOne, An Imprint of HarperCollins Publishers, 1987), p. 25.
2. Ibid., p. 30.
3. Ibid., p. 30.
4. Ibid., p. 31.
5. Ibid., pp. 31–32.
6. Ibid., *Part II The Addictive System as a Hologram*, p. 37.
7. Karl Rahner, *The Theology of Risk*, The Furrow, Vol. 19, No. 5, May 1968, p. 268, footnote 4.
8. Anne Wilson Schaef, *When Society Becomes an Addict*, pp. 18–19.
9. Ibid., pg. 33.

Chapter 17
Recovering the Lost Biology of Christian Spirituality

1. C. Otto Scharmer, *Theory U—Leading from the Future as it Emerges—The Social Technology of Presencing,* pp. xvi & xviii passim.
2. Eugene T. Gendlin, *Three Assertions About The Body,* in *The Folio: A Journal for Focusing and Experiential Therapy*, Vol. 12, No. 1, Spring 1993, pp. 29 & 31.
3. C. Otto Scharmer, *Theory U—Leading from the Future as it Emerges—The Social Technology of Presencing,* p. xvi.
4. Anne Wilson Schaef, *When Society Becomes an Addict*, p. 150.
5. C. Otto Scharmer, *Theory U*, Foreword by Peter M. Senge, p. xvi.

Afterword

1. John Muir, *My First Summer in the Sierra*, (Edinburgh, Cannongate Classics, 1988), pg. 8.